Velocette

Velocette

'TECHNICAL EXCELLENCE EXEMPLIFIED'

Ivan Rhodes

About the author

Having always had high regard for the technical merits of the Velocette, Ivan Rhodes has been fortunate to have met many of those involved in the design and manufacture of these fine machines, including most of the Goodman family, whom he can count amongst his friends. He served his apprenticeship as a motorcycle fitter with the reputable firm of Wileman's Motors in Derby during the late 1940s. There he was involved closely with a wide range of British motorcycles, including Velocettes, for which they were the main agents.

Ivan prepared and rode machines in all types of competition for many years before retiring from the sport so that his two sons could take over and continue. He was instrumental in the development of the Vintage racing scene and has given his full support to the Celebatory Lap of Honour in the Isle of Man. To date, with the exception of 1988 and 1990, he has provided at least three—sometimes four—machines on each occasion, ridden by such notable riders as Stanley Woods, the late Freddie Frith, Mick Grant, Bill Lomas, Steve Murray, his old friend Chris Williams and, of course, himself. As he has competed in a couple each of Manx Grands Prix and TTs, he is qualified to join in.

His speciality has always been the overhead-camshaft model, in particular the KTT. He was fortunate in collecting a wide range of ohc components, including some ex-works stock, from all quarters of the globe at a time when there was little interest in old racing motorcycles. Consequently, he has been able to build up an interesting and unique collection of Hall Green raceware.

These machines are not just static monuments to Veloce's past glory, however, but are frequently taken out and ridden in anger, on the principle that all good things should be shared and enjoyed.

First Published in 1990 by Osprey Publishing

Reprinted Spring 1997 by Osprey,
a division of Reed International Books Limited,
Michelin House, 81, Fulham Road London SW3 6RB
and Auckland, Melbourne, Singapore and Toronto

© Copyright Ivan Rhodes 1990

All rights reserved. Apart from any fair dealing for the purpose of private study, research, criticism or review, as permitted under the Copyright, Designs and Patents Act, 1988, no part of this publication may be reproduced, stored in a retrieval system, or transmitted in any form or by any means, electronic, electrical, chemical, mechanical, optical, photocopying, recording, or otherwise, without prior written permission. All enquiries should be addressed to the publisher.

British Library Cataloguing in Publication Data

Rhodes, Ivan
 Velocette.
 1. Motorcycles, history
 I. Title 629.227509
 ISBN 0-85045-717-3

Editor Ian Penberthy
Designer Geoffrey Wadsley

Filmset by Keyspools Limited, Golborne, Warrington
Printed in England

Contents

Foreword 6
Acknowledgements 7
Introduction 8

1 The formative years 9
2 The two-stroke of 1913 13
3 The early Kamshaft models 18
4 'Whiffling Clara' 24
5 Development of the Mk II KSS from the racing machines 29
6 The introduction of the M-series 36
7 Development of the M-series 44
8 KTT—Kamshaft Tourist Trophy 48
9 The speedway KDT 66
10 Stanley Woods' influence 67
11 Double ohc and Mk VI KTT 71
12 Mk VII and Mk VIII KTT 82
13 The Waycott ISDT outfit 92
14 The factory racing 500s 95
15 The Roarer 99
16 The Model O 114
17 The Velocette clutch 119
18 WD models and post-war production 120
19 The post-war works 350s 131
20 A new dohc 250 142
21 Viper, Venom and Thruxton 148
22 The 24-hour record 159
23 A new roadgoing 250 163
24 The demise 165

Appendices
1 Specifications 167
2 Engine, frame and gearbox numbers 178
3 Production figures 189

Foreword

It's a great pleasure to write a foreword for this book about Velocettes. More than 50 years have elapsed since I first became involved with the marque, and I feel that I can take some credit for bringing the company's fortunes back from the doldrums after their great successes in the late 1920s.

I made certain suggestions around 1935 as to how their race machines could be turned into winners. Mind you, I had to be careful how I did that. The Goodmans were clever engineers and very innovative, but they liked to do things in their own way.

I used to go to the factory from time to time, and George Denley, who was married to Ethel Goodman, said quite early on, 'We'll go round the factory first, then to the boardroom for morning coffee. Then we may look at the experimental shop, and back to the boardroom for lunch.

'During the day, you may have some ideas to put forward. Wait until we have afternoon tea and just say something like, "I wonder what would happen if we did so-and-so?"' He told me to leave it at that. In a month or so, it would have taken root, or they'd have tried it and rejected it.

They were very kind people, top drawer, you couldn't meet finer, and they were always trying to do something new. The KTT was a wonderful racing motorcycle, although my personal choice was the 500.

In recent years, I have been able to renew my acquaintance with this model through the generosity of the author of this book, Ivan Rhodes. The years rolled away when I saw my initials stamped on the cambox!

There is no doubt in my mind that Ivan is the leading authority on Velocettes today. I met him first at an early Vintage Race of the Year at Mallory Park where I was a guest. They gave me a Cotton to ride and it wasn't very good. Then he offered me a ride on the Velocette and instantly I felt at home. The Island Lap of Honour—or the 'geriatric TT' as I call it—was a milestone in my life.

Ivan has been instrumental in resurrecting the supercharged twin. He has the detailed knowledge of the machines, and the drive and enthusiasm to see projects through to a fitting conclusion. Mind you, he has great back-up from his charming wife, Rene, and the two boys, Grahame and Adrian. It's not a solo effort!

They are all Velo enthusiasts, and I wish Ivan every success with this book.

Stanley Woods
Downpatrick
March 1990

A historic occasion—the rebirth of the Roarer at Borrowash on 7 May 1989. Standing, left to right: Len Udall, Grahame Rhodes, Ivan Rhodes, Rene Rhodes, Peter Goodman. Stanley Woods is sitting on the bike (*Nottingham Evening Post*)

Acknowledgements

When preparing a manuscript of this size, inevitably one is dependent on others in various ways. I have been particularly fortunate to gain first-hand information from many 'who were there' at the time. I am delighted to give my grateful thanks to Australians Frank Mussett and Phil Irving who have been extremely helpful, as have works race mechanics, Jack Passant and the late Frank Panes.

My senior and valued friend Arthur Wheeler, also Les Archer, Bill Lomas, and the late Freddie Frith were all riders with a contribution to make to the book.

I spent many an interesting hour with Tich Allen, particularly when he was compiling his *Velocette Saga* for *Motorcycle Sport*, some 20 years ago.

Charles and Len Udell are names that will need no introduction.

I make no apology for the fact that Stanley Woods figures strongly in this book. Quite apart from being a close friend of my family, he was the astute master of his craft when Velocette were in the doldrums before the war. He was instrumental in turning their fortunes to the benefit of us all. Stanley Woods (b. 28 November 1903) passed away a few years after first publication of this book. He was a man greatly to be admired.

If I was to consider to whom I should dedicate this book, it would be to Stanley, Freddie and their contemporaries who campaigned these fine machines.

A very special word of thanks must go to the Goodman family—Peter, Bertie and his wife Maureen. They have helped immensely in various ways, with advice, photographs and human stories. This is quite apart from the friendship shown to me, and their dedication to the cause which enabled the honourable flag to be flown for so long.

Over many years I have been in contact with Dennis Quinlan of Australia, who probably has as much detailed knowledge of Velocettes as anyone. He is always delving into technicalities, particularly of the racing machines, and has kept me aware of much that otherwise might not have been recorded.

Bob Murney and George Mason of Derby compiled technical details of various models so that specifications could be included.

The Velocette Owners' Club kindly allowed me to use some of their photographs and other archive material, as did Brian Woolley and Phillip Tooth of *Classic Motorcycle*.

David Davies of Brigg, East Yorkshire, the VMCC Overseas Correspondent, who is well-versed in motorcycling matters, has applied professional expertise to reproduce photographs and slides so that we can have a record for posterity.

Geoff Dodkin has an immense knowledge of the models through working on them over a long period — what better! His wife Desne worked at Veloce for many years. Both have contributed to the book and read the manuscript.

Another good friend of some 30 years is Gordon Small, better known as Gordon Cadzow, the editor of *Classic Motorcycling Legends*. He once owned Mk VIII KTT 1040. He very kindly offered to sub-edit the book when I needed help. Without Gordon, I would have been stuck.

Two ladies at Wilkinson's the Derby coachbuilders typed up my scrawl, Mrs Hilary Goodman and Mrs Joyce Novak. Thank you Frank Gilbert.

Mrs Betty Griffin, the daughter of the late Tommy Mutton, sent many personal photographs.

My wife Rene has given me her full support. Not only has she put up with the Roarer being spread around the front room in pieces for years, but the study was scattered with paper, photographs and books for the same length of time. Few women would stand for it, and I shall be forever grateful for her indulgence.

I give my thanks and warmest gratitude to these fine people. Without them, this book could not have been written.

The author and the publishers are pleased to note the name Velocette and the spirit of the marque still continue strongly today. Following the liquidation of Veloce Limited and satisfaction of its creditors in 1971 the assets were acquired by Matthew David Holder. He then established The Velocette Motor Cycle Company.

Now based in the world-famous Meriden Works, Birmingham Road, Allesley, Coventry CV5 9AZ (Tel: 0676 22066) the company is ably run by David Matthew Scott Holder, son of the founder. The Velocette Motor Cycle Company is able to provide an enormous array of parts for Velocette, Vincent HRD, Scott, Royal Enfield, and a host of other prestige marques.

The name Velocette is the trademark of D M S Holder and is used with his kind permission.

Introduction

It was at the 1983 TT Riders' Association Lunch that I was asked by Tim Parker, the then editorial director of Osprey, to consider writing a book on the rather specialized subject of Velocettes.

I had taken a strong interest in the marque, particularly the overhead-camshaft models, since I had been a schoolboy. My first Velocette ride was on a 1929 KTT, engine no. 179. To me, there was a magical ring in the letters KTT, just as there is in Rolls-Royce, and that magic is still there. On leaving school, I followed my own instincts and found a job in the motorcycle trade, gaining experience which proved to be very useful later on.

I competed in all types of events on a 1926 350 (Big Port) AJS in the late 1940s and early 1950s, not only because I couldn't afford anything better, but also because I enjoyed the challenge of competing in modern events with an older machine. Eventually, KTT 179 came into my hands and I used it with some success in early VMCC and other road race events at a time when few Velocettes were entered.

My name seemed to become linked with camshaft Velos, and various people began to approach me with bits and pieces, and even with complete machines, some of them historical. In this way, I acquired much of the ex-works racing stock in the form of special engines, frames and components, and a couple of pre-war 500s which were eventually rebuilt and used. We were also offered—and we bought at great sacrifice—the Roarer because the previous owner felt that my family would be the most likely people to get the machine to run again.

In between building Velocettes, preparing them for racing and earning a living, I started to put the book on paper. It took a long time, but it is my account of the machines produced by this small family concern. I am privileged to know the Goodman family and to have had access to some of the special machines, quite apart from the 'bread-and-butter' production models.

Veloce—pronounced *Veeloce*—were first with many things, including the positive-stop foot change in 1928, the dualseat which was patented before the war, and the first effective swinging-arm rear suspension, as we know that it was used by Veloce in the 1936 TT.

The manuscript has been checked by the Goodman family, and by Geoff Dodkin and his wife who worked at Veloce for many years. Len Udall, who also was with Veloce for many years, has agreed it.

The manuscript was sub-edited by Gordon Small, who writes under the name Gordon Cadzow and is editor of *Classic Motorcycling Legends*. We have been friends for 30 years.

I have found the time taken to produce the book pleasurable and hope that my story of Veloce will give enjoyment and some assistance to those sufficiently encouraged or intrigued to buy it. Velocettes were considered to be among the finest motorcycles produced in their time, and I am in great debt to the family who made it all possible.

Ivan Rhodes
Fell Side
Borrowash
May 1990

CHAPTER 1

The formative years

Johannes Gütgemann, having left Germany for England at the age of 19 in 1876, eventually met Elizabeth Ore, a policeman's daughter and a direct descendant of Thomas Ore, a highly reputable 18th-century watchmaker, married her in 1884, and settled in Birmingham. Soon he ventured into business with a Mr Barrett who, it transpired, had inherited a pill making concern called Isaac Taylor and Co.

Gütgemann adopted the name John Taylor, having acquired the business from Barrett, and ventured into the manufacture of bicycles and fittings. He then met another cycle maker, named William Gue, and between them they set up a partnership called Taylor Gue, which was based at Hampton Works, Peel Street, Birmingham. Here they were to produce the Hampton bicycle and later, among other things, rickshaws, becoming a limited company at the turn of the century. Eventually, they were to manufacture the frames for the Ormonde motorcycle which housed a Belgian Kelekom engine.

Bicycles enjoyed a boom at this time and Taylor Gue were expanding rapidly. By 1905 they had bought out the entire assets of Kelekom Motors and, thus, were able to produce a complete machine.

The trade name Veloce was chosen and a 2 hp machine produced, but it was not a success and the venture soon collapsed. Meanwhile, however, John Taylor had formed an association with a chain wheel manufacturer named Williams who financed the new company of Veloce Ltd, having acquired premises in Spring Street, Birmingham, where they were to continue manufacturing chain wheels, cranks and other cycle fittings and to offer a metal plating service to the trade.

John Taylor's marriage to Elizabeth produced two sons: Percy and Eugene. Percy had been apprenticed to a pattern maker and had spent many of his early years in India, where he was to become involved in the sale of Wolseley motor cars and sheep-shearing equipment, while brother Eugene had been apprenticed in the toolroom of New Hudson in Birmingham.

There were also three daughters: Ethel, Adele and Dora. Ethel became company secretary and married George Denley, while Adele, the eldest, married during World War I and her husband was killed on active service next day. Dora, the youngest, married Dick Hillman who worked in the Veloce planning department—both are now dead.

When Percy returned from India in 1907, he and Eugene set up a company called New Veloce Motors and produced a prototype 20 hp car in 1908, but despite the fact that the car was of sound design and construction, orders failed to materialize. 'Bread-and-butter' business continued with the bicycle fittings and plating service, plus the manufacture of roller skates and a range of bicycles for which they had established a healthy export market.

Percy Taylor's fertile mind was soon to turn to the manufacture of motorcycles, however, and the design of an advanced unit-construction engine/gearbox assembly. This featured a large outside flywheel, geared primary drive (and consequently a crankshaft that ran backwards like a Moto Guzzi), two-speed footchange

Johannes Gütgemann, otherwise John Goodman, in 1909

THE "VELOCE"

2 h.p. Motor Cycle.

25 Guineas.

Weight from 65 pounds.

This machine has been designed by a motor expert, and is equal to any 2½ h.p. heavy weight motorcycle. The weight of engine, tanks, etc., has been placed low, thus **obviating side-slip.**

Send for particulars
TAYLOR, GUE, Limited,
52, Wells Street West.   Works:
London.   Birmingham.

A few 1904 Ormondes 3 h.p. at Reduced Prices.

Abridged Specification.

Frame—Entirely new design, long wheel-base, 22 or 24 in. Girder forks 10/- extra.

Wheels—26 in. 1½ in. Heavy Roadster Tyres.

Engine—New design 2 h.p., with outside fly-wheel. Built in our works. Hardened steel bearings.

Ignition—Double wipe, make and break, E.I.C. Trembler Coil and Accumulator.

Carburetter—Float-feed Spray.

Control—Front Rim Brake, Back Coaster Hub, Exhaust Valve lifted by Bowden Cable from handle-bar. Timing and Throttle Levers operated from top tube.

General—2½in. Mudguard. Middlemore's Saddle. Petrol capacity ½ gallon. Enamelled Black and Lined. Usual parts heavily plated.

gearbox and belt final drive. The engine was of 276 cc with a bore and stroke of 68 × 76 mm, and it had an overhead inlet and side exhaust valve layout—although initially it was laid down with an automatic inlet valve.

Lubrication, from an integral sump, was via a non-adjustable mechanical vane type oil pump, not unlike that used in most car engines today.

The lack of response from potential customers made it apparent that such a design was far ahead of its time. The lubrication system, dispensing with the need to give the customary shot of oil by the accepted method, was the cause of much suspicion. The design was shelved while a more conventional machine was produced. This was based on the simple and acceptable sidevalve single cylinder of 499 cc with a bore and stroke of 85 × 88 mm and a direct V-belt drive to the rear wheel. That such a design should resemble that of the Triumph of the period was perhaps more than coincidental, since the Triumph was a well established favourite, and I have been told, on good authority, that even the cams were interchangeable between the two models.

The new machine was known as the VMC (Veloce Motor Company) and sold well at 40 guineas. As far as is known, only two have survived, and at the time of writing both belong to women. One is owned by a Mrs Harrison living near Melbourne, Australia, while the other is in the hands of Maureen Goodman, wife of Bertie, Percy Taylor's son. (In 1911 John Taylor made a successful application to the Home Office to become a naturalized British subject, but it wasn't until 1917 that the whole family changed their surname by deed poll to that of Goodman.)

Left **An early advertisement extolling the virtues of the 2 hp Veloce**

Below left **Enjoying the seaside, left to right: Eugene Goodman, Mrs Goodman, Ethel Denly, George Denly** (*Pauline Arculus*)

Below **Eugene Goodman relaxing after a hard day at the factory, 1940** (*Pauline Arculus*)

Left The rather tatty remains of an early Veloce—so it reads on the timing cover of the conventional side-valve engine (*Velocette Owners' Club*)

Below left In 1908, the Goodman brothers—or Taylor brothers as they were then known—designed and built a prototype motor car which they called the Veloce Auto Car. A sales brochure was prepared, offering an 18–20 hp and a 24–26 hp vehicle with a choice of body. Though of sound design and construction, the venture came to nothing and it's believed that the sole example was eventually driven to the scrapyard

Below A technical picture of the interesting $2\frac{1}{2}$ hp IOE Veloce combined engine and gearbox unit of around 1910–12. The engine ran backwards and used a rotary oil pump. Note the detachable sump and rocking two-speed gearchange pedal

CHAPTER 2

The two-stroke of 1913

In 1913 the company launched the Velocette (it meant, simply, the diminutive Veloce), Percy Goodman having designed and developed a neat little two-stroke machine. Its oil was carried in a separate although integrally cast sump, fed under pressure from the exhaust system, and controlled by an adjustable metering screw, into a drilled mainshaft along which it travelled to the plain phosphor-bronze big-end. The mainshaft was long for adequate support within the main phosphor-bronze bearing and, in turn, the cylinder axis was set well over to the right-hand side of the machine, in an attempt to gain adequate cooling.

The spark plug had to be slightly offset to clear the bottom right-hand side of the fuel tank, although the tank itself was cut away slightly to allow the plug to be changed. Bore and stroke were 62 × 73 mm, giving a capacity of 206 cc. The carburettor was a tiny Amac instrument. The magneto was by Bosch, driven by a fine chain, with a manual ignition control lever mounted on the tank top on the right-hand side; this was very much a necessity when paddling-off the direct belt-drive model A.

The frame was a single tube, full-loop cradle with additional support for the steering head and was very robust, although the engine was mounted simply by the use of two cast-aluminium clamps. The front forks were of the single blade, side spring Druid pattern accommodating a stirrup front brake. The rear brake was operated by heel to an adjustable shoe pressing on the belt rim in the then conventional fashion. The wheels carried 24 × 2 in. Dunlop or Hutchinson tyres, but one could have 26 in. tyres to order, for a nominal extra charge. The finish was in black enamel with a two-tone green petrol tank, lined and lettered in gold leaf. Total weight was 112 lb. The machine was priced at

As far as is known, this is the only complete example of the circa 1912 2½ hp Veloce that exists—certainly in the UK. A further machine has been built in New Zealand around an original power unit

25 guineas. A deluxe version with a two-speed gearbox and chain drive was also available.

In order to rationalize production even in those days, the two models shared a common frame and power unit, the standard A model having provision for the little cast-iron, two-speed gearbox of the deluxe version, which was supported by a single $\frac{1}{2}$ in. diameter stud. On the deluxe machine the engine drive pulley of the A was replaced by a sprocket behind the outside flywheel, and a primary drive was taken to a chain wheel on the input side of the gearbox. A large chainwheel on the rear wheel was aligned to a detachable final drive sprocket, fitted to a keyed taper on the gearbox mainshaft which formed the output shaft. Thus was introduced a feature peculiar to all single-cylinder Velocettes to the end of the line in 1971!

Rear brake operation on this model was moved to the right-hand side where the adjustable shoe operated

Right and below In the early days there were red tanks and green tanks. The example of lettering on this 1913 Model A—stamped 'Prov-prot' (provisionally protected) on the crankcase—no. 123 is probably the only record of the original finish remaining. The tank is in two-tone green with gold lining. Note the cutaway for the sparking plug

on a dummy belt rim. Weight was increased to 122 lb and price to 30 guineas.

The standard Model A continued unchanged for 1914, whilst the deluxe two-speeder was to sport an all-black tank with gold lining and a new Velocette logo, initially on a cast plate, which was to become so well known.

This little gem of a machine was soon to become popular. A third model was announced specially designed for ladies and having a dropped frame and an aluminium dress guard over the cylinder head as an encouragement to the gentle sex. It also appealed to reverend gentlemen whose attire restricted them to this choice of mount when going about their business.

A Veloce publicity booklet, produced during World War 1, was headed *The delights and economy of Velocetting by those who have tried it*, and referred to the ease of handling, fuel economy and general excellence in design and workmanship of the Velocette miniature motorcycle. All of this underlines the fact that the machines had many endearing features which were to establish the marque head and shoulders above the others in their class.

Soon they were to introduce a revised and more positive method of lubrication, based on the same separate oil compartment theme, in addition to which, in order to take the jolt out of taking off and gearchanging with the all-chain, clutchless model, a spring-loaded cushdrive arrangement was incorporated in the back sprocket. But little more developed for the time being.

Following its introduction at the 1921 TT, where it proved to be unsatisfactory, a three-speed gearbox was redesigned and marketed for the following year's production, along with a clutch that was simple, effective and narrow enough to fit inboard of that final drive sprocket, which was now securely located dog fashion on to the shaft.

A three-cam scissor arrangement was devised to operate a thrust bearing which, in turn, lifted an adjustable spring carrier threaded into the outer plate—via three short $\frac{3}{16}$ in. diameter pins, evenly spaced and located in the back plate. Thus, it allowed the clutch chainwheel, which carried a number of cork inserts, to spin freely on its bearing between the two pressure plates when parted, the whole assembly being less than 1 in. in width.

Meanwhile, the frame had been redesigned, incorporating duplex tubes that ran from the steering head, under the engine and terminated at the base of the saddle tube, allowing for more substantial engine unit mountings and, thus, obviating the possibility of it

The year 1913 and the two-stroke Velocette, in single- and two-speed versions, arrives

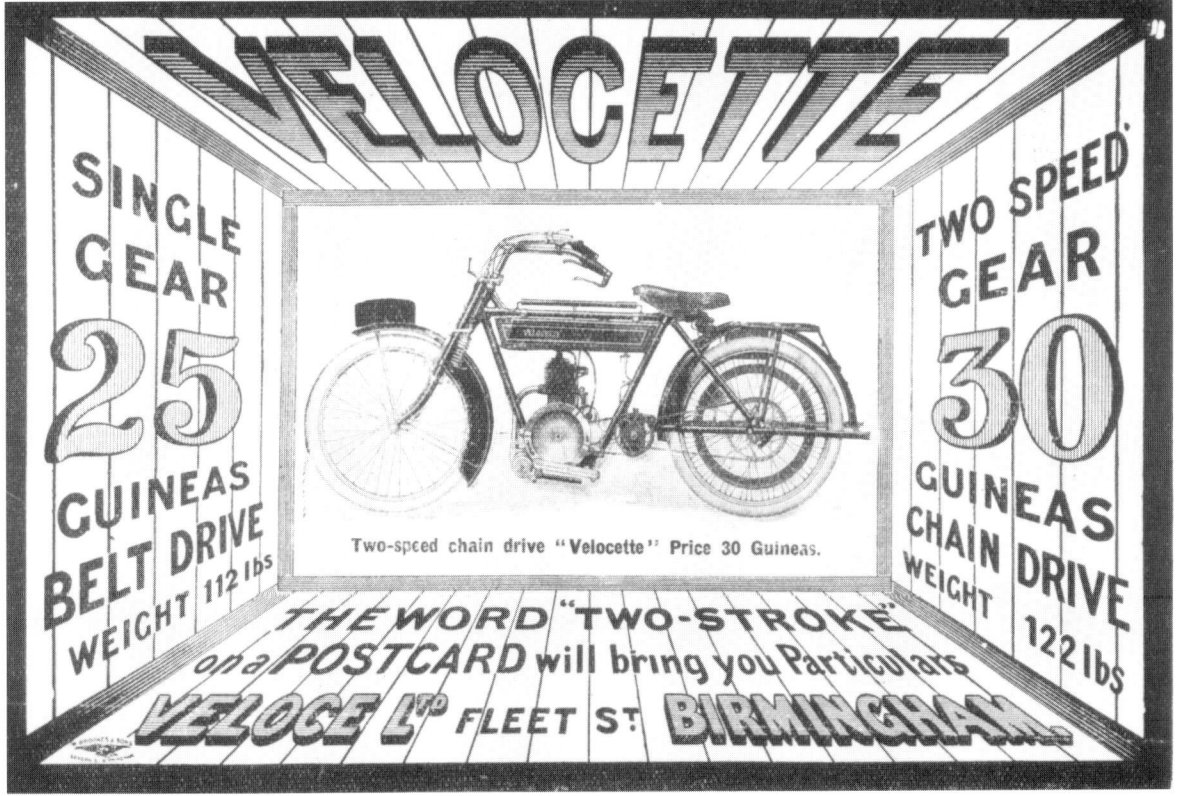

THE DELIGHTS OF "VELOCETTING."

Newquay Reliability Trial. We are pleased with the way the little machine ran over the rough roads of Dartmoor; in fact the machine held first place until nearly home, when we ran nearly ten miles off the course.

LONDON.

Will climb any hill.

I am riding every day in all sorts of weather. . . . She will climb any hill.

KENDAL.

This photo represents my sister, who has successfully ridden a Velocette during 1915 season. Many tours have been made throughout the Lake District, Lancashire, and Cumberland, without any mechanical trouble.

BREWOOD, STAFFS.

3,000 Miles—137 m.p.g.—A quart of oil lasts 3 months.

I have just noticed the pulley of my "Velocette" is considerably worn after having done 3,000 miles.

I have used the machine constantly during all the bad weather and it has behaved splendidly. I now average 137 m.p.g. As for oil, the consumption is exceedingly low—a quart of oil lasts me about 3 months. My last purchase was early in October and this is not yet exhausted.

OLDHAM.

2,000 Miles per Gallon of Oil.

I have ridden the machine 2,500 miles and am very pleased with it. I get 115 miles per gallon with 24 jet, riding short journeys in all weathers over vile roads (cobbles). I got 2,000 miles out of the last gallon of oil.

6

working loose, as had been experienced with the earlier method of fixing; no doubt aided by the tendency for a rocking couple on an engine with overhung crank considerably offset to the right.

The economy A and B models were continued in production for a while, using the old single front downtube but with revised engine mountings. Front brakes also came in for some marginal improvement, since their replacement, a tiny Webb device designed by Goodman, was so small that conventional return springs (as we know them) could not be accommodated. Instead a large circlip that fitted into a slot around the outer edge of the shoes was covered by the lining material and served to keep the shoes together satisfactorily, and whilst it performed little better or indeed as effectively as the old stirrup brake, it was, at least, less dangerous.

The reader may question the need to go into brief detail about the early two-stroke models, but remember that even the name 'Velocette' was derived from the need to distinguish the diminutive machine from the bigger Veloce, and of course the technicalities of the unique final drive and clutch designs emanated from these superb machines, quite apart from the high repute the company were to gain during that early period.

If one was to mention the name Velocette to the average man in the street, he would probably remember the silent watercooled machines used by the police, or he might recall that his father owned an MAC or even a KSS at one time and that the name was connected with racing and riders like Woods, Frith and Lomas. Mention the two-stroke and he might refer to the GTP, which latterly had a separate throttle controlled oiling system, probably not aware that this was the last of the two-stroke singles which, in fact, was preceded by a range of delightful little mounts developed in the early and mid 1920s. These were the models E, G and H series, and the rare S models, all with overhung cranks, separate magnetos and two or three speeds.

VELOCETTE.

SINGLE GEAR MODEL.

Engine	Veloce single cylinder valveless two stroke, 62 × 73 mm, désaxé cylinder, outside flywheel.
Lubrication System	Veloce patent exhaust pressure feed.
Carburettor	Amac or Senspray.
Magneto	Bosch or U.H.
Silencer	Cast aluminium expansion box with extension pipe, rendering the machine very quiet.
Frame	Built of very heavy gauge steel tubing, so as to give an enormously stiff construction even without the stiffening afforded by the crank case. The head is a one piece casting, with a stiffening bar. Ground clearance 6in.
Forks	Druid patent.
Wheels	24in. × 2in., fitted with Dunlop or Hutchinson tyres. We build a model with 26in × 2in. wheels to special order at a nominal extra charge.
Stand & Carrier	Of weldless steel tube. The stand is fitted on a stud independent of wheel spindle.
Saddle	Lycett's No. L110.
Tool Bag	Pannier leather bag in steel case, with complete tool kit.
Mudguards	3in. front and rear, with side wings.
Tank	Of stout sheet steel. Capacity 1⅛ gallons.
Oil Compartment	Cast with crank case. Capacity 200-250 miles.
Transmission	Dunlop ¾in. belt.
Gear Ratio	6 : 1.
Control	Carburettor, front brake, and compression release from handle bar, magneto control from tank.
Foot-rests	Arranged to give a comfortable riding position Footboards 12/6 extra.
Brakes	Bowden front brake, and pedal belt rim brake.
Total Weight	112lbs.

Price — 25 Guineas.

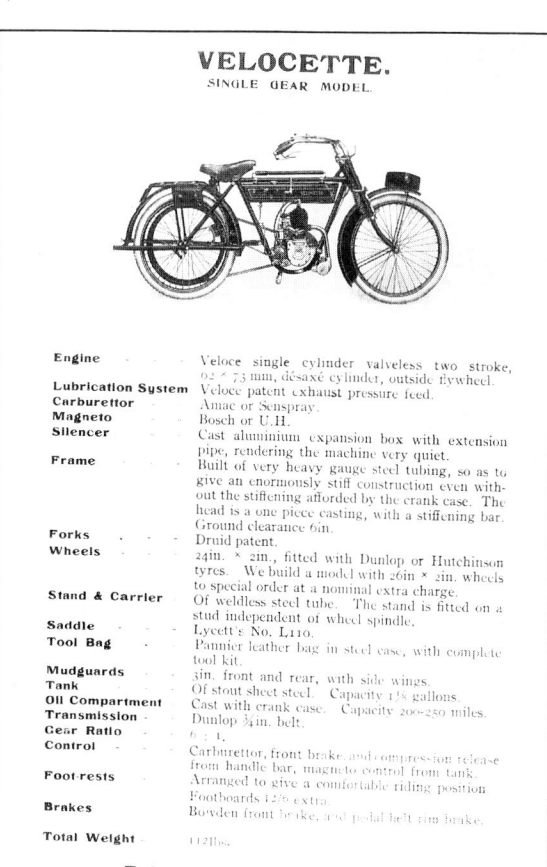

Maker's specification of the 1913 Model A, the first Velocette

During World War I, Veloce produced this booklet as a publicity exercise. Titled *The Delights & Economy of 'Velocetting' by people who have tried it*, it contained a large number of complimentary quotes from satisfied customers

CHAPTER 3

The early Kamshaft models

It was during 1924 that the company looked to new horizons. No doubt it was taking note of the growing popularity of certain other manufacturers' products with 'new' overhead-valve engined designs that were showing great promise. Thus a decision was made to draw up an engine incorporating the latest desirable features and, at the same time, to take into account the need to accommodate such a design within the limits of their well-established rolling chassis—to use a modern term.

When I say that a decision was made, I have no record suggesting that this was a company policy decision, or that of one man, namely Percy Goodman himself. However, it is said that Percy would spend his spare time at home preparing drawings for a new engine, drawings that I believe were carried out in the bedroom of his then four-year-old son Bertram.

AJS, JAP and Calthorpe, among others, had settled for a bore and stroke of 74 × 81 mm, and their engines performed well. Meanwhile, Herbert Le Vack was enjoying considerable success in racing a pair of double-overhead-camshaft, JAP-based engines designed by Val Page, which he had developed and used in a variety of frames, including those of Coventry Eagle, Zenith and Excelsior, depending on whom he was contracted to for a particular event. Another rider, the wily Dougal Marchant, was also achieving great success with a home-brewed overhead-camshaft Chater Lea.

A rare picture of the actual prototype 1924 pre-production machine. The vertical drive shaft was splined, with one blind spline to help retiming. Rollers were incorporated in the rockers—they suffered from lubrication problems (*Dr Helmut Krackowizer*)

The early Kamshaft models | 19

Above The prototype cammy Velo of 1924 with Druid-pattern forks and oil compartment in the petrol tank. Soon the forks were changed to Webbs and it became urgently necessary to redesign the engine

Left A publicity shot of the first cammy engine of 1924/5. The reciprocating plunger oil pump, taken from the two-stroke, can be seen on the end of the cambox

The existing Velocette frame and transmission design determined the need to keep the engine as narrow as possible in order that it could be accommodated, with the added potential bonus that if the width of the crank and bearings was less than the diameter of the cylinder bore, any possibility of flexure of the crank at relatively high engine revolutions would be minimized.

Thus the new overhead-camshaft Velocette was born and shown for the first time at Olympia in 1924. Total weight of the new model was 215 lb, the Brookes racing saddle height, 28 in., and the 650 × 65 mm beaded-edge wheels had 3 in. section tyres. There was a B&B carburettor and an ML or BTH magneto or Lucas Magdynette which gave an electric lighting facility. Forks were by Druid, and in common with most other machines of the period, the oil was contained in a separate compartment within the main fuel tank.

The frame was of the open diamond type with the engine suspended between the lugs at the bottom of the duplex front downtubes and the gearbox mounting bracket. The crankcase lugs were 3 in. wide at the front and only $1\frac{7}{8}$ in. wide at the back, dimensions that were to remain unchanged on all single-cylinder four-stroke Velocettes from then on—with the exception of the

MOV/MAC which had 2 in. lugs at the rear and was derived from the sidevalve Model M.

The cast-iron flywheels carried a single-row, $\frac{5}{16} \times \frac{5}{16}$ in. roller big-end assembly, the flywheels themselves measuring a mere 2.2 in. between the supporting main bearings, and the bevel drives to the overhead camshaft and the primary drive were taken only a fraction of an inch from those bearings, making the whole assembly relatively rigid.

Cylinder and head in cast-iron were fairly conventional, but there was a lapped joint between the two. An alloy cambox was mounted atop the cylinder head securing bolts, which had extended hexagonal heads with suitably threaded holes. The vertical drive shaft to the camshaft was splined to the top and bottom bevels, although one spline was blind to facilitate retiming when the engine was dismantled, any fine adjustment required being provided by the use of elongated holes in the top crown bevel where it was mated with the camshaft by four $\frac{1}{4}$ in. studs. The rockers were retained in the cambox by detachable hardened pins and carried a roller on the camshaft end, while the opposing end contained a threaded collet and convex taper-headed tappet which gave line contact on the valve. A conventional hemispherical combustion chamber and valves giving knife-edged seating, returned by duplex coil springs and retained by split collets within steel spring collars, were used.

The total–loss lubrication system was different in that an oil pump driven by skew gear from the end of the camshaft was of the adjustable reciprocating type, identical to that used on the two-stroke models, and controlled by a spring and ball feed—as the later models. A $\frac{1}{4}$ in. spring-loaded ball prevented oil from seeping into the engine when at rest. Oil was fed through a gauze filter into the cambox casing (where the cam dipped into the supply) and thence into the vertical drive shaft casing, on into the lower bevel housing (which also housed the magneto drive pinions) and then to the big-end via a crankshaft opening which aligned with the feed only on the upward stroke when crankcase depression was at its best.

The whole design was ingenious to say the least and typical of the brilliant Goodman, but it proved not to be a success, particularly when three models entered in the 1925 TT broke down through mechanical failures caused by faulty rocker forgings. So it was back to the drawing board for Percy Goodman. His basic design was fine, but he was quick to realize the need to recirculate the oil through the engine rapidly to dissipate heat. Therefore, he incorporated an immersed gear pump, to some extent following Sunbeam, whose racing machines used a similar pump bolted directly on to the timing cover, thus rendering it a dry sump.

The Veloce pump fitted snugly into a close fitting machined housing and was driven by a toggle to allow for a slight eccentricity in the drive from the secondary gear, which also served to drive the magneto chain. The vertical drive shaft was changed by introducing a pair of Oldham couplings to allow for flexure and accommodate machining tolerances. The drive shaft cover tube was retained at both ends by castellated gland nuts with asbestos string as a sealant. This had proved perfectly satisfactory in service on the detachable threaded doors and primary compression sealing crankcase stuffers on the little two-strokes.

The fully enclosed pump meant that there were no external oil pipes, except for main feed and return to a now separate tank, and an odd cambox return to the crankcase on the timing side, soon to be changed to the drive side, controlled by a clack valve in an effort to evacuate the cambox and thus minimize overspill. Because the oil was circulating at the rate of 10 gallons per hour, careful assembly was called for. It was controlled at the recommended pressure of 10-12 psi by the use of a bypass valve consisting of an adjustable spring and $\frac{1}{4}$ in. ball, using the Rolls-Royce principle. In order to maintain this pressure and, at the same time, lubricate the cam gear, a slot in the revolving camshaft lined up, once per revolution (every two engine revs) with another slot, passing sufficient oil under pressure to lubricate the cams. The driveside of the camshaft was supported by a phosphor-bronze bush with an outer dimension of some $3\frac{1}{8}$ in. which, in turn, was trapped, spigot-fashion, between the face of the upper bevel box and the cambox casting.

Oil feed to the big-end was controlled by another spring and $\frac{1}{4}$ in. diameter ball located in the hollow timing side mainshaft, the ball seating on a left-hand threaded cap nut, drilled radially to pass the oil under pressure, at the same time retaining the reduction gear which drove the oil pump and magneto drive pinion, and the lower bevel drive to the overhead camshaft.

Following the lubrication redesign of 1925, the scavenge hole was positioned midway along the base of the sump, which caused a surplus of oil to collect to the rear of the hole when the machine was on the move. However, the collection point was subsequently revised to a rearmost position which satisfactorily effected a cure.

Another clever feature of this revised engine design was the introduction of a hunting tooth to the overhead-camshaft drive bevel gears in order to distribute the load and wear on all the teeth except, of course, the lower drive bevel. The use of a bevel gear with 22 teeth driving a mating gear with 23 teeth, while at the cambox end a further 23 toothed gear drove the 44 toothed crown bevel, meant that only after 23 engine revolutions did the same pair of gear teeth match up. This was to prove a headache to some owners accustomed to removing cylinder heads for decarbonizing purposes at fairly frequent intervals, and was the cause of a good many potential owners fighting shy of obtaining such a model.

The only Velocette entry in the 1924 TT; this very special 'beehive' 250 finished tenth in the Lightweight event in the hands of George Povey. Listed in the works records as the 1924 TT Racing machine—using a poppet-valve engine, no. R1/24, and frame no. B5206—it was eventually broken up and the engine used by the Cope family of Bearwood as an auxiliary engine driving the rear wheel of their BSA three-wheel trials car

However, the smooth power delivery and relatively good performance allied to excellent reliability and machine handling soon offset this possible disadvantage, and discerning riders were quick to realize the merits of such a design, especially when Alec Bennett, having already won a couple of TTs, approached Percy Goodman with a proposition that he couldn't refuse. Having tried out a machine prior to the 1926 TT, Bennett requested the use of the model on the basis that if he didn't win he would ride for nothing. That he won by ten minutes, despite his customary slow first lap to allow the castor oil to warm up and pass through the small-bore plumbing—and having dropped it at the Nook on the last lap—is surely sufficient testimony to the genius of Goodman.

When the new ohc Velocette was introduced to the trade, it was called—once again—Veloce. The Velocette name only applied to the diminutive two-stroke. However, the agents quickly told the factory that they preferred the well-established Velocette name for the new model.

Preceding paragraphs have made reference only to the design of the engine, but equally the rest of the model was treated with the same thoroughness of design, workmanship and development. This becomes clear when one considers that all the Goodmans—Percy, Eugene and sister Ethel—rode the machines they produced and, in consequence, were to carry out gradual 'seat of the pants' improvements along the way.

Veloce had entered teams in the Tourist Trophy event and reliability trials, initially with the two-stroke models and later the new K design, and in consequence handling had been developed to a very high degree at a time when speed wobbles were the norm. There were 7 in. brakes front and rear, and a good stiff brake plate and shoes at each end meant rapid retardation compared to a good many of the opposition who still relied on a dummy belt rim or an internal expanding type of puny dimensions.

There is no doubt that the 1926 TT win was the turning point in Velocette fortunes, and orders for this superb machine, or machines like it, began to flood in to the extent that they just couldn't cope. Thus, a decision was made to move to new premises at York Road, Hall Green.

A. J. Stevens took their new chain-driven overhead-camshaft machines to the TT in 1927, but found them lacking in performance. They had overlooked the fact that flexure in the valve gear, allied to a certain amount of valve bounce, on the previous year's overhead-valve engines assisted in gaining a few horsepower, whereas the better control of the overhead camgear necessitated a revised cam and timing to get them going properly. Percy Goodman had made use of a stroboscope to get the Velocettes motoring to good effect, so during the 1927 TT period he sent a message round to Harry Stevens at the AJS camp, offering to assist in the development of their engines, but his offer was courteously declined.

Meanwhile, the company was joined by Harold Willis. Willis' father was a master butcher in Birmingham and when, with the move to Hall Green, Veloce needed to fund the expansion operation by placing a large block of shares on the market, Willis senior bought a fair slice and obtained a seat on the board of directors for Harold. He was to find himself the only outsider in this erstwhile family concern.

Harold Willis had served in the Royal Navy and subsequently had been apprenticed to a firm of marine engineers. Although he had suffered the consequences of salt water inhalation after being torpedoed, it didn't stop him becoming a successful TT and Brooklands rider. His role was to take control of the racing department and develop and ride the machines on suitable occasions. He was soon to be instrumental in

Above Alec Bennett was so impressed with this fine piece of machinery that he made Veloce an offer they could not refuse. He said he would ride it for nothing unless he won, which he did with ten minutes to spare—Veloce's first TT win, the Junior of 1926. Bennett was sympathetic to machinery and had a neat, easy riding style which inspired Stanley Woods, who modelled himself on Bennett

Willis, Hicks and Baker on the occasion of their record-breaking spree at Montlhèry in France during 1928. Note the bulbous cambox cover, the special fuel tank, strutted forks and evidence of a drop of oil!

OP 7931 was Harold Willis' first TT Velocette, and he called it 'Roaring Anna'. Later, she was fitted with the first positive-stop footchange. She is still around

preparing and riding machines to break several records at Brooklands, to finish second to Freddie Dixon in the Junior TT, and then to go on to a further record breaking spree at Montlhéry in 1928 which included the coveted one hour at 100.3 mph, with another second in the Junior TT of that year. Prior to that TT, the company had produced a one-off sprung-framed machine for Alec Bennett, their number one rider.

It is well known that this bike's rear end was of Bentley & Draper design, with a triangulated rear fork supported by coil springs and friction damper controlled, the design being such that it grounded on corners and was only used for practice. Willis called it 'Spring Heeled Jack'—the machine is still intact and in full working order.

Willis' own machine, with which he finished second in the TT in both 1927 and 1928, and which I believe is the machine he also used for his successful record attempts at both Brooklands and Montlhéry, he nicknamed 'Roaring Anna'. It was 'Anna' to which he affixed the world's first positive-stop footchange mechanism, which gained him useful seconds during that 1928 TT ride.

In 1929, however, having fulfilled her primary purpose as development test-bed for the new KTT model, 'Anna' became the property of H. C. Webb & Company, manufacturers of the famous Webb forks and friends of the Goodman family. It was used as a general hack by the company's representative when visiting the scenes of its former triumphs, such as during race week in the Island. 'Anna' was used for such tasks for many years before being passed on to an employee of Webb—I believe for a while it towed a sidecar around. Then came salvation. At a *Motor Cycling* magazine Donington day in 1939 Grahame Walker, the then editor, who had laid on the very first vintage race that day, overheard Harold Willis, who had been invited as a guest, remark that if only 'Anna' had been there she could have given the rest of the field a lap start and have been decarbonized before the others had finished. There and then, Willis vowed that if 'Anna' could be found, she would show her paces at the next Donington day. But alas, Willis was to die from meningitis in little more than a month later, on the day before Stanley Woods won his last TT, the Junior of 1939, with the latest of Harold's engines.

In later years, however, 'Anna' was to fulfill her role when she was to win a vintage race at a *Motor Cycling* Silverstone Saturday meeting in 1949; and she is still around to this day, albeit slightly modified. The same engine with that peculiar bulbous top bevel housing is still there; the same frame; the same cast-aluminium primary chaincase which someone has seen fit to cut about to make only a top run over the chain, but the basic machine remains.

CHAPTER 4

'Whiffling Clara'

In his quest for improvements in 1928–30, Harold Willis built a long-stroke KTT engine of 68 × 96 mm bore and stroke which he immediately dubbed the 'bicycle pump'. These dimensions were subsequently to be used for the MAC high-camshaft pushrod engine of later years. The reason for this departure was aimed at improving combustion, but it performed no better than, if as well as, the standard 74 × 81 mm KTT and after one outing in the TT was dropped.

At the same time, Willis had produced an experimental four-speed gearbox, drawn up by the young Charles Udall. In common with all the KTTs, it used his positive-stop mechanism. Meanwhile, Eugene Goodman, quite independently of Harold Willis, produced a prototype four-speeder which was very different in that it housed a large circular camplate that must have presented problems with inertia. It contained a gear train with relatively long shafts which caused it to hang very lopsided in the frame. No doubt, it would have produced a few cornering problems.

The conventional—or unconventional—Velocette clutch arrangement remained, but its operation differed from the normal Veloce bell crank arrangement, in that it used a long $\frac{1}{4}$ in. diameter pushrod passing through the back of the box which was activated by a normal adjustable operating lever, like BSA and a good many more manufacturers. Additionally, this box housed a conventional kickstart arrangement, again similar to BSA, Burman, etc.

Reference to sales literature of 1932 models will show an artist's impression of this peculiar box. Only the

Veloce won the team prize in the 1928 Junior TT. Here, Percy Goodman proudly stands alongside Harold Willis, who was second, with winner Alec Bennett and Freddie Hicks, who was fifth

A Veloce sales promotional picture, based on an artist's impression, showing the new KTT for 1931 with the proposed four-speed gearbox based on Eugene Goodman's prototype. Note the thick-base barrel. As far as is known, no such machine ever existed

prototype remains, however, and was used mainly by Bob Burgess on his sidecar outfit. It was not heard of again until it turned up, somewhat incomplete, a few years ago.

Bearing in mind that the overhead-camshaft engine had been designed in 1924 and developed to a pretty high state of tune even by 1930, doubts were beginning to form about its potential for further development without the need for a drastic redesign of the bottom end. This is understandable considering the relatively small main bearing dimensions, despite the fact that the narrowness of the crank gave a stiff assembly. Already it had been found necessary, through the preceding years, to increase the dimensions of the rockers, to reduce the base circle of the cam and thus reduce the operating speed of cam against skid (only on that first engine of 1925 were rollers used). Increased compression ratios had determined a need to increase the thickness of the cylinder base flange, and even then the odd blow-up had been caused by those pushing the ratio up to astronomical values. The likes of German hillclimbers, for instance, were the guilty parties; they caused the production of a cylinder with a base flange so thick that the retaining nuts were to be seen halfway up the cylinder.

Big-end assemblies had changed from $\frac{5}{16} \times \frac{5}{16}$ in. crowded rollers, to $\frac{5}{16} \times \frac{3}{8}$ and even $\frac{5}{16} \times \frac{7}{16}$ in. crowded rollers, until eventually they settled for a caged assembly using 16 $\frac{3}{16} \times \frac{9}{16}$ in. rollers. This was to form the basis of all single-cylinder Velocette big-ends from then on, except that the 500 with a bigger diameter assembly used 18 rollers, and the 250, 14 rollers. Con-rods were improved and became standard in basic design.

The question was whether or not the basic engine design would stand an increase in power output which, at that time, was 22 bhp. Phil Irving had the bright idea of assisting atmospheric pressure on an engine on the test-bed by using the blower of an industrial vacuum cleaner used around the works. Having duly rigged the unit with the aid of a biscuit tin, he soon proved that the little extra puff produced had a tremendous effect on the power output by upping it to 30 bhp. There was much jubilation in the engine test department, known to the staff as the 'din house'. This historic engine was numbered KTT 240.

By referring to the factory records, we can determine the name and address of the agent to whom a machine was invoiced on a particular date and subsequently, in the case of most of the customers in the UK, the name, address and date of invoice of the purchaser. In the case of KTT 240, the records merely state, 'Mr Willis'. No doubt, having built this particular engine, he decided it should form the basis of further experiment and the records were amended accordingly.

The drawing office was put to work, and Willis soon had a design laid out which incorporated a blower mounted low down in front of the engine and a large tank fitted to the rear chain stays on the right-hand side. This he called the 'Official Receiver'. The fuel tank was an unusual 'pistol-grip' type which had what was described by Willis as an 'udder', not unlike that used on the racing New Imperials of the period. It had the effect of increasing the capacity and keeping an

adequate head of fuel above the taps, blown motors being notoriously thirsty. The frame was basically standard KTT with some KTP-like lugs added to make use of the horizontal rear tank mounting arrangement on the two-port camshaft models available at the time. The gearbox used was the original Willis four-speeder with rack-and-pinion selector operation. Without going into a lot of detail, a great many problems had to be overcome, and through development the arrangement of the carburettor being between blower and engine was changed so that the blower was between carburettor and engine. Additionally, overheating caused problems until the original cast-iron head with coil valve springs was changed for a new alloy-bronze type with hairpins. This was to become standard on the Mk IV KTT later on. The gearbox was also changed for the new constant-mesh box which had been developed and proved satisfactory in production.

Apparently, there was a need to release the built-up gases that were a potential hazard to the rider and this was achieved by the fitting of a rather 'hush-hush' flame-trap device that Amal produced and which, I believe, had been developed for use by the Air Ministry. This was controlled by a valve lifter type lever, and was particularly useful when one considers the apparent delayed action of the throttle. There was no instant

Don Bain sitting astride what is undoubtedly an ex-works KTT, probably ridden by one of the Mitchell brothers who favoured Brampton forks. Just visible below the rider's toe is a vertical boss at the front of the gearbox end cover, which houses the rack for the selector drum mechanism of the Willis four-speed box. Note also the special thick-base cylinder with retaining nuts above fin no. 6. Works Velocettes invariably had flat alloy mudguard stays at the front. Bain won the 1932 Australian Junior TT on this occasion, on the old Vale Circuit at Bathurst, NSW (*Dennis Quinlan*)

throttle control because of the time taken by the gases to travel round the extensive plumbing. With the motor gassed up following rapid retardation for a corner, for instance, it was necessary to clear its throat, as it were. A quick tug on the lever released the 'pig's dollop', as Les Archer called it (though he was less polite), and it would be chiming again and away.

'Clara' (as the machine was known) was ridden in two TTs, once by Willis and once by the South African Lind, in addition to which she was ridden on at least one occasion by Archer in the Ulster when he retired with the remark, 'I am not a fish', referring to the typical Ulster weather. Archer, of course, rode 'Clara' on

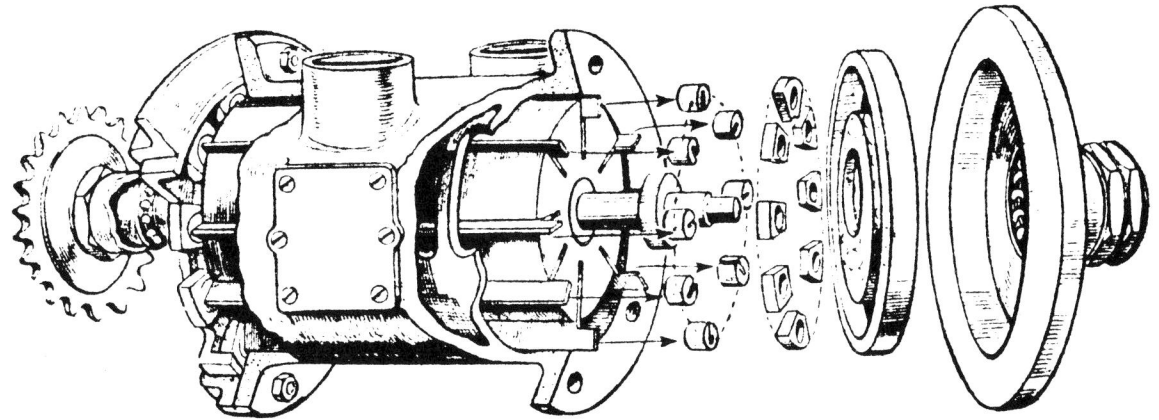

Above Harold Willis' 'Whiffling Clara' was built around this Foxwell supercharger, which was based on a vacuum cleaner designed for use in cinemas. Willis liked the method of blade location—at both ends— which minimised drag (*The Motor Cycle*)

frequent occasions at Brooklands. The only recorded trouble in these events was a broken frame in the TT and the loss of the carborettor main jet nut when ridden by Lind.

'Clara', we are sure, is still around. At least KTT 240 still exists. She doesn't sport a blower anymore, but she has that peculiar frame with an assortment of lugs for

Below A rare shot of 'Whiffling Clara' being refuelled during the Brooklands Grand Prix of 1933. Les Archer is bending over to check the sticking control valve below the pressure tank. It was necessary to clear the 'pig dollop', as Willis called it, at times during a race to release the pent-up gas. The whole operation is being overseen by Bemsee marshall Gus Grose (in trilby). Archer's mechanic and sometime sidecar passenger, Dennis Offord, is in charge of the pit whilst dad, J. C. Archer, carries the can. Note the funnel-like air intake above the blower and the 1932-type four-speed gearbox (*Les Archer*)

Whenever Harold Willis had a cold, he would take a trip in his old aeroplane, a de Havilland Moth, kept at Castle Bromwich. Willis called it 'Clattering Kate'. He would fly to Wales on holiday. He spoke the tongue like a native

mounting the big gas tank on the rear fork stays, and similar lugs for mounting the special oil tank on the other side. She has a one-off gearbox mounting lug, heavily reinforced, which is where one would imagine the frame broke in that TT outing—that lug being the weak spot of early KTT frames. She has the aluminium-bronze Mk IV type head and the bronze top and bottom bevel housings that Willis seemingly preferred to the earlier cast-iron housings or the bronze-bushed steel housings also used during that period and beyond. And, of course, she still sports that 'pistol-grip' fuel tank.

The original blower was produced by Daniel Foxwell Ltd of Heaton Chapel, Stockport. I believe the blower they produced was primarily designed for commercial vacuum cleaners, as used in cinemas and industrial premises, but Willis rather liked it because it had proved both efficient and reliable. It suffered only minimal frictional losses by way of its unique design of blade location within special end drums, thus eliminating the usual centrifugal pressures experienced with other basically similar designs.

Harold Willis was well-known as a dry humorist, and his comical sayings were legion.

He referred to the long-stroke KTT of 68 × 96 mm as the 'bicycle pump', and the Bentley and Draper sprung-framed machine of 1928 was called 'Spring Heeled Jack', after the comic-strip character of the period. 'Whiffling Clara' was so named because after she had been run and left leaning against the garage wall, peculiar wheezing sounds were emitted for a while as the pressure within the plumbing subsided. And, of course, the de Havilland Moth that he occasionally flew from Castle Bromwich was named 'Clattering Kate.' When someone asked what GTP stood for, he replied 'generally tight piston', and his own TT machine, to which he added the first positive-stop footchange mechanism in 1928, he called 'Roaring Anna'.

Aluminium bronze was referred to as 'doorknob metal', and magnesium alloy as 'electrified dirt'. 'Lamp post iron' meant cast-iron.

The one-piece racing seat was called 'The Loch Ness Monster', and a horse was a haymotor. A plug was a 'candle', a valve a 'nail', and a piston a 'bung'. An exhaust pipe was a 'long hole', and a cam a 'knocker'— hence the term 'double knocker'.

Detonation in an engine, which caused the eating away of a piston, Willis referred to as the 'death-watch beetle'.

It was Willis who introduced the hollow-stemmed, sodium-filled exhaust valve, and separate valve seats shrunk into the cylinder head, used on the works racing machines in the late 1930s, including the blown shaft-driven twin which he called 'The Roarer'.

Tragically, he died from meningitis, aged 39, on the eve of the 1939 Junior TT. The race was won by Stanley Woods on a machine on which Willis had lavished much care. In tribute, a bench seat was erected outside the works at Hall Green, funded by the management and workers at Veloce. After the works closed in 1971, members of the Velocette Owners' Club rescued the seat and had it re-erected at Ballaugh, on the course that Willis regarded as the ultimate Grand Prix circuit.

'Spring-heeled Jack', a works 1927 KSS no. 928, used experimentally during the 1928 practice period and equipped with Bentley and Draper rear suspension. It was put aside because it caused a few cornering problems! It still lives near Birmingham (*Phillip Tooth*)

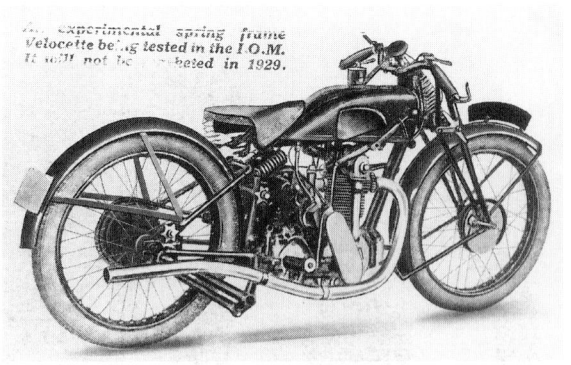

CHAPTER 5

Development of the Mk II KSS from the racing machines

So far I have mentioned a little of the development of the production overhead-camshaft models. Inevitably this has involved the racing machines, because racing, especially TT racing, improved the breed.

Detail development was taking place all the time—the fact that the Goodmans and Willis all rode the machines they produced, far enough and hard enough to get to know their every whim, ensured that any weakness was attended to. The con-rods and big-ends have been mentioned, the three-speed gearboxes, though adequate, left much to be desired, mainshafts were increased in diameter and the number of splines was changed from six to eight. Kickstarters, making use of spring-loaded rollers for engagement, were changed from one roller to three rollers and, finally, to two rollers, until eventually the four-speed box, introduced in 1932, had a completely different arrangement which was to remain unchanged; it was right, at last. Steering head dimensions were also increased in size from 1928 on because the old ex-two-stroke races used hitherto tended to work loose and chip. To overcome the occasional breakage of the malleable cast gearbox mounting lug, it was replaced by a forged lug in 1930 or thereabouts, which eradicated the problem.

In line with most other manufacturers, a variety of models was produced, from soft touring mounts to high-performance sports machines.

In 1930 the old company slipped up because they fell for the fashionable trend for upswept, twin exhaust pipes and produced the KTP, with a two-port head, pipes up or down, and coil ignition. It wouldn't pull the skin off a rice pudding, but it did have a new frame, with the forged gearbox mounting lug, a straight top tube and a very hefty saddle nose cum rear tank mounting lug, which was used on all subsequent overhead-camshaft machines until 1935.

During the period of severe austerity, it became necessary to review production methods and for the company to become more cost-effective.

Lighter and cheaper Webb pattern forks were chosen, and there was increased use of stampings for components such as wheel hubs and brake plates. The nice cast-alloy oil bath primary chaincase, used during

The standard Model K of 1927 (£65), which had a slightly increased fuel tank capacity over the previous year. Note the neat, black enamelled alloy primary chaincase

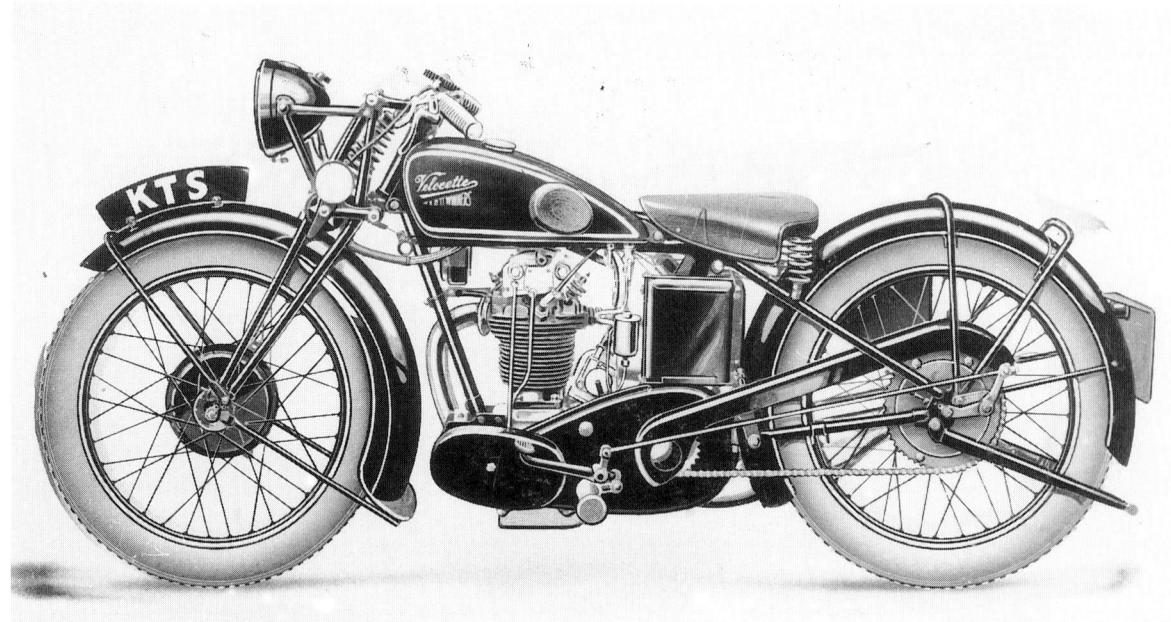

the 1920s and briefly during 1932 to use up old stock, had already departed, to be replaced by a neat and oil-tight two-piece pressing, held together by a multitude of $\frac{3}{16}$ in. screws.

Production rationalization effectively reduced the range to just three camshaft models for 1930: the KSS, KTT and, of course, the KTP. In the late 1920s, a wide number of variables had been available, such as the KS (sports), the KSS (super sports), KT (touring), KE (economy)—with the occasional KES (economy sports)— and the KN and KNS (normal and normal sports). There was also the rare KNSS (normal super sports)—some marked KCR used the latest cam and rocker design.

Show time in 1931 indicated the end of the touring KTP, which was replaced by the KTS, this being a touring

A KTP with a standard camshaft engine became the KTS, which replaced the twin-port model in 1932, initially making use of some of the old alloy primary chaincases. This is the 1933 model

version of the KSS, or a KTP with conventional engine. The three-speed gearbox continued with hand-change operation, but a four-speed version was at the design and development stage and was introduced on production models in late 1932, having as an optional extra what had become known as the Willis positive-stop foot-change. For the time being at least, this was mounted on the top of the end cover.

positive-stop mechanism was to become standard ware on all models to the end, in 1971. The discarded mechanism was sold to Scott.

No mention has yet been made of the pushrod models, which had been introduced by this time, but as we delve further into the development of the KSS, we will come across the 500 MSS which, for the sake of expedience, shared many features.

The MSS engine was based dimensionally on the factory racing 500s with a bore and stroke of 81×96 mm. The gearbox was that of the MK V KTT with an internal operating mechanism mounted behind the gear cluster, allowing for more clearance for the bigger crankcases.

This must have been a particularly difficult period for Veloce, and for most other manufacturers, too. The company's sales could not have been helped by the machines having a lower power output due to a lower compression ratio to make use of some early old-stock cylinder castings, and their small fuel tanks lacked the style of previous models. It wasn't until 1934, with the introduction of the deeper tank and the resulting cobby look, that things began to improve.

Also at this time, a further development of the four-speed gearbox had taken place. The use of its internal

Veloce publicity photo of a 1927 KSS, the first of the saddle tanks with a straight, lower tank tube and small steering head. It cost £75

Veloce publicity picture of the 1929 KN (Normal) Standard 350, which sold at £62 10s 0d. The 'water bottle' silencer, designed by Cheswick and Wright, was the forerunner of the fishtail

The MK V KTT also provided the geometry of the new model's frame and forks, which were much heftier than before, with a stout vertical saddle tube, a single front downtube and a full cradle into which the engine/gearbox could be dropped and firmly secured.

The new KSS engine, designated the MK II, quickly followed and dropped into the MSS frame. The new KTS, basically an MSS with KSS engine, was introduced at the 1935 show. Freshly-designed, with an all-alloy cylinder head and fully-enclosed valve gear, the KSS and KTS (both were stamped with the KSS prefix) had

The French-built Rovin, which appeared at the 1932 Paris show, appears to be based on the twin-port KTP engine and three-speed gearbox, both obsolete Veloce stock at that time. Since the KTP head (identifiable by the vertical finning between the exhaust ports) accommodated a flange-fitting carburettor, presumably this clipped-on carb is fitted to a flanged stub to clear the rather tall magneto. Quite a number of KTPs were supplied to order with magneto ignition (*Brian Woolley*)

crankcases with common fixing points to the MSS and shared the same frame and basic cycle parts.

The MSS and KTS used touring 19 in. wheels and heavily-valanced mudguards, but the KSS Mk II, introduced in early 1936, sported 20 and 21 in. wheels together with the narrower sports mudguards of the old Mk V KTT.

The hubs were basically those of the older KSS, being of the pressed type with brake plates produced in a similar manner. The rear brake anchor was improved by incorporating a 10 in. arm with a key slot locating with a button on the frame. This was another KTT feature which was both simple and foolproof.

The company were soon to introduce a new rear wheel with separate hub and brake drum and a substantial two-piece spindle, allowing the wheel to be removed while leaving the brake drum and drive in situ. This became a feature of all roadgoing models.

The double-damped forks were superseded by a single damper, as used on the discarded KTT Mk V.

The performance of the new KSS seemed slightly docile when compared with its predecessor, the machine being somewhat heavier for a start. However, the sweet refinement, allied to robustness and impeccable handling, endeared it to its new followers. The complete enclosure of the valve gear, with subsequent oil tightness, and the alloy head ensured that the owners of previous models were soon clamouring to buy this latest model. Some, no doubt, were disappointed, whilst others thought it was the best bike they had ever ridden.

I have briefly mentioned the MK II KTS, but it is well known that this was basically an MSS with a KSS engine. It was produced intermittently until 1939, and continued briefly post-war.

Occasional valve spring breakage had occurred with the camshaft engine, albeit only after considerable mileage, and usually with prolonged wide throttle openings. However, this tendency increased following the introduction of the MK II engine. Since the springs were fully enclosed, it became necessary to look closer at the problem, and it was found that spring surge was the cause.

Development of the Mk II KSS from the racing machines | 33

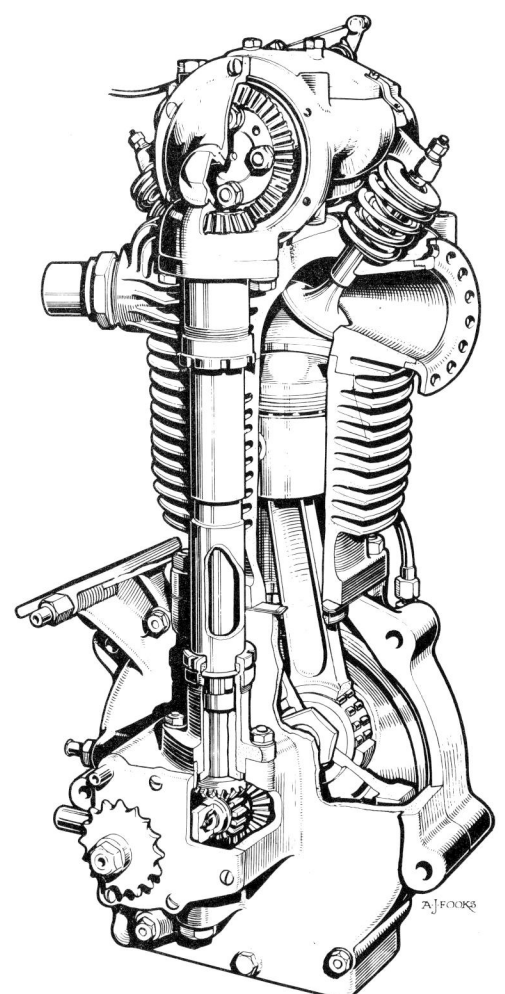

An almost standard KSS engine of around 1932 with a thin-necked cylinder and a caged big-end. Artistic licence allows for the double-row big-end rollers and machined con-rod, which were not quite correct (*The Motor Cycle*)

This was simply overcome by producing an inner spring that was wound in the opposite direction to the outer. The two springs fitted closely together, and the rubbing contact between them completely eliminated the vibrations which had caused the breakages. A suitably modified collar completed the set which, once proven, was applied to the rest of the single-cylinder range.

Further development on the MK II series included the replacement of the full-skirted piston with one of the slipper design, with a higher ratio. The cam was changed, and the lubrication to it, by a jet which occasionally became blocked, was superseded by the simple rotating groove feed, via the alloy camshaft bush as on previous production camshaft engines.

Provision for an additional breather was initially made in the form of a boss at the top end of the timing cover. Since this proved unnecessary, however, the boss was soon discarded.

Below **The 1931 catalogue picture of the KSS in full road trim, complete with electric lighting, electric horn and licence holder (£62 10s 0d). The speedometer illustrated (with drive enclosed in the front wheel brake) was 13s 6d extra if specified**

Above Only 33 Mk V KTT models were produced between October 1934 and October 1935. The cycle parts formed the basis of the MSS and KSS Mk II series, which allowed the use of existing jigs and fixtures until 1948

Below Evolved as a means of continuing the use of existing stock and tooling from a soon-to-be-discarded Mk V KTT, this MSS was introduced in March 1935 and extended the range of M-series production models. Its bore and stroke of 81 × 96 mm matched the Senior class works racing machines

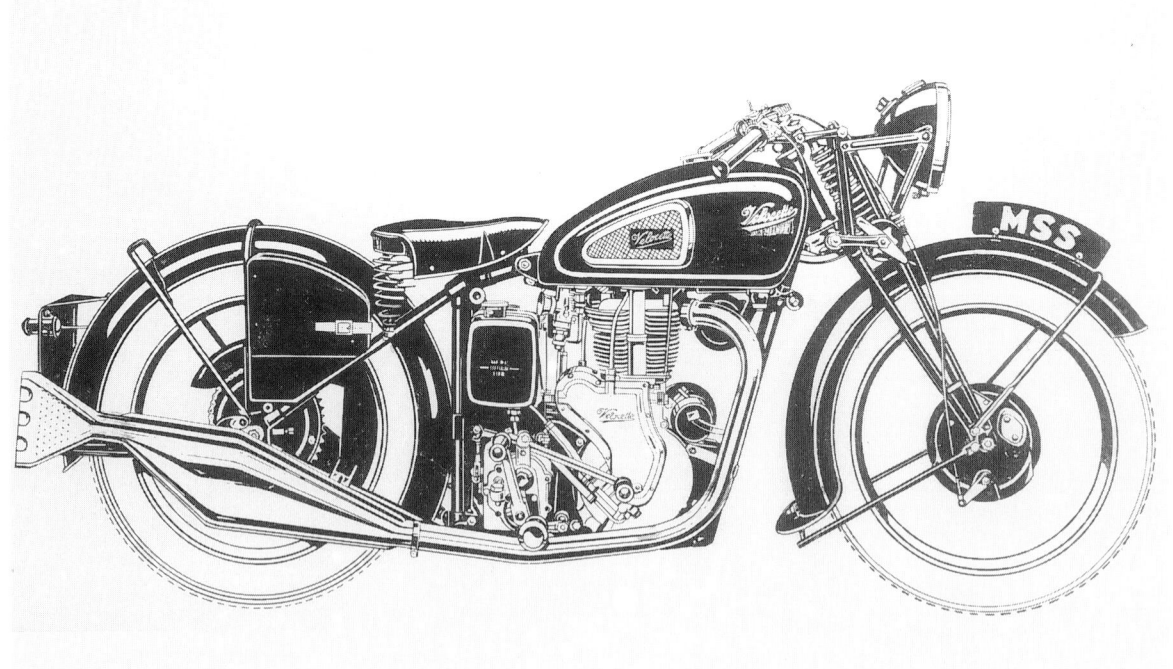

The KSS Mk II, introduced early in 1936, shared many cycle parts with the MSS and KTS. Being based on the discarded Mk V KTT, it was race-bred from its inception

CHAPTER 6

The introduction of the M-series

To recap a little, we have seen how the company grew from small beginnings, taking great pains to develop on positive lines, sound engineering principles and yet produce unique design features that were 'right'; the workforce was immensely loyal and protective of their peers. There was never, as far as I can ascertain, even during the most trying times, any thoughts of 'industrial muscle' being applied. Lighting within the factory in the 1920s, for instance, was by gas and even candle-light, and if a worker required another light to attend to something away from his workbench, he had to go to a Mr Hardy. This gentleman was, it seems, a general factotem about the factory and kept a tight rein on such things. He would give the worker a small piece of candle—not the whole candle, since that would have been extravagant.

Machine tools were driven by belts and overhead line shafts which, in turn, were driven by three 65 hp Dudbridge single-cylinder gas engines. It wasn't until Harold Willis arrived that they were to connect to an electrical lighting and power supply, having purchased

The ex-Waterloo Colliery, Browett and Lindley winding engine, reconditioned and converted for use in the power house by Harold Willis. It had a bore and stroke of 19 × 21 in.

two 400 hp Browett & Lindley engines which were apparently of enormous dimensions, having four cylinders of 19 in. bore with a 21 in. stroke. These were in poor condition when purchased, for they had seen much service as the main winding engines at Waterloo Colliery, and Willis was responsible for the reconditioning of one of these and its subsequent rigging to a

The only side-valve, single-cylinder Velocette produced experimentally in 1931, and discarded because it lacked torque. The frame came in handy for the immortal MOV

240 volt AC generator.

Willis, however, had miscalculated the weight of the flywheel, and his lifting tackle was not up to the job, so he left and went on holiday. I gather Eugene came to the rescue, and with the aid of chains and levers he manipulated it into position where it more or less fell on to the shaft.

Having gained such a tremendous reputation for fine workmanship and superbly engineered machines, the company rode out the Depression, won three TT races and numerous Grands Prix and captured a worldwide market with agents in just about every country of the globe. Percy Goodman's brother, Eugene, was works director, while sister Ethel was in charge of the purse strings, attending to the buying of raw materials, castings, and ancillary equipment, such as carburettors, magnetos, tyres, chains, etc, as well as being responsible for keeping the records of machines sold.

Left **The one and only Model M 350 side-valve engine in the custody of Ralph Seymour and on loan to the Stanford Hall Museum, near Lutterworth, Leics**

Below **A Veloce publicity picture of the first MOV, engine no. 1, frame no. 1, which was invoiced to Billy Tiffen in 1933. It's still around**

Above A dinner given by Eugene Goodman. Top table, standing under the lamp, Eugene and Mrs Goodman and, to their left, Harry Thorne and Mr and Mrs Chivers. Seated: Percy Goodman, Ethel and George Denly and Harold Willis. Front row seated is Billy Tiffen (*Veloce*)

We have seen a change of production from the two-stroke models to the overhead-camshaft range, the latter becoming the mainstay, while the two-stroke range diminished to just one model, the GTP. Eugene Goodman, as works director, meanwhile, had always dreamed that the company would produce a motorcycle that would suit everyone, a simple, well engineered machine that was relatively economical to manufacture with a sweet, yet docile, performance.

A surplus of old K components, such as cast-iron flywheels with a slim rod and crowded roller big-end, plus an abundance of low-crown pistons, was undoubtedly a contributory factor in choosing the design of a simple 350 sidevalve of low weight, thus qualifying for a reduced road tax levy in the middle of the early 1930s' Depression.

Phil Irving was responsible for the design of a prototype which also incorporated the reciprocating plunger oil pump from the old two-stroke and cleverly operated both valves with a single cam. A splined drive shaft for the engine shock absorber was used for the first time on this engine and was to become a standard feature on all subsequent designs emanating from the factory.

The assembly shop in late 1936, showing KSS, MOV, MAC, GTP, MSS and KTS machines being assembled

Right Machine shop C in 1932, showing the overhead line shafting. Three-speed and four-speed gears are in production. Cold saw and saw bars in foreground, others are Barber and Colman horizontal hobber, a Phanter vertical hobber and Brown and Sharpe gear and sprocket cutter, plus two Fellows gear shapers, according to Peter Goodman (*Betty Griffin*)

The unit was initially placed into a GTP frame for development purposes and while this work was taking place, the drawing office, under Irving's guidance, was busily engaged in laying out a suitable frame which had to be light and strong. It was of a full cradle design, based on known and proven Velocette steering geometry. The gearbox was mounted on a crosstube between the lower frame rails. Using this as a pivot point, with an adjuster securing the top mounting, provided a simple and effective method of maintaining primary chain tension.

The sidevalve engine, incorporating that now traditional narrow crank with inboard primary drive to match up with the existing GTP cycle parts, again continued those design features which had emerged back in 1913.

The prototype sidevalve machine was assembled late in 1931, development testing followed and while it proved to be light, easy to handle and docile, it lacked any sort of performance and was soon discarded. However, the idea of draughting a motorcycle-for-everyman was carried on by a young engineering apprentice, Charles Udall, while the rest of the staff were at the TT! Udall had joined the company in 1928 and had graduated through the repair shop, where much was to be learned about accessibility and the need for simplicity of assembly, to the drawing office where he had been engaged in draughting the ideas of Mr Percy, Mr Eugene and, indeed, Mr Willis.

Bearing in mind that the Veloce company had been involved in the production of Rolls-Royce engines during World War 1, and that Harold Willis was running a Riley car, which had a pushrod engine with camshafts high up in the block, hemispherical combustion chambers and good performance to boot, it is no wonder that the engine to replace the sidevalve should turn out to be the M, Overhead Valve of 68 × 68.25 mm bore and stroke dimensions—the bore size was probably determined from experience gained with the pre-war inlet-over-exhaust two-speeder. This machine remained simply the M model until the 350 MAC version arrived, when it became the MOV.

Despite its relatively small capacity, and a 250 in those days was looked upon as a mere toy, the prototype gave a good account of itself right from the outset. Timing gears were straight cut spur gears with an idler that was adjustable for mesh triangulated between the crankshaft gear and camwheel, for simple yet fine meshing, and the whole train was supported by a steel outrigger plate containing a trough in which a reservoir of oil collected to ensure adequate cam lubrication. The very short pushrods were operated by a pair of light, bottom rockers, sharing a common pivot point, and the top rockers, of equally light, yet immensely rigid, hollow construction, were supported simply between the two halves of the rocker box which, in turn, was bolted to the head at three points.

Lubrication was basically the old K-type gear pump, mounted on a cast-iron plate and located securely in the crankcase, albeit at 90 degrees to the crankshaft, from which it was driven by a skew gear. It gave positive lubrication to the big-end, camshaft and eventually rocker gear, with adequate scavenging of the usual relatively quick-circulation, dry-sump system. The magneto drive gear was made of Tufnol to keep tooth noise to a minimum. This new, little engine would fit the sidevalve frame, for which it was admirably suited.

It was decided to put this machine into production, and the first batch rolled off the production line at the end of May 1933, being invoiced to agents throughout the UK, and indeed worldwide, by early June. By the end of the year, some 430 machines had been sold. MOV no. 1 was used for development purposes and was to become the basis of a trials machine used successfully by that exclusive Velocette rider/agent from Carlisle, Billy Tiffen. It remains intact to this day.

As one might expect from the enterprising Goodman concern, the 250 was soon followed by a 350 (MAC) sharing many common features. This was achieved by simply stretching the stroke to 96 mm. After all, Willis had produced and tested in the 1929 Junior TT that long-stroke camshaft engine; and the old oil-cooled Bradshaw engine of the late 1920s with the same 68 × 96 mm bore and stroke, gave a good account of itself!

Production and tooling costs would be shared between the two models in the range, and soon they were rolling off the production line to be in service well before the 1933 motorcycle show, where they were to make quite an impact.

An excerpt from the show number of The Motor Cycle, dated 30 November, reads: 'World famous on road and track, Velocettes are well known as exponents of overhead camshaft. Recently however, the makers have introduced 250 and 350 pushrod engines. They have kept the pushrods short by raising the timing gear, and taken special pains to ensure mechanical silence. The valve gear is enclosed. The frame is of the cradle type, and both models are of typical Velocette excellence. The price of the 250, with electric lighting £47–10–0 and the 350 £49–10–0.'

Veloce had moved into a new era – here were machines that were light, easily handled and of good performance, all much to the chagrin of the overhead-camshaft brigade, and they were of clean lines and comparative simplicity. They were to become the mainstay of production for years to come. Inevitably, detail design changes were to take place in line with development since the company were always looking for improvement.

The timing gear train of straight cut gears, having been perfectly satisfactory on the prototypes, was to become embarrassingly noisy on production models. This was put down to the fact that the prototype crankcases, handcrafted with much more metal, absorbed the noise. Production cases, being somewhat lighter, acted as sounding chambers, so a fine helical tooth form was substituted whereupon the problem was eliminated. A damping plate was tried for a short period without success while tooling up for the helical gears. Later the tooth angle was to be changed from 15 to 11 degrees, before finally settling at 16 degrees,

The last of the open-frame cammies, the iron-engined KTS of 1935 (*Velocette Owners' Club*)

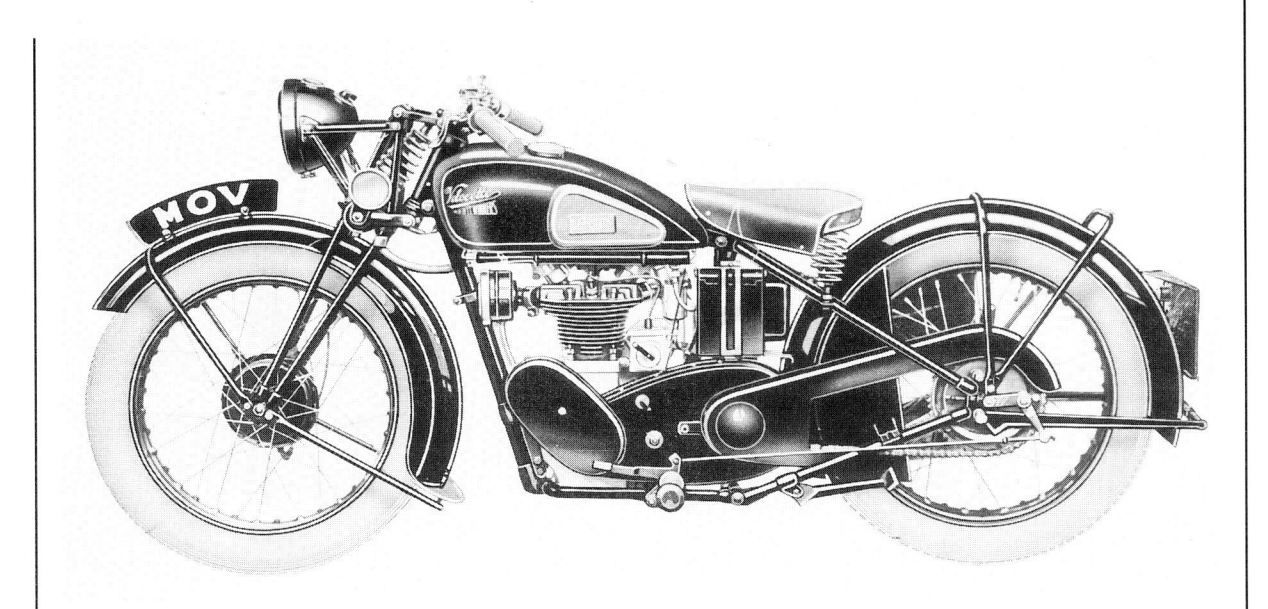

Driveside of the 1933 MOV no. 1

which was to remain to the end of the line in 1971.

Common components in the MOV and MAC were plentiful. They shared most cycle parts, the gearbox and engine features such as the crankcase, bore size and piston, valves, valve gear, etc. The heads, however, while being interchangeable, differed in the size of the inlet tract, and obviously the flywheels differed in stroke. The con-rod of the 250 was based on that of the early camshaft model and, indeed, the KTT, having the same centre-to-centre measurement, but it used a 14-roller caged big-end assembly, whereas the MAC rod, needing to be that much longer (some $\frac{3}{8}$ in. to be precise), used the 16-roller caged big-end inherited from the KSS and KTT. This same rod was also to be used in the KSS Mk II when introduced late in 1935.

Shared primary drive features of the two models differed from the overhead-camshaft machine, yet cut the cost of production. Use was made of some old stock, since the single-plate clutch chosen was simply that discarded in favour of the more robust multi-plate following that initial TT win in 1926. It used a much simpler shock absorber arrangement on the engine shaft and incorporated a splined mainshaft. This design emanated from the side-valve prototype, where the engine sprocket located directly up to the drive side main bearing, and a five-lobe (later to be changed to a three-lobe) cam, was splined to the shaft and retained by a flanged nut and spring. It was effective, but because the side thrust was loaded directly at the bearing inner race, there was always the tendency for the bearing to move on the shaft and wear a groove in the flywheel on later high-performance models, and for that matter gradually to tug the shaft out of the flywheel, despite the pegged interference fit of the two. The depth of the drilled and tapped hole and, consequently, the length of peg differed depending on whether or not the flywheels were for standard production or the racing models.

By contrast, the old K-type shock absorbers, designed to do the job when cost was of relatively little importance, consisted of a substantial boss fitted to a plain taper on the mainshaft. Percy Goodman was of the opinion that there was no need for the addition of a key, since the taper was of sufficient dimensions to hold firm if correctly assembled clean and dry; and he was right. To the boss was fitted the engine sprocket, which was free to rotate, and there was a fibre friction damper interposed between the two pressure faces. Against the sprocket was located a sliding dog, splined to the main boss and a five-lobe cam locating with the sprocket.

Added to it was a large-diameter, square-section coil spring and retaining ring, with a fine left-hand male thread, to the inside diameter on the outer end of the boss. The ring enclosed the main nut flange, thus facilitating easy removal of the whole assembly when required. This arrangement, when securely fitted—a 'hammer-tight' form of spanner was provided in the toolkit—was extremely effective, and provided there was a minimum of ten thou. between the back of the boss face and the crankcase, it worked completely independently of the main shaft and bearings. It did, however, need to be assembled and maintained with oil, which is why Veloce chose to take a drain pipe from an overspill cavity in the cambox to this assembly in preference to taking the feed to the exhaust valve guide.

In those days, any valve fortunate enough to receive positive lubrication was invariably the inlet, since this was kept washed dry by the incoming charge of

Above Fettling shop in 1937, showing a batch of KSS/MSS frames having been bronzed up and a pile of flywheels over to the left awaiting heat treatment. Next door and far left are the polishing spindles used prior to plating. Obsolete early frames and back stands are over to the right. Three generations of the Ridge family were the mainstays in the frame building shop (*Betty Griffin*)

combustible gasses, whereas the exhaust valve was considered sufficiently well cared for by the oil-laden exhaust, particularly so in the case of wet-sump engines which were prevalent in the 1920s.

In my opinion, however, there is a definite advantage in drilling the exhaust valve guide and lubricating directly via an $\frac{1}{8}$ in. OD copper pipe from that cambox overspill cavity. Valve guide wear then becomes minimal. The crankshaft shock absorber can be lubricated periodically with an oil can.

The primary chaincase used on the MOV/MAC was of the now well established pressed-steel type with paper jointing and a quantity of 2BA screws to hold it together but, again, the company had been expedient in using the very same tooling as that used on the camshaft model from 1933 on. The only difference arose in the location of the dynamo drive cover retaining pins, since the dynamo was fitted well to the front on the pushrod models, as opposed to being straight ahead on the pre-1936 camshaft machines. Of course, there was no need for the two holes amidships where footrest bar and brake pedal pivot shaft protruded on the earlier model, but simply one hole to facilitate the clamping of the cases—with a suitable tube for keeping them apart while anchoring the assembly firmly to the driveside engine plate. All details, perhaps, but part of development and cost effective production engineering at which Veloce was good.

Apart from the introduction of an automatic advance and retard system and other slight modifications,

Right 'Dan's Do' was a great occasion in the 1920s and early 1930s. Dan Bradbury, the Sheffield dealer, held an annual event at the ballroom in Glossop Road. As a major shareholder in both Veloce and Norton, he carried some weight in the trade. This photo, taken outside his premises in Sheffield, shows, left to right, Freddie Hicks, Percy Goodman, Harold Willis, Percy (Tim) Hunt, Dan Bradbury and Charlie Dodson

such as the elimination of an oil feed to the base of the cylinder, a change of engine breather from a clack valve to a hole in the driveside mainshaft, and variation in angle of tooth form of the helical gears as previously mentioned, these models were to remain basically little changed through the 1930s.

Just as there was a change to a quickly-detachable rear wheel on the new MSS and KSS referred to earlier, likewise the two smaller models were to benefit from the same feature. From the first MOV produced to the end of the same year some 430 models were sold, whereas production of the MAC, which came along a bit later, was only 72 to the end of 1933.

BRADBURY.
THE UNAPPROACHABLE
Norton
MOTOR CYCLES
O.H.V. MODEL

CHAPTER 7

Development of the M-series

It was usual for the next year's model changes to be introduced around September/October, after the works' annual holiday, so we can assume that 1934 production included some machines made in 1933. Therefore, from MOV no. 1 to 30 September 1934, and there is a line drawn across the record book at that point, that first year's production was some 1039 machines. For the MAC, from its introduction at the end of October 1933 to 30 September 1934, and again a line is drawn across the book, the number is a mere 630 machines.

The following year, however, the figures are reversed to some extent, because we find 624 MOV models produced from the end of October 1934 to the same period in 1935, whereas MACs accounted for 851 machines produced. In both cases, however, the records are frequently marked '1936 model' well before the end of September model change date appears, which suggests that some agents had more pull than others by commanding the very latest specification to satisfy their customers. We find the same system applied to the new MSS introduced in May 1935, for the 1936 season, whereas the Mk II KSS and KTS were not produced until February 1936, although a KTS prototype existed in October 1935, using MSS parts. This serves as another example of Veloce's policy of rationalization of production. One model led naturally on to another.

The M-series models had been established well and truly, and with the 500 version added to the range, Veloce Ltd were in a favourable position to accommodate the requirements of most riders, including those of the family-man, since this beefy yet docile pushrod engine was ideally suited to pulling a sidecar.

The 500 cc MSS bore and stroke dimensions, at 81 × 96 mm, were identical to those used on the works Senior race machines, as indeed were the flywheel blanks and big-end assembly, still with 18 caged rollers. While the timing side mainshaft and matching ball race remained dimensionally like those of the MOV and MAC models, and indeed as those of the K-series, though the shafts differed in length between the K and M, the drive side mainshaft was a full 1 in. in diameter and was supported in a double-row lipped roller bearing like the works racing 500s.

The by now obligatory speedometer is evident, while chrome rims with black centres suggest that this is a 1937 KSS Mk II. Sweet and docile, yet capable of being cruised in the high 70s, they were a joy to ride

Veloce publicity photo of the 1938 MSS

The design of the whole engine was based on that of the two smaller ones with a good many parts, such as timing chest components and oil pump, being interchangeable. The cam differed though, being designed specifically to suit the required power characteristics of its 500 cc. The piston was fully skirted with a low crown and two compression rings plus two stepped scrapers. The inlet tract was small at 1 in., and the use of a special adjustable throttle stop in conjunction with an automatic advance/retard unit, developed jointly by Veloce and BTH specifically for this model, ensured easy starting and clean, reliable, yet soft, low-down power.

The model was capable of a good 80 mph plus with nothing more than a whisper from the valve gear, a bit of suction noise from the carburettor and that characteristic low subdued exhaust note from the fishtail silencer. This was manufactured by Cheswick & Wright Ltd, whose motto was 'silence is golden'. They had developed the original 'water bottle' silencer for Veloce in the mid 1920s. The system of baffles used in this and subsequent Velocette fishtail silencers proved effective in reducing noise levels while marginally improving performance, quite apart from producing that distinctive note.

One other feature that had been introduced with the MSS and which was to continue on all models up to the

The 1938 KTS—wheel rims with black centres were only used in 1937

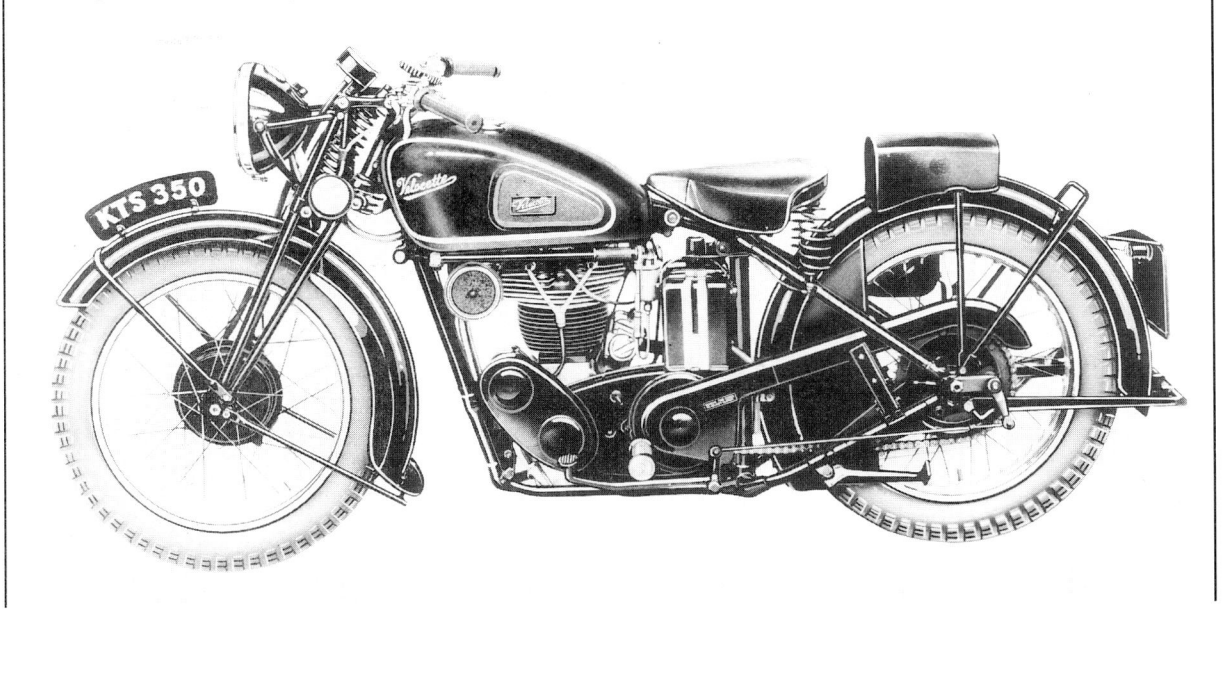

war was the push-pull twistgrip. This was free to rotate on the handlebars, without the need for any form of tensioning device (other than an anti-rattle spring and pad) to keep the throttle set, since there was no provision for a throttle return spring. The cable was a special, heavy-duty Bowden, more the size of a speedometer cable, which was securely clamped at both ends of the outer between adjustable split ferrules. Such a device sounds most unnecessary, but once one had become used to such a nicety, which allowed a rider fingertip control, one didn't want any other. It became yet another refinement for which the Velocette was noted.

The crankcase breather, from the early K-models had been in the form of a hole through the drive side mainshaft, terminating radially on the outside of the main bearing location, 180 degrees of which was covered by an extended boss to prevent ingress of foreign bodies on the upward stroke. This was not used initially on the MOV and MAC, a clack valve being used instead. However, the MSS used the hole through the mainshaft system (which had continued unchanged on all the overhead-camshaft models, except that the extended boss was dropped when the redesigned shock absorber became standard), with the bonus of lubricating the moving parts of the shock absorber. This

A rather nice publicity shot of George Beresford, *The Motor Cycle* artist, with a 1939 MSS and Watsonian Continental sidecar. We know it's 1939 because the front brake adjuster has moved down the forks and on to the brake plate. New, stronger, fork links would also have been fitted at that time (*Chris Wright*)

The 1938 MAC. In keeping with Veloce practice, it was sold complete with pillion and footrests

arrangement subsequently became standard on the MOV and MAC models, too.

Another detail worth mentioning is the gearchange operation. A long tubular lever, which was adjustable, was clamped to a substantial pivot shaft. An arm with an elongated slot was used to provide further adjustment by varying the arc in relation to the rider's foot. Emanating from the need to use a down-for-bottom and up-for-top arrangement on the old three-speed K-box, this system was continued on all subsequent gearboxes up to the war years, except for the KTT. In this case, although the same camplate was used, the lever pivot was mounted to the rear of the box and this had the effect of reversing the arrangement. In due course, however, with the trend towards up-for-bottom and down-for-top, all post-war Velocettes were to have a complete reversal of the pre-war settings which, in some cases, meant redesigning the camplate. On the MAC and MOV, the desired effect was achieved by a gear lever pivot redesign incorporating an extended engine bolt, suitably drilled for a greaser, on which the lever operated, and a spring-loaded ball locating on the actuating arm. This was a direct result of the need to standardize WD-issue machinery. Phil Irving was responsible for the rearrangement, following the supply of an initial batch of machines to the MoD with the original, pre-war equipment; confusion among new recruits was rife.

Veloce did not list their engine and frame numbers logically—engine numbers were consecutive, frame numbers diverse, to say the least. For instance, MOV engine no. 1, being a prototype, was matched with frame no. 1, however engine no. 2 was fitted into frame no. 19 and frame no. 2 appeared with engine no. 14. Right through the factory records this form appears and is doubtless due to the fact that frames were produced in batches and numbered consecutively prior to enamelling, after which they were put into store and taken out at random. Later in MOV production, following the introduction of the MAC model, it is not uncommon to find what should have been an MOV frame by consecutive numbering fitted to an MAC.

In concluding this chapter, a couple of power output figures might be of interest. Engine number MAC 6476 was bench-tested by Phil Irving on 9 February 1940 and gave 15.7 bhp at 5500 rpm. A few days later, MSS 4447 gave 20.8 bhp at the same revs.

CHAPTER 8

KTT—Kamshaft Tourist Trophy

Probably the most famous of all Velocettes was the legendary KTT, which was arguably the first commercially practicable racing machine. The KTT was a direct result of TT wins in 1926 and 1928, when Veloce announced that aspiring TT entrants could purchase a replica of the 1928 TT winning machine which had been ridden by Alec Bennett.

Harold Willis had himself taken part in competition to the extent that he was to finish second in the Junior of both 1927 and 1928, and he was responsible for the development and preparation of factory models for international competition. Already well established as manufacturers of a fine range of two-stroke models and by this time having quickly built up a fine reputation with the advent of the Model K 350 overhead-camshaft design introduced in 1925, the company had the confidence to back up their TT wins by laying down a batch of replica models.

Announced at the 1928 Olympia Show, the new TT machine was described as being 'an exact replica of Alec Bennett's TT winning mount'. It had a specially tuned engine with stiffened crank and a special cam giving a top speed of 85 mph. Mention was also made of an additional pump to force oil into the cambox. In fact, the pump referred to was an additional scavenge pump to take oil from the cambox and return it directly to the oil tank instead of to the crankcase, as was standard K practice, via a clack valve arrangement. This pump had been introduced on the works TT models and found to be a definite improvement.

Olympia Show 1929, Percy Goodman seated, the TT trophy is on the table. This picture was one of three removed from Bertie Goodman's office on the factory closure (*Veloce*)

Harold Willis (left) was famed for his sayings and descriptions of parts. 'Don't believe everything you hear and only half of what you see,' Willis would say. And he added, 'The quickest way to do a job is get it right the first time.' By contrast, Percy Goodman (right) was quiet and retiring, a perfect gentleman and a genius

The term 'exact replica' was not quite correct either, since lessons learned and, no doubt, selling aids were incorporated in the new model. For example, mention of the stiffened crank really meant that the hitherto smooth crankcase exterior of the previous models (indeed, the 1928 TT machines) was to give way to a crankcase with extra stiffening webs which were to become an identifiable feature of all KTTs from then on. These webs, incidentally, were added to the original K-model case patterns, which were further modified

The first KTT, introduced for the 1929 season and based on Alec Bennett's 1928 TT winner. They were sweet, fast and reliable and could be ridden on their wheel rims

afterwards. This made it necessary to manufacture a new set of casting patterns for the production KSS when a reduced bottom bevel chest was introduced in 1929.

KTT flywheels, unlike the standard models, were in steel with a con-rod machined all over and dispensing with the use of a small-end bush. This allowed the hefty 0.8233 in. diameter gudgeon pin to run directly within the rod without any problems. This is where the odd pin size came from!

A new type of cam gave a more suitable valve timing for competition work in conjunction with a long straight-through exhaust pipe. Rockers, which had previously been known to flex or break, were stiffened, and the exhaust valve reduced in size to suit a special cylinder head with a slightly shallower combustion chamber. This gave a compression ratio of 7.5:1 on 50/50 petrol/benzole. An alternative piston was listed for a ratio of 9:1 on Discol–dope fuel.

Initially, valve collets were of the three-groove variety, although these, were soon changed to a single-groove type. Earlier K-model collets had a multitude of small grooves for location, somewhat reminiscent of a 26 tpi thread!

A catalogue picture of the 1930 KTT. The 1929 models had their tool boxes on the one-piece, rear mudguard stays

The gearbox of the new TT model was basically the three-speed type, but with a special close-ratio cluster. Gearchanging was achieved with the new positive-stop arrangement, which Harold Willis had introduced for the 1928 TT and which was to set all other manufacturers working on the same lines.

The all-welded fuel tank had an extended filler neck and 1 in. bore balance pipes down below to join the two pannier halves and facilitate quick filling. An oil tank of one gallon capacity was mounted on the saddle tube and supported underneath. The filler was on the nearside so that the rider could have the cap off ready for a refill as he approached the TT pit area. A tap was fitted to the tank to prevent seepage of lubricant past the oil control valve into the sump, which was a good idea, provided one remembered to turn it on before starting the engine. Many people don't even today!

The rider's footrests were rear set, and mounted on substantial brackets running between the rear engine plates and the forward end of the rear chain stays. These brackets carried the rear brake pedal on the left-hand side, and also stiffened the main frame. Frame flexing had been known in the gearbox mounting lug area, resulting in some breakages.

All other basic components were standard KSS, except the front forks which were to become a distinguishing feature of the KTT.

Strutted Webb forks, originally designed to give additional rigidity for use on sidecar machines, were fitted. These forks were extremely strong, which was a selling point, although they suffered the disadvantage of adding to the unsprung weight.

One of the Webb family, over in the Island for the 1925 sidecar TT, was somewhat horrified to witness the considerable flexing that took place on fork blades when cornering an outfit at speed. On his return to Birmingham, the factory was instructed to produce a pair of forks with additional struts in an endeavour to eliminate such bending. The forks were eventually offered for use with sidecars and speedway and other track machines, but the extra few pence added to the

Willis sits astride his naked record breaker in 1928 trim with the new stronger frame, a pair of strutted Webb forks and a piece of bent, flat strip (just visible) as the only means of braking, coming directly off the rear brake plate (*Velocette Owners' Club*)

The first Japanese rider to compete in the TT was K. Tada, Veloce's Tokyo agent, who finished 15th in the 1930 Junior (*Veloce publicity*)

Webbs eventually talked their way out of continuing production. Instead, they offered a much heavier standard blade for the MSS and KSS, which became the basis of subsequent forks for the KTT.

However, when using the strutted forks, a special front brake plate with an extended fulcrum pivot bearing was produced so that the fulcrum boss would clear the lower ends of the additional fork strut. The front brake drum was increased in width to facilitate the use of a 1 in. wide shoe instead of the standard $\frac{3}{4}$ in. item.

KTT no. 1 (engine only) was supplied to an agent in south Durban in October 1928, and KTT no. 2 (a complete machine) was sent to the Milan Show in December. I assume that this was the Olympia Show model. Approximately 100 machines were despatched during June, up to TT time.

The works team for 1929 was Harold Willis, Alec Bennett and Freddie Hicks, a new boy who had made his name as a dashing rider at Brooklands. He was particularly noted for the meticulous preparation of his machinery (which he always insisted on building himself) as well as being a member of the successful record-breaking team that included Willis and J. A. Baker in 1928. Additionally, private runners (including

initial purchase price to a manufacturer was such that few, in fact, were to take it on.

However, Veloce used a pair on their successful Montlhéry record breaker in 1928 and Percy Goodman rather liked the idea of incorporating them on the new KTT introduced for 1929. Certainly, they added a sort of charisma, so a deal was arranged and the strutted forks became standard ware on all KTT models until the mid 1930s.

They were rather difficult to manufacture, however, and almost impossible to straighten once bent, so

Broadsliding *par excellence* by Dr J. Kelly Swanston on KTT 128 at Petter Sands, Scotland, during the Rudge Whitworth meeting in June 1930 (*Alastair Alexander*)

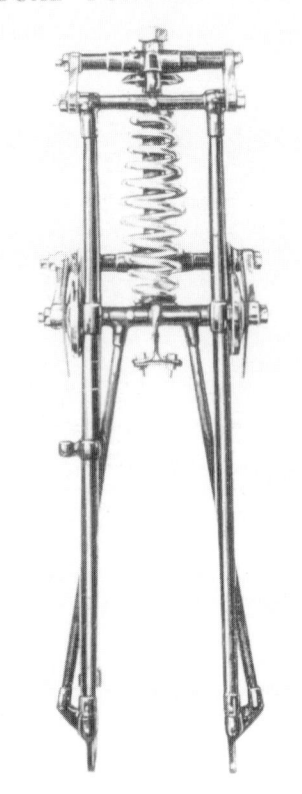

Publicity brochure for the Webb dual-purpose strutted fork that became a distinguishing feature of the Velocette KTT

Don Hall, the South African who had won the 200-mile South African TT) made a total of eight machines entered in the Junior race. Six of these machines were to contest the Senior too.

New boy Hicks, third in the early stages of the race behind Jimmy Simpson (AJS) and Stanley Woods (Norton), was to find himself leading by lap three, Jimmy having blown up his motor, while Stanley had also become sidelined with mechanical bother. Bennett was lying second and Handley (AJS) third. Willis lay fourth, but was soon to fall and damage the bike. Handley broke the lap record, passing Bennett in the process. Hicks responded by turning up the wick still further, raising the record and putting himself some 40 seconds in hand, despite clouting the wall at Glen Helen on the last lap. He was to become a popular winner in what was only his second TT—he was fifth in 1928—when Veloce took the team prize. Bennett finished third, with other production KTTs in fourth, sixth, tenth and eleventh spots, while Hicks was to finish fifth on the same 350 in the Senior race.

Freddie Frith was to make his first trip to the Island that year for the Manx GP in September, as mechanic to Eric Foreman of Grimsby, who had entered a new KTT, no. 106. Freddie was so fired with enthusiasm that he entered for the 1930 event in which he was to finish in third place in the Junior—Velocette took the first eight places in this event.

KTT production continued throughout 1929 as the demand grew on the strength of the successes gained throughout the season, and in the latter part of the year an increasing number were invoiced to agents overseas. Some 180 machines were produced and sold by the end of the year, most of which were prepared for the following season of events.

Here, at last, was a machine that had been carefully built, was soundly engineered and had road holding of such a forgiving nature that it was to put many a young lad on the ladder to stardom. Used intelligently and not meddled with, it could be relied upon to give results far beyond the wildest dreams of many a new boy and to rejuvenate a good many older hands, too.

The Velocette three-speed gearbox, directly descended from the two-stroke, was probably the Achilles' heel of the model. However, with the TT close ratios and the Willis positive-stop footchange, cog swapping could be carried out quickly and relatively noiselessly. Furthermore, the 1930 TT box benefited by the use of a larger diameter $\frac{13}{16}$ in. ten-spline shaft, which was more capable of coping with the job in hand than the old six-

Left Another fine picture of Australian Don Bain after his success in the first Australian Junior TT at Bathurst, New South Wales. The machine is an ex-works experimental machine with Bentley and Draper front forks, a special cylinder and a special Willis-designed four-speed gearbox (*Dennis Quinlan*)

The inscription on a magnificent solid silver rosebowl, proudly displayed in the Goodman household, reads as follows:
'Presented to P. J. Goodman as a mark of appreciation for the wonderful achievement of the VELOCETTE, in the 1929 TT.

RIDERS
F. G. Hicks—Winner

A. Bennett	F. G. Craner	T. Simister
W. S. Braidwood	D. Hall	E. R. Thomas
S. A. Crabtree	J. W. Shaw	H. J. Willis'

Percy Goodman was a quiet, shy man who found it somewhat embarrassing to be lifted shoulder high by those present shortly after this photograph was taken. Left to right: Willis, Percy Goodman, Thomas, Dan Hall (possibly), Simister, Freddie Craner and Jimmy Shaw—seated, of course, is Freddie Hicks on the winning machine

spline shaft of $\frac{3}{4}$ in. diameter, since this tended to suffer from severe flexure and occasional breakage under extreme conditions.

Aware that some of the opposition at least were using four-speeders, Willis set to and produced his own box with this number of ratios. It was quite unlike anything Veloce had produced before, or since for that matter, and incorporated a four-speed cluster operated through a barrel-type selector shaft, similar to contemporary BSA mechanisms and, of course, later Burman gearboxes. The selector shaft, in turn, was operated by a rack-and-pinion arrangement in conjunction with his own, Veloce patent, positive-stop mechanism. Detail design drawings were produced by the young Charles Udall.

The prototype four-speeder, of which I believe two were made, was undoubtedly a step in the right direction, although the ratios were not ideal and it lacked the constant-mesh of all gears (the next stage of development, as is turned out). In consequence, the gear teeth of second and third suffered from the crash operation that had existed with the old three-speeder.

At about this time, Sturmey Archer produced a superb, cleverly designed constant-mesh four-speed gearbox with an internal camplate. It incorporated a toothed quadrant that meshed with a small-diameter gear wheel combined with the camplate and thus was capable of traversing the whole range of ratios with minimal movement of the operating lever.

Like any development engineer worth his salt, Willis, and no doubt Percy Goodman himself, realized the advantages of the internal camplate mechanism. He took it a stage further by simplifying the method of

54 | Velocette

Left The author riding KTT 179—the first Velocette he ever rode, as a schoolboy, and which he later acquired for £5. Subsequently, it gave much pleasure and success in early vintage road racing events. The machine is now campaigned with equal success by his elder son, Grahame. The special Willis rack-and-pinion-operated four-speed gearbox is in evidence in this picture

Below The experimental supercharged 350, which was nicknamed 'Whiffling Clara' by race boss Harold Willis. In her earlier form, with cast-iron head and coil springs, she would eat sparking plugs by making them incandescent, which kept her going long after the electrode had burned away. Here she is with a bronze head and hairpin valve springs. Engine number KTT 240 can clearly be seen on the crankcase in the original photograph. The machine is still around (*EMAP*)

ously it had taken the form of an adjustable, indeed detachable, lug. Likewise, a froth tower was added to the top of the oil tank, which overcame the tendency for excessive amounts of oil to pour down the breather pipe on to the rear chain and even on to the tyre.

One significant improvement that took place late in 1930, however, was the introduction of a barrel with a thick base to give added rigidity where it was most needed, especially when a machine was set up with a high compression ratio for use with alcohol fuels. The original K-KSS cylinders of the late 1920s had been carefully designed to give as much strength as possible around the area of neck between the lower fins and base flange, since it was an obvious potentially weak point. Veloce had retained the flange radial thickness fore and aft, as well as port and starboard, where most other manufacturers reduced it to form a neck, yet this only highlighted the need to increase the flange

operation using, in effect, a peg in a T-slot to achieve the same end. By redesigning the gear cluster to give constant-mesh, yet retaining the short rigid shafts and gear centres of the original Willis four-speed box, Veloce were to produce a gearbox that was to remain virtually unchanged from then on because it was right.

Other developments of the KTT also took place, in the quest for improvement, although these were marginal detail changes. For example, the saddle nose pivot lug was positively fixed for 1931, whereas previ-

Left J. H. Blythe of Kircaldy proudly displays his silver cup for 12th place in the 1932 Junior Manx, which he achieved riding this Mk III KTT no. 344 (*Alastair Alexander*)

thickness to a full 1 in. before the weak point was eliminated.

At this time, too, the traditional Velocette big-end was introduced. The original crowded roller assembly, which had been changed in detail only between 1925 and 1930 and which still had been found lacking in reliability and longevity, gave way to a new design with an increased roller track diameter, a duralumin bearing cage (located on the pin itself), and carrying 16 $\frac{3}{16} \times \frac{9}{16}$ in. needle rollers. The design was an immediate success and was to become standard on all models from then on except, of course, that the pin diameter and, in consequence, the number of rollers varied from model to model depending on capacity.

For good measure, con-rods were also beefed up, not only on the racing models, but on the touring K and later M, which were to enjoy the benefits of a good quality forging that, in fact, produced a stronger rod than that of the KTT. The latter had a limited life, as has been found by those continuing to run the old Mk IV and V rods in more recent years.

KTT production for 1930 commenced at no. 180 and ended at 270, which was listed as an engine only. This was sent to South Africa for Don Hall, one of the many colonial riders who enjoyed a little support from the company. Some of the other names are interesting, too. Craners Garage of Derby supplied a machine for Frank Swindells, Fred Craner having been the prime moving force behind Donington Park and Derby Motor Club. Chepstow Motors of London features regularly and supplied winning machines to the late D. J. Pirie. Tommy Blumfield, the Birmingham hub manufacturer, took delivery of a roadgoing KTT to KN spec; Tommy

Above Veloce had their own loading platform adjacent to the works. Eight standard KTTs are lined up for despatch to the 1933 TT. A 'works' bike is about to go up the ramp. They finished in fourth, fifth, sixth, seventh, eighth, ninth, tenth, 13th, 14th, 15th and 16th places (*Goodman Collection*)

Les Archer astride KTT 402, the MK IV model with which he had just won both Junior and Senior Brooklands Grand Prix races in July 1933. It was on this machine that he gained the honour of being the first rider to cover over 100 miles in one hour on a 350 cc machine on a British track, when he took first place in the Hutchinson 100 event the following month (*Les Archer*)

A Mk IV KTT, no. 502, belonging to a gentleman in West Germany. This one has a 19 in. rear wheel—originally it was 20 in. The weak point, if any, was the gearbox mounting which stressed the gearbox shell that tended to crack

rode in the TT in 1912 on a machine bearing his own name, and was for many years, I understand, the rep for Homer petrol tanks.

Other well known names include Somerville Sykes, a Brooklands *habitué*, Billy Tiffen, Austin Munks, Tommy Simister, and Bert Parrish of Grimsby for Eric Foreman, with whom Freddie Frith was to travel as mechanic to the Manx. Harold Hartley of Hull, noted Rudge exponent, also took delivery of a KTT (no. 130), a machine which is now in the hands of David Ward from Rugby.

The Cann Brothers, Maurice and his brother Tommy, were to feature prominently on KTTs in the very first race meeting at Donington Park. KTT 241 was secured by dealers Earnshaws of Huddersfield for one of the Mitchell brothers for the TT, and 240 was a spare machine for Harold Willis which, with the registration number OG 1965, was to become the experimental blown 'Whiffling Clara'. Contemporary photographs of 'Clara', however, show her wearing OX 8922 which was the number from Willis' 1928 TT mount—the practice of swapping plates was not uncommon in those days. Freddie Frith took delivery of his first KTT, no. 256, in July 1930 in readiness for the Manx, while Lamacraft collected the last of the official 1930 stock, no. 266, complete with lighting set in October of the same year. A fair percentage of these models were sold in full road trim, while in accordance with usual Velocette practice, a good many more were distributed throughout the world.

Production for 1931 officially commenced with KTT 267 in November 1930, the last official 1931 machine being KTT 333 in September. Bearing in mind that some were listed as engines only, the quantity per season was diminishing. The technical specification remained basically the same, except in a few cases, particularly the works or semi-works models to which larger petrol tanks were fitted.

Some of the riders' names mentioned previously appear again, since they took delivery of up-to-date models, while additional notable names begin to appear, such as Gilbert Emery, Brewster, Les Archer and Wilfred Harding, via the Salisbury Garage in Douglas where machines destined for use in the Island events

TT Notes and News for 25 May 1932 depicts the new Mk IV cylinder head incorporating the use of hairpin valve springs and a 14 mm sparking plug. It is quoted as being capable of being run at 8000 rpm for quite a long time!

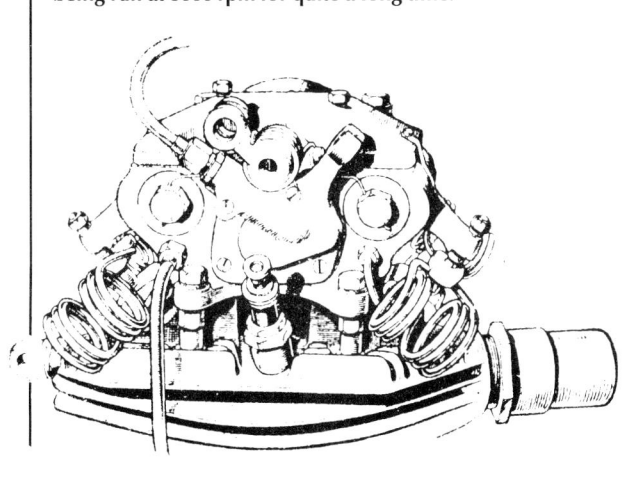

58 | *Velocette*

An extremely rare machine is this 'dog kennel' engined 350 of 1933, which has what is best described as a Mk IV frame with a single front downtube. Yet it retains the underslung, bolted-up four-speed gearbox and the bolt-on subframe of the Mk IV. The rider is L. J. Archer rounding Governor's Bridge. This was a second-string works bike offered to Les Archer in 1934, on which he finished sixth (*Archer Collection*)

were deposited as late as possible prior to practice. Having been 'well arranged' by Willis, they were delivered with instructions that they were not to be meddled with.

Another name of note was Alec Bennett who, as a rider/agent, distributed many of the KTTs quite apart from the other factory products, and had previously ridden works machines prior to KTT introduction in 1929. Then there was H. B. Tew of Swindon, J. H. Blyth who rode in the Manx for many a long year, J. Fothergill Cooke, and Tom Bryant, another name that was to become synonymous with Island racing and sponsorship through the years.

The closing months of 1931 and the first quarter of 1932 saw a run-down in production of the 1931 specification model, some 32 machines in all, ending at KTT 366. Of these machines, 14 were fitted with the new four-speed constant-mesh gearbox.

Development had been taking place with the works models and included lessons learned from Les Archer's 100 mph stint at Brooklands, quite apart from various sessions with 'Whiffling Clara'. This work had determined changes in design and other technical details that pointed the way to a general re-arrangement of the KTT, thus creating the need to identify it with a form of mark reference for Veloce stores reference. Therefore, it was logical to call the new model a Mk IV. According to the Veloce record books, Mk I referred to 1929–30 models (engine nos. 1–266), Mk II the 1931 machines (engine nos. 267–333), and Mk III those for 1932, that is engine nos. 334–366; 367 to 400 were not used, and the Mk IV commenced at no. 401. This was issued to Billy Tiffen prior to the 1932 TT, but was not invoiced to him until January 1933. Mk IV production ended at no. 549.

The Mk IV had the new four-speed gearbox, initially with Willis-type positive-stop gearchange mechanism mounted externally, and was to benefit from a new design of cylinder head. While still of cast-iron, this used a 14 mm sparking plug for the first time, being favourably positioned to give improved combustion. To allow for the repositioning of the plug, it had been necessary to redesign the cambox and the little scavenge pump that returned excess oil to the oil tank. The original pump, a reciprocating plunger type, protruded from the left-hand side of the cambox and prevented any change, however desirable, in the position of the plug.

Left to right: Billy Tiffen Jnr, Ernie Thomas, H. E. Newman, Harold Willis, Les Archer and Walter Handley. The machine is probably MT5001, the first of the 500s of 1934 with the 'dog kennel' type of cambox. Note the experimental rubber buffers just below the wing nuts of the front locks

By eliminating the use of a camshaft securing nut, and designing a neat, narrow gear pump to screw directly on to the end of a trimmed cambox, not only was it possible to re-arrange the plug position, but by further trimming it was possible to fit hairpin-type valve springs. These were made under licence from Sunbeam and allowed an increase in maximum engine revolutions when used in conjunction with a new type 30 cam. By deepening the spigot of the cylinder-to-head joint, it was possible to provide an increase in compression ratio without recourse to adding more meat to the piston crown.

The inlet tract was opened to some $1\frac{1}{16}$ in. from the normal 1 in., while the bottom end had already been dealt with as previously mentioned.

While cycle parts were to remain unchanged for the time being, the fuel tank mountings, by 'ears' fore and aft, were soon to be changed to rubber buffers on what were generally referred to as lowered tank rails, the tank itself being a deep four-gallon unit. The frame numbers of these models were prefixed KTL, the 'L' referring to the lowered tank rails.

Later in the year, and directly as a result of the work carried out on the machine used by Les Archer during his high-speed lappery of Brooklands, the Mk IV model was fitted with a subframe as standard that ran from the engine, under the gearbox and was bolted on to the rear stand mounting lugs. Meanwhile, development of Willis' 'Whiffling Clara', with her Foxwell blower, had caused problems of overheating of the cast-iron head. This led to the fitting of a bronze head to Mk IV specifications, which not only overcame the problem, but then became standard issue on the Mk IV model.

Some 148 Mk IV models were produced between June 1932 and October 1934, after which the Mk V KTT was introduced. This was based on the works racing machines that had been undergoing general development and had a new frame, incorporating a single front downtube, a hefty vertical saddle tube and a full cradle supporting the engine and gearbox. The last was mounted much more rigidly than hitherto, being surrounded by mounting plates with the usual facility for primary chain adjustment. Initial stages of development, however, involved a couple of unusual frames. One, with the suspended gearbox with two-pin fitting, had a single front downtube and bolt-on subframe,

Left Another photo of the Mk V KTT which gave many an aspiring racer a step up the ladder of success. They were quick, reliable and quite predictable

Below Gilbert Emery was down to ride this new 'dog kennel' 500 in 1934, but was injured in practice. The bike was offered to the up-and-coming Les Archer (seen here), who finished a creditable fourth behind team-mate Walter Rusk on a similar machine. They were notoriously doubtful in the handling department, requiring all the road at times. Yet no one dared to give more than a hint of this to race chief Harold Willis until Stanley Woods eventually tried one for a lap in 1935. Stanley was forthright in his comments, and he put the company on the road to success. According to Archer, once Stanley's frame was in use, and with no more power than that previously available, a good half a minute per lap was gained (*Archer Collection*)

Don Bain working on his Mk IV KTT, which has the earlier four-speed box with Willis positive-stop footchange, but the later deep tank and extra frame rails and centre stand. Note the standard Amal no. 6 carburettor and oil breather pipe clipped to the exhaust pipe (*Dennis Quinlan*)

while the other had the new full-cradle with heavy vertical saddle tube, but retained the normal dual front downtubes.

The engines of the works models had benefited from a need to reduce the amount of oil, previously under pressure around the bevel gears, while maintaining a sufficient supply of lubricant to the vital parts. This was done by simply transferring the feed, through a redesigned inner timing cover, via a filter and drilled galleries, to jet oil where it was required, namely through a close-fitting quill located inside the timing side mainshaft and thence to the big-end.

At the other end of the oil gallery, an external pipe, bolted on, directed oil through jets to the top bevel and the cam itself, sufficient lubricant being provided for the remaining bevels as the oil drained back into the lower chamber. One other feature of the new design, also incorporated in the Mk V and subsequent models, was the use of through-bolts to secure the cylinder and head. These, in conjunction with a deep locating cylinder base spigot and in consequence a deeper crankcase mouth, eliminated a potential weak spot around the cylinder base neck, a feature of the M-series range introduced in 1933.

The Mk V KTT was to benefit from all these points, while retaining the bronze Mk IV head, although the camshaft bearing oil supply, no longer under pressure from the bevel drive, passed through a $\frac{3}{8}$ in. diameter hole drilled in the camshaft support bush. The cam itself was fed directly by jet as previously referred to.

The new Mk V gearbox, having already been established on the works motors, used the same ratios as the Mk IV, although the now well proven internal positive-stop mechanism was placed at the back of the box allowing the operating lever to mate with rear-mounted footrests. It also allowed a bigger crankcase when a motor was stretched to 495 cc. Bear in mind, too, that the later MSS, KSS and KTS Mk II series were to use the same gearbox, frame and cycle part design. It is likely that these factors were taken into consideration at the time.

Meanwhile, the works motors had progressed to a

Above Wal Handley rode this 'dog kennel' works 350 during 1935 TT practice. However, he caught a finger in the chain when attempting to adjust the rear brake on the move, which gave Stanley Woods an introduction. Note the experimental snubbers around the lower fork links—presumably to allow for some slight movement before actuating the usually well-tightened damper plate

Left A rare 'dog kennel' 500, no. MT5002. It's all-alloy, except for a magnesium cambox, and was listed for Ernie Thomas for the 1936 Senior TT. Note the M-type features in the design of the downdraught cylinder head and the engine shaft shock absorber incorporating the splined mainshaft (Ken Reddish)

new head design, with a downdraught inlet tract which was based directly on that of the high-camshaft, pushrod-engined M-series production model—the MOV and MAC—and indeed these racing engines were known as MTT. However, since it was deemed necessary at that time to expose valve springs to the elements to keep them cool, and in an endeavour to keep the oil inside the cambox, a new casing was designed which completely enclosed the rockers. These acted directly upon the valves, eliminating a tendency to tilt the valve with the normal wiping action. Tappet adjustment was effected by the use of eccentric rocker spindles retained by lock nuts and locking plates.

64 | Velocette

Left One of those rare 'dog kennel' engined 500s. This is the 1935 TT machine which, despite encouraging results the year before, had gained more weight and handled even less well. It retired in the capable hands of Ernie Thomas. Note the rocking pedal heel-toe gearchange lever, the hand-made timing cover and the stub-fitting carburettor (*Dennis Quinlan*)

Below left The equally rare 'dog kennel' 350, also of 1935 with which Pirie, Nott and Thomas finished fourth, fifth and sixth. Count the number of fins on the cylinder and compare with those on the 500! (*Dennis Quinlan*)

Right Yet another 'dog kennel' 350, this time a 1934 model featuring the full cradle frame and fully supported gearbox. Note the hand-made timing cover. The Mk V was produced from this one, as were the MSS and KSS Mk II series

Below No apologies for another picture of the Mk V KTT, this time of the driveside

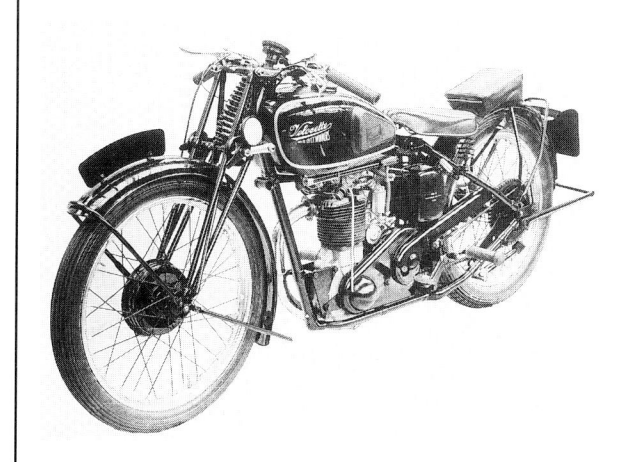

These engines were comonly known as the 'dog kennel' engines—another of Willis' terms—since the shape of the cambox matched that of the gable end of the traditional dog kennel.

As these early works MTT race engines were essentially development units, the outer timing covers were hand beaten, usually from brass or aluminium, since the need for a cast cover did not become necessary until the advent of the Mk V production KTT and subsequently the KSS Mk II, which used the same component.

There is evidence that these units enjoyed the benefit of an included valve angle of 60 degrees. Against the standard Velocette 70-degree valve angle, this must have assisted the breathing.

CHAPTER 9

The speedway KDT

Since Hall Green Speedway was but a stone's throw from the Velocette factory, it is not surprising that they produced a batch of machines specially for this purpose during 1929.

A total of 21 machines are recorded as having been sold, all with a special short frame with a multitude of odd-legged chainstays, a very upright steering head and a pair of Webb speedway forks based on the Harley Davidson Peashooter design. One further engine is listed, but this was fitted to a standard KTT frame and despatched to Milan.

Based on the KTT, the speedway engine was of 407 cc, making use of an 80 mm bore yet retaining the standard 81 mm stroke. The cylinder was a special casting, as indeed was the head, suitably sphered to match the bigger bore, while the webbed KTT crankcases had to be opened out slightly at the mouth to accommodate the larger-diameter spigot at the base of the cylinder.

The steel flywheels carried a standard KTT con-rod with crowded-roller big-end, but were balanced specially to match the rather heavy piston with its high crown for use with dope. Lubrication was by the usual dry-sump system, the oil being carried in a small compartment at the front of a special small fuel tank slung between the top frame tubes.

Transmission was via the normal multiplate clutch and, according to the record book, a standard three-speed gearbox which, presumably, was run devoid of a layshaft cluster and bottom gear pinion, rendering it a single-speed countershaft unit. Overall gearing was taken care of by a huge rear sprocket with 72 teeth, hence the need to offset the lower chainstays to clear the chain. This sprocket was in one piece with the rear brake drum, which was of standard dimensions. No front brake was used, and the final ratio selection was determined by changing the final drive sprocket in true Velocette tradition.

Ignition was by the usual square ML magneto, while carburation was handled by a $1\frac{1}{16}$ in. Amal track instrument with twin floats.

Cam gear was standard KTT with a special cam which gave a good spread of beefy power, peaking at 6000–6200 rpm. If all was correctly set-up, 7000 rpm was possible, but at the risk of blowing the motor apart if prolonged.

One original dirt track Velocette is known to exist in

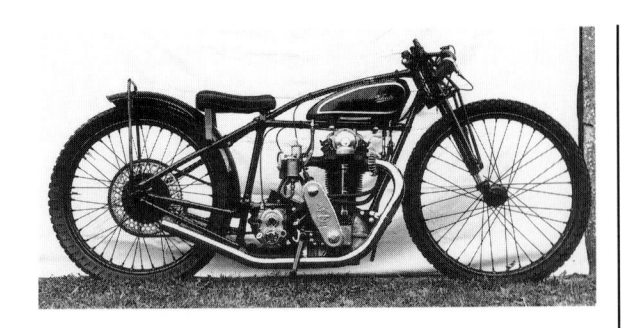

This is the only known example of a dirt-track Velocette, other than a machine with a standard KSS engine. This machine, engine no. KDT 149, belongs to Jeff Clew, the well-known motorcycle author

the UK, but it has a standard early KSS engine fitted, while motorcycling author Jeff Clew has a replica machine with many original parts, including a genuine 407 cc dirt track engine (no. KDT 149), which was originally used by Bert Clayton.

Two further engines exist in the UK, one of which was originally purchased by Maurice Cann of Leicester for occasional use in his early KTT. It was campaigned at Donington and other local events in the early 1930s.

While I have no record of the compression ratio used with the original Veloce dope piston, this particular engine has a Martlett piston fitted and runs satisfactorily on a ratio of 10:1, which I regard as the optimum for this engine, taking into account the stretched dimensions and the method of retaining the rather narrow-flanged barrel to the crankcase.

Three more engines are known to exist in the Antipodes.

In October 1986, Peter Goodman told me that his father, Eugene, used one in a standard KTT frame as a road hack for a while and rather liked it. He arrived home one day with it, carrying an assortment of grass and undergrowth around the footrests and control pedals. It transpired that he had been travelling rather rapidly, as was his wont, up a long hill in Henley-in-Arden. As he topped the rise, at over 80 mph, he found the road blocked with vehicles after an accident. Eugene took immediate avoiding action through the hedge bottom to stay out of trouble and simply pressed on!

CHAPTER 10

Stanley Woods' influence

Stanley Woods had, on more than one occasion, offered his services to Percy Goodman, only to be politely turned down. Being the shrewd, freelance operator that he was, Stanley was always on the lookout for potential winning machinery and he knew full well that Velocettes were always in with a chance in the Junior class.

For the 1935 TT, he had secured rides in the Lightweight and Senior with Moto Guzzi, and it was towards the close of practice that, to his surprise, he was approached by Percy Goodman, 'to take one of the works Velocettes out for a practice lap'. It transpired that Wal Handley, a works runner at that time, had attempted to adjust the rear brake while in motion, and damaged his hand in the process—the brake adjuster being at the front of the brake rod, adjacent to the final drive sprocket with which he had become entangled. It seems, too, that it was Handley who had been firmly

Stanley Woods passing through Parliament Square in what he calls the Geriatric Parade. He's on his old bike, another of the ex-works 500s, which carries his initials on the engine. This is fitted to the actual frame which carried the 350 double-knocker engine that failed on its first lap in 1936

against Stanley riding a Velocette and the reason why Percy Goodman had rejected Stanley's previous offers. Woods completed only one practice lap on the Junior Velocette, but it was sufficient for the maestro to make a critical analysis; 'It's a good motor, but the handling is poor, the brakes are poor, and the gear ratios are all wrong.'

It is well known that he won both the Lightweight and Senior events that year for Moto Guzzi, and before the month was out, he had received a letter from Goodman requesting a meeting to discuss plans to 'secure the services of a rider such as yourself' to assist in developing a machine for the following year. The outcome was that Stanley's services were secured. He insisted that quite apart from the need to improve the brakes and modify the gear ratios (he stated his required ratios), a form of rear suspension was of the greatest importance, and he had firm ideas of what was required in this direction, too. It seems that Willis, no longer riding himself, would not accept that the race models did not handle properly, but was always concerned with developing more 'urge' from the engines, while tending to neglect these other factors.

Rigidity of the rear fork and its pivot bearings was of paramount importance, as was the positioning of the power unit relative to the wheel centres. Earlier racing Velocettes (1926–34) had the engine well forward of the centre-line drawn vertically between the wheel centres, but more recent developments had seen a tendency to move the engine to a more central position, which had resulted in the rather doubtful handling. Since there was a difference of opinion between design staff and riders on this point, it was decided to take a couple of machines over to the Island in the autumn of 1935 for a fact-finding session.

It seems that Harold Willis had contemplated placing the engine further back in the frame, in order to put more weight on the back wheel to keep it down. Stanley and Percy Goodman had other ideas, however, since Goodman had seen Walter Rusk struggling to keep his machine under control while in mid air at the 13th milestone. He had come to the conclusion that what was required were first principles applicable to aviation. One of those first principles was to keep the air pressure behind the centre of gravity. Thus moving the power unit forward rather than backward would have the desired effect.

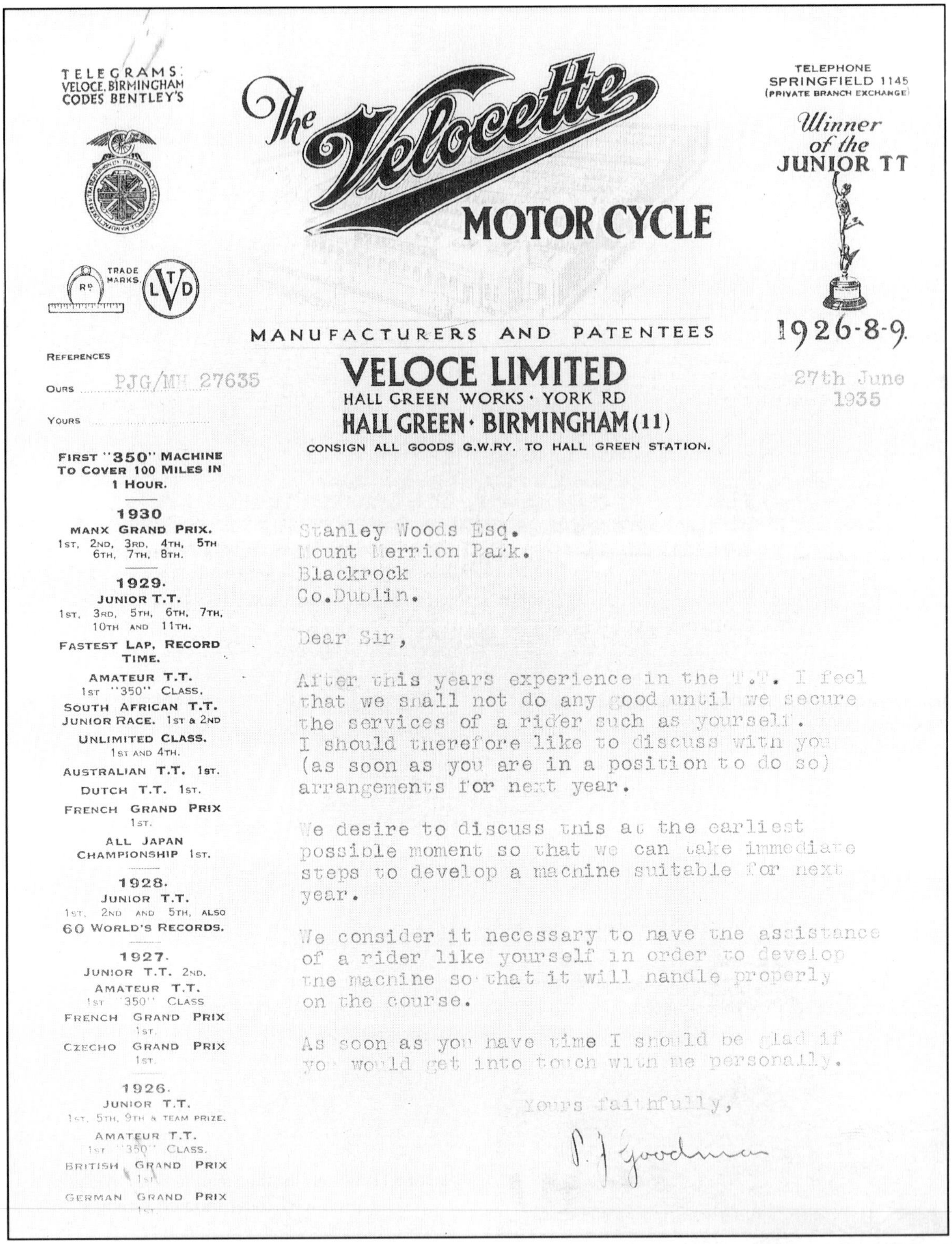

```
                                                              TELEPHONE
  TELEGRAMS:                                                SPRINGFIELD 1145
 VELOCE, BIRMINGHAM         The Velocette                  (PRIVATE BRANCH EXCHANGE)
 CODES BENTLEY'S
                            MOTOR CYCLE                      Winner
                                                             of the
                                                           JUNIOR TT

          TRADE
          MARKS.
                    MANUFACTURERS AND PATENTEES            1926-8-9.
 REFERENCES
                        VELOCE LIMITED                      27th June
 OURS   PJG/MH 27635    HALL GREEN WORKS · YORK RD            1935
 YOURS                HALL GREEN · BIRMINGHAM (11)
                      CONSIGN ALL GOODS G.W.RY. TO HALL GREEN STATION.
 FIRST "350" MACHINE
 TO COVER 100 MILES IN
      1 HOUR.
                              Stanley Woods Esq.
       1930                   Mount Merrion Park.
   MANX GRAND PRIX.           Blackrock
 1ST, 2ND, 3RD, 4TH, 5TH      Co. Dublin.
    6TH, 7TH, 8TH.
                              Dear Sir,
       1929.
     JUNIOR T.T.                    After this years experience in the T.T. I feel
 1ST, 3RD, 5TH, 6TH, 7TH,     that we shall not do any good until we secure
    10TH AND 11TH.            the services of a rider such as yourself.
 FASTEST LAP, RECORD          I should therefore like to discuss with you
       TIME.                  (as soon as you are in a position to do so)
    AMATEUR T.T.              arrangements for next year.
   1ST "350" CLASS.
 SOUTH AFRICAN T.T.                 We desire to discuss this at the earliest
 JUNIOR RACE. 1ST & 2ND       possible moment so that we can take immediate
   UNLIMITED CLASS.           steps to develop a machine suitable for next
    1ST AND 4TH.              year.
  AUSTRALIAN T.T. 1ST.
    DUTCH T.T. 1ST.                 We consider it necessary to have the assistance
  FRENCH GRAND PRIX           of a rider like yourself in order to develop
         1ST.                 the machine so that it will handle properly
     ALL JAPAN                on the course.
  CHAMPIONSHIP 1ST.
                                    As soon as you have time I should be glad if
       1928.                  you would get into touch with me personally.
     JUNIOR T.T.
 1ST, 2ND AND 5TH, ALSO                                  Yours faithfully,
  60 WORLD'S RECORDS.
                                                         P J Goodman
       1927.
   JUNIOR T.T. 2ND.
    AMATEUR T.T.
   1ST "350" CLASS
  FRENCH GRAND PRIX
         1ST.
  CZECHO GRAND PRIX
         1ST.

       1926.
     JUNIOR T.T.
 1ST, 5TH, 9TH & TEAM PRIZE.
    AMATEUR T.T.
   1ST "350" CLASS.
  BRITISH GRAND PRIX
         1ST
  GERMAN GRAND PRIX
```

Following a one-lap appraisal of the Junior Velocette at the end of the 1935 TT practice, Stanley Woods received this letter from Percy Goodman. It was the beginning of the turning point in Veloce racing fortunes (*Stanley Woods*)

Above A post-race picture of Stanley Woods with the new 500 springer of 1936, on which he finished second to his best friend and former team-mate, Jimmie Guthrie (Norton). Stanley put up the fastest lap, but was eventually slowed by a misfire caused by a carburation upset due to flexing of the oil tank on which the float chamber was mounted (*The Motor Cycle*)

Stanley spent some time at the factory during the autumn of 1935. The experimental frames were produced and machines built for himself and Ernie Thomas. They were taken to the Island for some early-morning high-speed testing. By adding lead weights to strategic points on the frame, a new geometry became firmly established.

A revised frame design, incorporating rear springing, was drawn up under Goodman's guidance. Initially, this was produced for Stanley's Junior and Senior mounts for the 1936 season. A new steering head lug was developed which enabled the front downtube to run very close to the front mudguard, thus allowing the engine to be positioned as far forward as possible.

The hefty vertical saddle tube carried an additional malleable cast lug which, whilst also serving as the engine/gearbox plate mounting as well as the oil tank support, was to form the basis of the rear fork pivot bearing. It accommodated a couple of cup bearings, the same bearings, in fact, that had been used on the earlier KTT models for the steering head. A pair of rear forks were produced using tapered tubing with substantial lugs at both ends. The forward ends were

Stanley Woods and Mildred at his pit alongside the 'dog kennel' 500 no. MT 5002, which he used at Phillip Island, Victoria, during his Australian tour between December 1936 and February 1937 (*Dennis Quinlan*)

Jock Leyden kindly gave us permission to use a copy of his superb pencil sketch of one of the 'dog kennel' engined machines of 1935. Willis described the big fuel tank as being 'like a barrel of ale'

splined and clamped on to a pivot shaft of equally substantial dimensions for rigidity, the whole being finely adjustable by the use of large nuts and dust covers. These were identical to those used on the steering heads of the previous models (1928–35), later models being slightly smaller in diameter.

A pair of simple telescopic suspension units were supported by a triangulated subframe that was dowelled and bolted to the main frame under the saddle, and to the lower end by a close-fitting spindle within the swinging fork pivot shaft. This was supported additionally by outrigger bearer plates carrying footrests, gearchange and rear brake pedals, the last operating the brake by means of pushing an outer cable instead of pulling a rod.

The newly designed rear brake incorporated a long aluminium torque arm that was retained by a special anchor pin. When tightened, this allowed the facility of wheel movement for chain adjustment without the need for slackening and the potentially disastrous risk of not re-tightening.

The resultant rear suspension design, to be modified in detail over the following years, was nevertheless so advanced as to be the basis of the general layout of most subsequent swinging-arm suspension systems to this day. Not until the advent of proprietary rear dampers, however, such as those produced by Woodhead Monroe, Girling and Armstrong would motorcyclists see such a suspension in universal use. Lack of good dampers was the limiting factor.

During the late 1930s, though, Phil Irving, having rejoined the company following a spell with Phillip Vincent, had designed and produced three sets of damper units. These incorporated springs that were securely located at each end in similar fashion to the later Veloce telescopic fork spring fitting, and as a means of damping made use of a Ferodo-type friction material. One set was fitted to the prototype Model 0, vertical twin, which he also designed, while another was used for racing by the Austrian Franz Binder. The third set was employed on a one-off springer MSS, also built by Irving.

Back to 1936, however. In his rare days off, Willis flew a de Havilland Moth called 'Clattering Kate', which he kept at Castle Bromwich. While many such light aircraft relied upon nothing more than the flexure of the rudimentary undercarriage as a suspension medium, Willis had noted that some of the more up-to-date kites enjoyed the benefit of a telescopic system made by Dowty. This combined air and oil for suspension and, thus, was readily adjustable for load as well as providing the means of damping. Having become friendly with George Dowty, who co-operated by providing a pair of suitably sized telescopic legs, Willis modified the new frame layout to suit, enabling the development test riding to be carried out in the Island.

This was the beginning of an association that was to develop a useful sideline for Dowty, who hitherto had not been involved in the motorcycle industry, the famous Dowty Oleomatic rear legs becoming a notable feature on the TT Velocettes. When Webb began to run down the production of their equally famous girder fork post-war, Dowty set out to produce replacement telescopic oleo front forks, to Veloce design. These were to lay the foundations of Hall Green's own telescopic fork introduced on the LE in 1949, although as far back as 1937, layout drawings for such a fork had been produced for an advanced project involving a new concept of race machine. This was to be supercharged and be shaft driven—but more of that later.

Interestingly, Kawasaki aircraft were the first to use Dowty suspension.

The mounting arrangement of the Irving-designed spring/friction damper units on the one-off MSS. Note the adjustment slot at the top

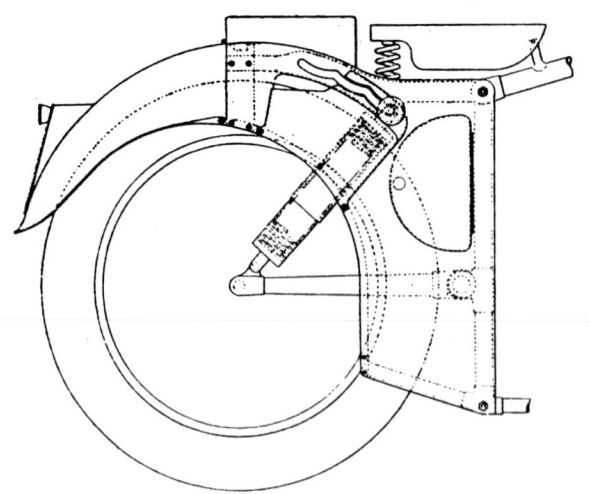

CHAPTER 11

Double ohc and Mk VI KTT

While all the frame development work was taking place behind the scenes, other projects of equal importance were also underway to provide competitive race machinery for their well established customers. Various factors came into play here. The works 'dog kennel' engine, with its alloy cylinder head and downdraught inlet tract, incorporating a narrowed valve angle, giving improved combustion, was one. The drawings of the new Mk II KSS were another. New casting techniques had been perfected for the KSS, allowing for the production of a complicated alloy head, incorporating a cambox and full enclosure of the rocker gear. Leading on from that, thoughts were put on to paper for a bigger alloy head which would house a set of hairpin-type valve springs. Like the Mk II and the 'dog kennel' engines, it would incorporate eccentric rocker spindles to facilitate tappet adjustment which had proved so successful with the works racing engines.

A new frame was devised, based on the Mk V design, but with revised geometry, allowing the engine to be moved as far forward as possible. No doubt, this was a result of data obtained from those Isle of Man trips and Stanley Woods' suggestions. The rest of the layout was, to all intents and purposes, as the Mk V, although the works machines had the magnesium alloy camboxes of the 'dog kennel' engines, and also the now conical rear hub. There was a new two-piece front hub and brake plate, while alloy rims were fitted to the front wheels only—painted black so as not to be so obvious to the eagle eyes of the opposition, which usually meant Norton.

Additionally, the new frame provided accommodation for a new, bigger oil tank, which was rubber mounted to a malleable casting brazed to the hefty saddle tube. The tank was also supported by adjustable rubber buffers from a mounting below and between the rear engine plates. A petrol tank of some four gallons capacity, which was both longer and deeper than before, was included together with a neat exhaust system which terminated in a megaphone that satisfied the regulations about exhaust pipe length, and at the same time contributed to top-end performance. From these ingredients came the KTT Mk VI, something that would have been quite startling and different, if it had all worked out as intended.

However, development work was going on in all directions and included the M-type racing engine, otherwise known as the 'dog kennel' design. The separate cambox bolted to the alloy downdraught cylinder head of this engine lent itself to the possibility of a double overhead-camshaft arrangement, which had not been overlooked by Willis.

In preparation for the 1936 TT, five new machines were laid down (two 500s and three 350s) using two of the new rigid frames with as much magnesium alloy as possible, along with three new sprung frames. The springers had alloy rims on the front, again discreetly painted black.

The 500s, one each for Stanley Woods and Ernie

Bore and stroke of the 500 were 81 × 96 mm, identical to the pushrod MSS. This engine was used in the machine which Stanley Woods took on his Australian tour in the winter of 1936–7 (*Ken Reddish*)

Austin Munks rode this 'unofficial' KTT Mk VI into a brilliant first place in the 1936 Junior Manx Grand Prix. Later in the week, he won the Senior MGP on a Norton. Austin had only one eye, having lost the other in a shooting accident during the previous winter. At first, the ACU were reluctant to let him ride, but his wins justified their ultimate decision

Thomas, had all-alloy, single overhead-camshaft motors of proven design, Thomas' engine being housed in a rigid frame, while Stanley's was in a springer. The 350s, however, had a new double overhead-camshaft arrangement that had been developed during the 'off' season and which fitted directly on to the existing works cylinder heads. It was described thus, 'The vertical shaft drives a top bevel in the ordinary way, but behind this is a straight-cut pinion. This drives two intermediate wheels, which in turn each drive a camwheel. The cams bear on very short hollow pushrods which slope downwards on to the ends of the valve stems. Very complete measures have been taken to ensure adequate lubrication. This form of valve gear is capable of running at very high engine speeds. Naturally the gear takes up rather more room than the normal type, and would in the case of the 500, with its necessary higher engine, interfere somewhat with the shape of the underside of the fuel tank.'

Well, as far as we know, there were no 500 double overhead-cam motors pre-war, but that there were three 350s there is no doubt. Thomas and Woods rode sprung-framed models, while Mellors' was housed in the new rigid frame, with which he finished third. Stanley, who started as hot favourite (he said that he expected to win at a canter) retired at Sulby Bridge on the first lap with a broken Oldham coupling, while Ernie Thomas, having been in second spot for a time, was relegated to fourth following a fall at Quarter Bridge. If only that coupling hadn't broken!

Later in the season, the same mounts were campaigned on the Continent by Mellors and Woods to very good effect, Mellors becoming European Champion for the Junior class that year, while Stanley Woods concentrated on the Senior class. More often than not, both Junior and Senior classes were run together.

Stanley himself was most impressed by the performance of the double overhead-camshaft motors. On one Continental outing, when riding one of the 350s, he was going like a dingbat, only to lose it when well in the

Left Ernie Thomas, on the second of the dohc works models, finished fourth in 1936 behind Mellors, following a fall at Quarter Bridge while lying second. Had he not fallen and had Stanley's motor not failed, they might have completed a glorious 1, 2, 3

Below Ted Mellors rode the third of the works double-knockers of 1936 into third place. It had the new Mk VI rigid frame which he preferred. (Engine no. 482/5, frame 6TT2)

lead, on a high speed corner, which had become waterlogged following a freak storm. He went backwards into a sandbank, which filled the carburettor with the stuff, and he retired.

That Junior TT failure, however, was an embarrassment to Veloce and the dohc project was hurriedly dropped, despite those other successes. It was established that too much rigidity in the vertical drive shaft was a contributory factor, this component being of a constant diameter throughout its length. Subsequent works drive shafts were waisted to allow for some torsional flexibility, while Oldham couplings were to be substantially beefed up in diameter. This necessitated the machining of slots in the bevel gear retaining sleeves, top and bottom, to accommodate them.

It's a pity that the company did not persevere with these engines, despite their findings, but such a failure had made Willis very wary of any further development in that direction. Furthermore, as much work was also going on with a hush-hush rotary-valve engine perhaps there was insufficient time available to take another look at the twin-cam project.

However, I understand that the engines and spares languished in the racing department until 1939 when Frank Mussett, over for a spell to prepare his own

Above H. E. Newman finished 11th in 1936 on this Mk VI which had conventional TT forks. (Engine no. KTT 620, frame 6TT3)

Left Stanley Woods on the 1936 dohc 350 with which he expected to win at a canter because it was so quick. Unfortunately, it broke an Oldham coupling at Sulby on the first lap. Engine no. was 483/5 and frame no. SF2. It was one of the first three springers introduced that year. The front wheel rim was alloy, discreetly painted black

Above **The first three sprung frames produced by Veloce for the 1936 TT incorporated Dowty pneumatic suspension struts, steering head races for the pivot bearing and a cable-operated brake. This is Woods' 500 with $\tfrac{5}{8} \times \tfrac{1}{4}$ in. chain (*The Motor Cycle*)**

machine for the TT and the Ulster, managed to prise them out and take them back to Australia just before the outbreak of war. In fact, after his TT jaunt, Mussett spent some time working at the factory and gradually developing his own Mk VIII, making good use of the Heenan and Froude dynamometer.

Mussett had a particularly good working relationship with Percy Goodman, who offered him Mellors' works TT 500 to take back to Melbourne, for £160. For good measure, he was also sold a hack 350 for a further £25. The 350 was supposedly the one and only Mk VI, so he took them both.

Additionally, remarking that there was going to be a war, Percy gave Mussett the keys to the experimental shop and told him to take anything that he wanted, so he helped himself to a fair assortment of useful spares, ramming the petrol tanks of both machines with parts small enough to go through the filler holes! Seeing the dohc bits languishing under a bench, he decided he

Below **Billy Tiffen failed to finish on this Mk VI in 1936. It had experimental side dampers fitted to the forks. (Engine no. KTT 622, frame 6TT4)**

would take those too, since they had been discarded.

Works mechanic Tommy Mutton remarked that he doubted whether Mr Percy would let them go—Willis had died from meningitis by this time—but was surprised when Mussett was allowed to take them. No doubt, Willis' death and the rumours of war had their effect on this decision.

Meanwhile, however, machines were being prepared for the Ulster Grand Prix, and it transpired that Stanley Woods' 350, which was entered for the Junior race along with that of Mellors, was without its gearbox. This had been removed and taken on to the Continent by Mellors as a spare where it had been 'conveniently' left

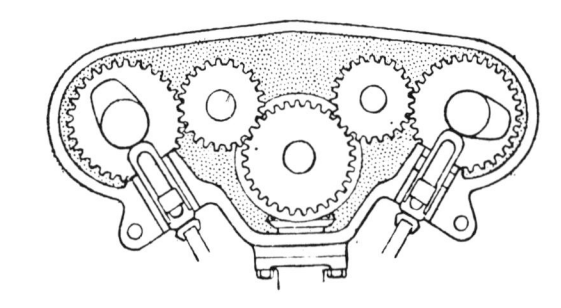

Above **The first double-knocker in Birmingham. The three 1936 works 350s all used this arrangement (*The Motor Cycle*)**

in a Belgian railway parcels office and forgotten! I believe that some rivalry existed between these two riders and when Stanley learned what had happened, he arranged for the removal of the gearbox from Mellors' Senior model, despite the fact that it had been sold, since it wasn't required in Ulster as both classes were run together.

Another Mk VI in the hands of Frenchman Roger Loyer, but he failed to finish. His model also has the experimental side dampers on a pair of strutted forks. (Engine no. KTT 623, frame 6TT5)

In the meantime, one of the mechanics had suggested to Mussett that he should ride Mellors' 500 in the Senior Ulster in place of his own 350. Frank replied that he wasn't used to the big bike and was not too keen to have his first gallop on it on such a long, bumpy circuit. Eventually, however, he agreed, subject to finding a suitable replacement gearbox. This was not easy, since the works gearbox had a very special set of ratios, peculiar dogs and a heavy 1 in. diameter mainshaft, quite apart from the magnesium casing.

Percy Goodman suggested that the spare box should be collected from Belgium, and that Frank could do this on the experimental Model O twin. This had a couple of geared crankshafts, but since the primary gears of these had tended to rattle when running at idling speeds, they had been made of Tufnol in an endeavour to quieten them. As Mussett set off, Percy Goodman's parting words were that he should 'try to break it'. Frank did collect the gearbox and on his return journey, somewhere in Kent I believe, and without trying too hard, persuaded the teeth to fall off the Tufnol gears — the rest of the journey had to be completed by train.

The 350 box was fitted to the 500 which was duly taken to Ireland where it performed admirably. Mussett soon accustomed himself to aviating the big 'un along the Clady Straight but, alas, it stuck in bottom gear at Clady Corner, smack in front of Percy Goodman who was spectating there. Mussett was forced to retire. When the gearbox was stripped, it was found that a small piece of metal that had chipped from one of the dogs had become firmly wedged in the internal footchange mechanism. Possibly, it had been in the bottom of the box for some time, but had become dislodged during its Continental travels.

Students of Velocette history will recall that it is generally understood that only one Mk VI KTT was ever produced, and this was used by Austin Munks to win the 1936 Junior Manx GP. It was known as 'the little rough 'un', but was it, in fact, the only one?

Ernie Thomas rode the bike on the Continent, and while he could not remember much about it, he stated that it performed and handled well, and had a long, comparatively narrow, deep petrol tank. It was, he said, an odd machine that Veloce used to loan to riders seeking a bit of factory support. It had a bit more than average performance. Billy Wing, of Daybrook, Nottingham, recalls that he once rode a factory 350 over in

A family picture of Ted Mellors with his wife, daughters and mother-in-law. The machine is the rigid dohc 350 of 1936 which took him into third place in the Junior (*Maurice Wear*)

the Island that had a KSS Mk II head and which, he assumes, was the same machine.

It has been recorded that Willis had become so frustrated at the non-appearance of the promised new cylinder head castings, that he had gone into the stores, collected a new Mk II KSS cylinder head, opened up the ports, fitted a bigger inlet valve and dropped it on to one of the new alloy barrels that were intended to mate with the new, as yet unavailable, square finned head.

That no new production KTT should have come out of Hall Green between October 1935 and March 1938 is, to my mind, significant. A huge gap in the records between the last Mk V and the first Mk VII indicates that, quite apart from putting their efforts into things like the Aspin rotary-valve engine, the cylinder head supply must have been a contributory factor. Five Mk VI frames had been used in 1936, two for the official team (6TT1 and 6TT2), while the other three machines (6TT3, 6TT4 and 6TT5), all with big-finned alloy barrels and Mk II KSS cylinder heads, were ridden by Newman, Tiffen and

Loyer. The rest of the machine was to the Mk VI specification as mentioned earlier.

Frame no. 6TT6 does not appear in the records, but does exist—I have seen it and it is true to type; 6TT7 was also not recorded. However, the company's system of making a batch of frames, stamping them, enamelling them and then taking them from stock at random may have had something to do with this—it could have been left in the stores as a spare.

Finally, 6TT8, the last of the Mk VI type, was used by Mellors for the 1937 Junior and housed an engine bearing the 10 in. square head, known as the 'Huntley and Palmer' head (so called because it was said by Willis to resemble a Huntley and Palmer biscuit tin). This bike was the basis of the Mk VII, which was to become available to all in 1938. Other works runners, including the Senior models, were to use the new 10 in. square cylinder head layout in 1937, too.

The Mk VI and Mk VII frames, prefixed 6TT and 7TT respectively, were identical. Some of the earlier machines used strutted Mk V type forks with an experimental damper, whie others had the later, heavier type. It is my view that the Mk VI was intended to be the next production KTT. With delays caused by lack of suitable head castings and other factors, by the time it was all together, it had to be the next listed model, the Mk VII.

Could this be the 'little rough 'un'? The rider (bottom) is Cliff Ellerby from Lincolnshire – he bought the bike from a man named Binder (below) from the Manchester area and rode it regularly in the late 1940s and early 1950s. Then he sold it to an RAF chap who came from Kent. It was last heard of during the 1950s when it broke a rod at the Brighton Speed Trials. The machine was basically a Mk V KTT with Mk IV fork blades, a Mk V bottom half and a KSS Mk II head. The important details are the boss at the bottom front of the crankcase, into which the oil drained from the cambox which would normally be removed on the standard KTT, and the oil tank, which is undoubtedly of the square Mk VI/Mk VII type with the float chamber clipped to it—it would be carried on a heavy lug brazed to the vertical saddle tube (*David Davies*)

Above The author, as President of the Velocette Owners' Club, is occasionally called upon to assist in the judging of the concours at the club's annual gathering at Stanford Hall. He is seen here with the club's stalwart Chairman, Vic Pratley (right)

Developments in springing

With the advent of the sprung frame, much higher speeds were possible over bumpy surfaces, but fork spring breakages occurred frequently. One day, Percy Goodman remarked that it was not really surprising considering the bending that took place at either end of a fixed spring. He made his point by placing a bar under the top of the fork blade and over the top crown, demonstrating the movement.

Charles Udall was quick to design a mounting that accommodated the same spring, but was fixed at both ends into revised lugs containing silentbloc bushes and joined through the spring centre by a $\frac{3}{8}$ in. diameter rod and tube with a greasing point. This was to become standard racing practice from then on.

Prior to the introduction of the telescopic spring the breakages, which had left the forks in a dangerous, semi-collapsed state, had led to the fitting of bolt-on rubber snubbers as a safety factor. Mounted on the rear fork blade, the snubbers took the thump of the lower crown on full deflection. These, too, became a permanent brazed-on feature.

Above Ernie Thomas with yet another Mk VI KTT (Frame no. 6TT7) at the 1937 Junior TT

Below Presumably Ted Mellors was reluctant to give up his 'seat of the pants' ride on a rigid 350 in 1937, or was it that there were insufficient springers to go round at that time? This machine is the last of the Mk VI type, no. 6TT8, with new motor with the big head. This makes it the prototype Mk VII, the engine number being 485/7. The side lifting handle is, in reality, a stay to prevent the mudguard being hammered on to the tyre

Following the introduction of the sprung fame in 1936, when the rear brake was cable operated, it became apparent that the cable produced a rather spongy operation. Something had to be arranged that was more direct and reliable. It also became obvious that the pivot points of a brake rod and rear fork, being geometrically different, would cause the brake pedal to see-saw when travelling over undulating surfaces with the suspension working overtime.

Typically, Veloce came up with a clever two-piece brake pedal that made point contact smack in the

Left Having been embarrassed by the failure of one of the new dohc engines in 1936, Veloce quietly dropped them at the end of the season. Then they concentrated on a hush-hush rotary-valve development that seemingly had great potential. Only when six wasted months had elapsed did they look into building a new single-cam engine with a new cylinder head design for 1937. It didn't produce the required horses and Stanley could only finish fourth. Had he known that those dohc engines were still around and had used one instead, he says he could have won

Right Stanley Woods brought back a pair of Borrani rims when he returned from honeymoon on the Continent in 1936. He talked his way through Customs, so the tax was waived. He told them that the rims were important to British industry

Below A new front end was built up for Woods' 500 which included (for the first time) an alloy torque arm clamped to the front forks. It proved so successful in practice that the whole assembly was transferred to the 350 for the Junior race, (*Mr Alexander*)

middle of the swinging-fork spindle pivot point, which completely eliminated the problem.

For 1937, new sprung frames were produced, based on the 1936 prototypes. However, these differed in the area of the pivot spindle and rear fork. The spindle was of two diameters—with only a few thou. difference— and was a press-fit into the frame lug, from the left-hand side. The rear fork, now in one piece, was bushed and free to revolve around the fixed pivot. Both ends of the pivot shaft were threaded and retained the lower ends of the rear subframe with two nuts per side, thus allowing for some control of end movement.

Because of the addition of a bracing tube between the two fork legs, it became necessary to make these 1 in. longer, thus lengthening the wheelbase by that amount.

The Aspin rotary-valve project

Brief mention should be made of the Aspin rotary-valve engine, since Veloce were preoccupied with it for some time. An engineer called Frank Aspin had caused a stir in making great claims of high power outputs on low-grade fuel, using his own design of conical rotary valve mounted on the bottom half of a 250 Rudge. He claimed an output in the region of 24 bhp at some 12,000 rpm!

Frank Aspin approached Veloce, offering exclusive use of this design, for which Willis fell hook, line and sinker. It was agreed that the whole project should be kept quite secret, for Willis was convinced that a race engine, to be used for the 1937 TT, would be developed to produce some 35 bhp, an unheard of figure for a 350 in those days. According to Phil Irving, who gave me this information, Veloce would have had the exclusive rights to the design for one year, if it was successful.

However, it seems that Aspin had approached BSA with the same deal, after some six months' work had taken place at Hall Green; all to no avail.

Frank Aspin was a brilliant engineer— some even called him a genius who had a flair for marketing. He was known as the 'Wilmslow Boy,' having originated from that part of Cheshire, although his early working life was spent at the Lancashire Steel Company where he was employed as a draughtsman.

This background have him an insight into the use and application of various metals. He specialized in the manufacture of taps, dies and reamers used in the railway industry, as well as other specialized equipment for industry in general.

However, he was obsessed by the idea of developing his patent rotary valve. This obsession, together with the ability to sell the idea, brought large development fees from the leading car and commercial vehicle manufacturers. He was then able to offer suitable conversions, showing considerable savings in fuel consumption. Amongst his clientele were such well-known names as Freddie Dixon and Prince Bira.

Apparently, Aspin had good business sense and was highly respected by his happy team of workers. Frequently, they would be required to work long into the night to complete jobs that were required for testing first thing in the morning.

Above Number 110 is Werner Mellmann on a 350 dohc NSU alongside Ted Mellors with his works 350 in the rigid Mk VI frame. Taken somewhere in Germany, 1937 (*Dr Helmut Krackowizer*)

Above left The experimental Aspin rotary-valve version of a KTT dropped into a Mk V frame (*The Motor Cycle*)

Left The experimental Aspin/KTT engine mounted in a BSA frame and cycle parts for test purposes during the war

I believe that he embarked on a post-war 'people's car' project in conjunction with Monty Beaumont and Dennis Kendall of Grantham, but this came to nothing. He died only a few years ago.

CHAPTER 12

Mk VII and Mk VIII KTT

The new Mk VII KTT, although still rigid framed, in all other respects was endowed with the beneficial features developed on the works machines, and it handled very well.

The front brake, still basically as used on the Mk V and VI models, was improved by the addition of a new magnesium brake plate that was anchored by a long duralumin torque arm to a point well up the fork blade. This removed the bending stresses previously experienced by the fork end. Equipped with a wider pair of shoes, also in magnesium alloy, the whole assembly was very much stiffer and more effective.

Similar improvements were carried out at the rear end, where the ribbed brake drum was dished inwards to an angle closely related to that of the spokes, thus allowing for wider shoes, also mounted on a stiff magnesium brake plate. To this was riveted an abbreviated torque arm which otherwise was similar to that on the KSS, MSS and Mk V KTT models. With a compression ratio of 8.75:1, on petrol/benzole, the 9 in. square-finned, cool running motor would turn over like a turbine up to 7000 rpm, producing some usable horses in the process.

However, while established agents at home and abroad were expected to take at least one machine each for their favoured clients, and Stevens of London were to take more than most, the demand was not what had been expected. Only 37 of an intended batch of 100 machines were produced.

Four engines were marked 'S', signifying that they were special units which differed from standard. These had special forged pistons, with wedge-section rings, giving a compression ratio of 9.7:1. There was a different cam, giving higher lift, but using the same valve timing as the standard engine, and rockers fitted with return springs and floating bushes. These engines were supplied to Bryants of Biggleswade for an unnamed rider, McIntyre, Belfast, for J. E. Little, W. A. Wing of Daybrook for Bill Wing himself, and Stevens of London, again for an unnamed rider.

It is perhaps not surprising that the response was poor. Apart from the possibility that orders had been lost due to the delays in manufacture, the works teams had become well established with their springers. It soon became apparent that Veloce must lay down a batch of production KTTs for the 1939 season that were bang up to date.

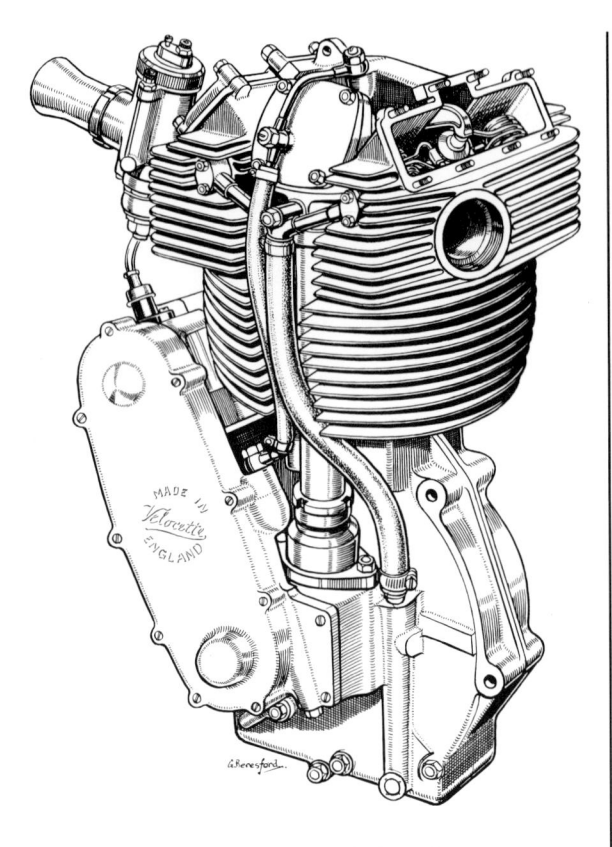

A full-blown 1937 works engine with the 10 in. square 'Huntley & Palmer' cylinder head—the same casting as used on the 500. The cylinder had ten huge fins, but 11 fins were used in 1938 and 1939 to accommodate longer con-rods. The large bottom bevel housing contained bearings instead of the usual bush. George Beresford was the artist, and he can be seen elsewhere in this book on a delectable MSS with Watsonian Continental chair

It came as no surprise, therefore, to learn that a new KTT—the Mk VIII—was to become available to selected riders for 1939. It would be virtually as the works machines which had been campaigned for the last couple of seasons. Having said that, the engine and gearbox were almost identical to the Mk VII in that the main castings were in aluminium. The works motors usually had crankcases and gearboxes in magnesium alloy, while the works cylinder heads, manufactured

Above **Northwest 200, Portrush 1937. Mildred, using the camera she was given as a present on their Australian tour, photographs Stanley, Tommy Mutton and Walter Rusk. Shortly afterwards, the works 500 was to have an alloy torque arm clamped to the fork blade for the TT** (*Betty Griffin*)

Left **Ted Mellors on the starting grid at Monza in 1938** (*Dr Helmut Krackowizer*)

from the same alloy castings as those used on the factory 500s, were a full 10 in. square. The production KTT head, for both Mk VII and Mk VIII, however, was a mere 9 in. square.

The new alloy cylinders were cast around a corrugated cast-iron core incorporating the square base, similar to the KSS. The works barrels were somewhat bigger all-alloy items, into which were shrunk thick-walled liners with substantial double-diameter spigots on the top for the cylinder head joints. In some cases, the fins completely enveloped the vertical drive tube.

An interesting experiment was carried out by Willis in an endeavour to establish the merit of alloy cylinders against those of cast-iron. He fitted immersion heaters

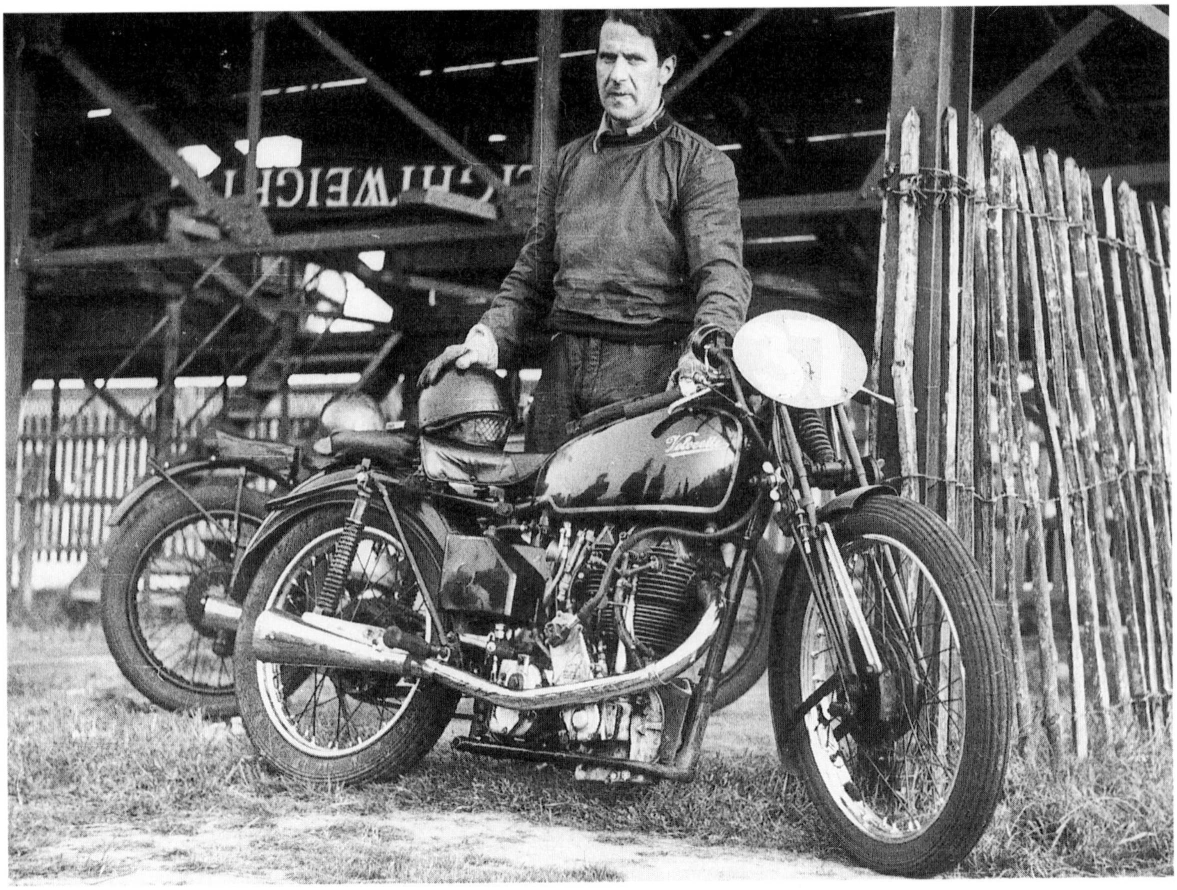

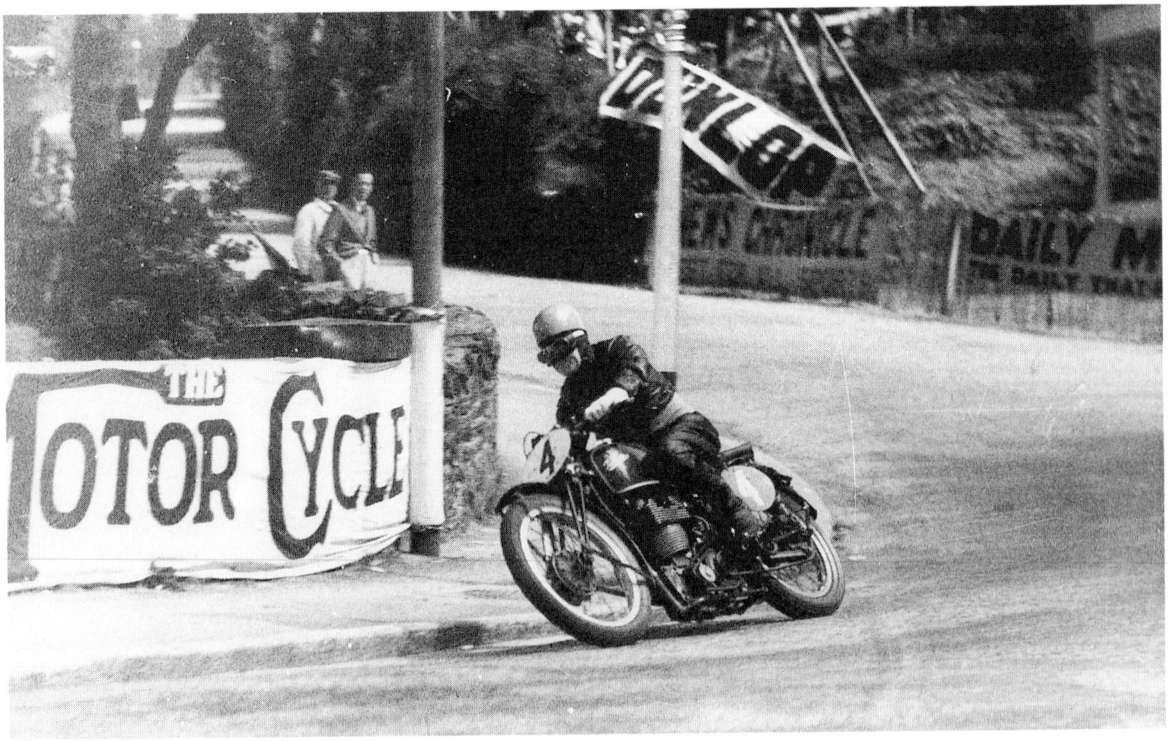
THE
OTOR CYCLE
DAILY M

Left Franz Binder with his 1939 Junior TT machine, a second-string works hack using Mk VII engine no. 702 and now owned by Dr Helmut Krackowizer. Note the Irving-designed, friction-damped rear suspension struts

Below left The inimitable style of Stanley Woods rounding Quarter Bridge during his victorious Junior ride in 1938

inside one of each type, plus a fan for cooling purposes, and proved beyond doubt that the cast-iron cylinder gave better cooling at the disadvantage of far too much weight.

In common with the Mk VI, the valve sizes of the new engine were $1\frac{11}{16}$ in. inlet and $1\frac{19}{32}$ in. exhaust. Lubrication and bevel gears remained unchanged in that the latter were identical to the KSS Mk II, the submerged oil pump coping amply with the return of oil from the cambox, in addition to that in the crankcase. However, this method had been the cause of some embarrassment at races with delayed starts, such as the TT, where plugs had to be changed for hard racing ones just prior to the 'off'. Frequently, the engine would fail to fire up due to the hard plug oiling up. This was caused by oil from the cambox draining into the crankcase which, particularly with an engine that had seen much service, was too much for the pump to cope with.

The answer to this was to blank off the camshaft drain into the case and divert it into the bottom bevel chamber, scavenging it independently by adding a

No book about Velocettes would be complete without reference to the Tiffens of Carlisle. Between them, this father-and-son team built up an impressive list of Six Days Gold Medals, riding camshaft models. Billy Jnr was a regular competitor in the TT from 1935 to 1939. This Mk VIII took him to 15th place in the 1939 Junior and 23rd in the Senior

Ted Mellors with his 1939 Junior model. The 11 cylinder fins suggest a taller-than-usual engine which, along with Woods' machine, used a longer con-rod. Note, too, the bolt head protruding from the bottom fins where an experimental cylinder wall feed had been tried and dispensed with (*Kieg*)

narrow gear pump between the lower magneto driving wheel and the inner timing cover. The last was suitably drilled to pass the oil back to the tank via an additional return pipe. Thus, the main pump dealt only with that oil in the crankcase. This modification had been carried out on the works motors, and while all standard Mk VIII engines before and after the war were manufactured without it, it became a modification regularly incorporated by private owners post-war. Such names as Tommy Tindle and Doug Beasley, for instance, were to use this idea as standard practice in their race preparation.

Bottom bevels had proved quite adequate up until then, but increased speeds made it necessary to introduce heavy-duty ones, as used on the factory 500s, first on the works machines, then as standard on all production KTTs.

The works machines, being largely experimental, often differed one from another. The production KTT would have the same frame, forks and general arrangement, but would be built around aluminium alloy castings rather than magnesium ones. They would have an identical and proven specification and be bench-tested to an acceptable level of performance. They would also have a good standard of finish, which was a secondary consideration as far as the works bikes were concerned.

The power unit, basically that of the Mk VII, used a crank pin with an increase in shank diameter from $\frac{3}{4}$ in. to $\frac{7}{8}$ in., similar to that of the racing 500s (and the production MSS). Apart from giving increased stiffness of the crank assembly, it enabled the compression ratio to be increased to 10.94:1 which had proved to be the optimum on the works motors on petrol/benzole. To cope with an improved cam form and rocker return springs, a deeper rocker forging was introduced with those heavier bottom bevels. All these factors were introduced directly as a result of the occasional failure during a considerable number of racing miles and test-bench hours. It was typical of the thoroughness with which Veloce approached the job.

The gearbox was a standard KSS/MSS casing with TT close-ratio gears and a camplate, like all KTTs, without a neutral notch. There was no provision for a kickstarter, of course, since that unit was discarded in favour of a

Right Probably the first production KTT Mk VIII for 1939 consumption. Note the valanced rear guard and Mosley air cushion, as used pre-war

Below right A fine action shot of Ted Mellors riding a works 350 in the German Grand Prix at Sachensring in 1938. Note the one-piece magnesium gearbox end cover and the hole-through-the-fuel-tank method of fixing at the rear. Note also the 10 in. square cylinder head and the unusual fork damper known as the Dene. This photograph has lain in archives in the USA for the past 20 years, only recently being identified by Dr Helmut Krackowizer, and was kindly presented to the author

Below One could call this a work of art; the delectable KTT Mk VIII as it was introduced at the 1938 show. Pretty and business-like, it could be relied upon to complete a full season's hard racing, and more, without any major attention

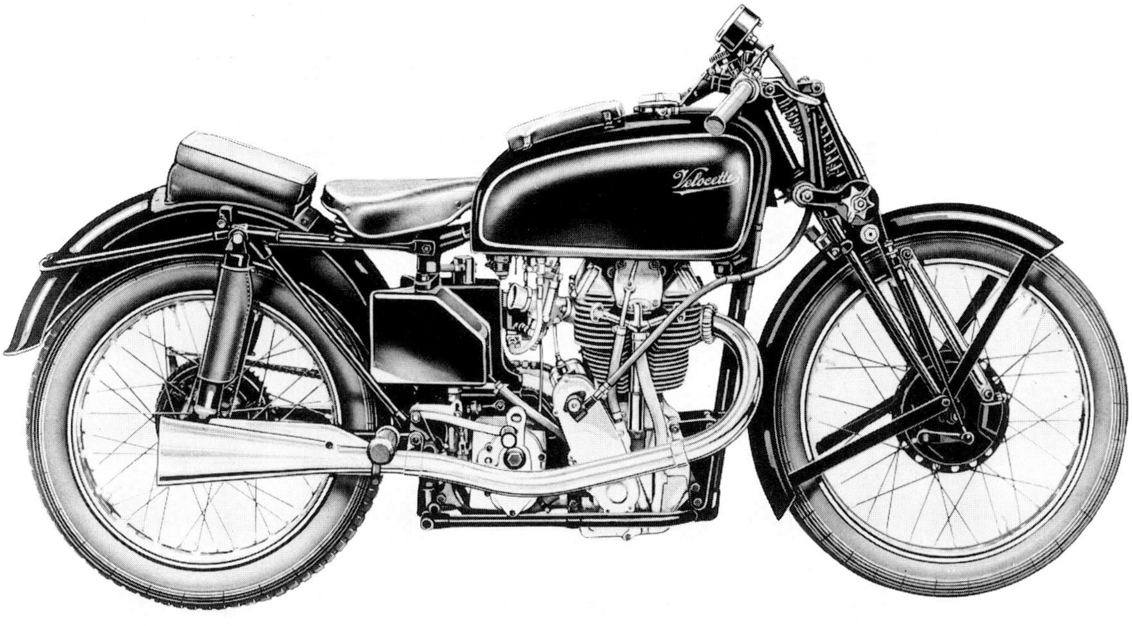

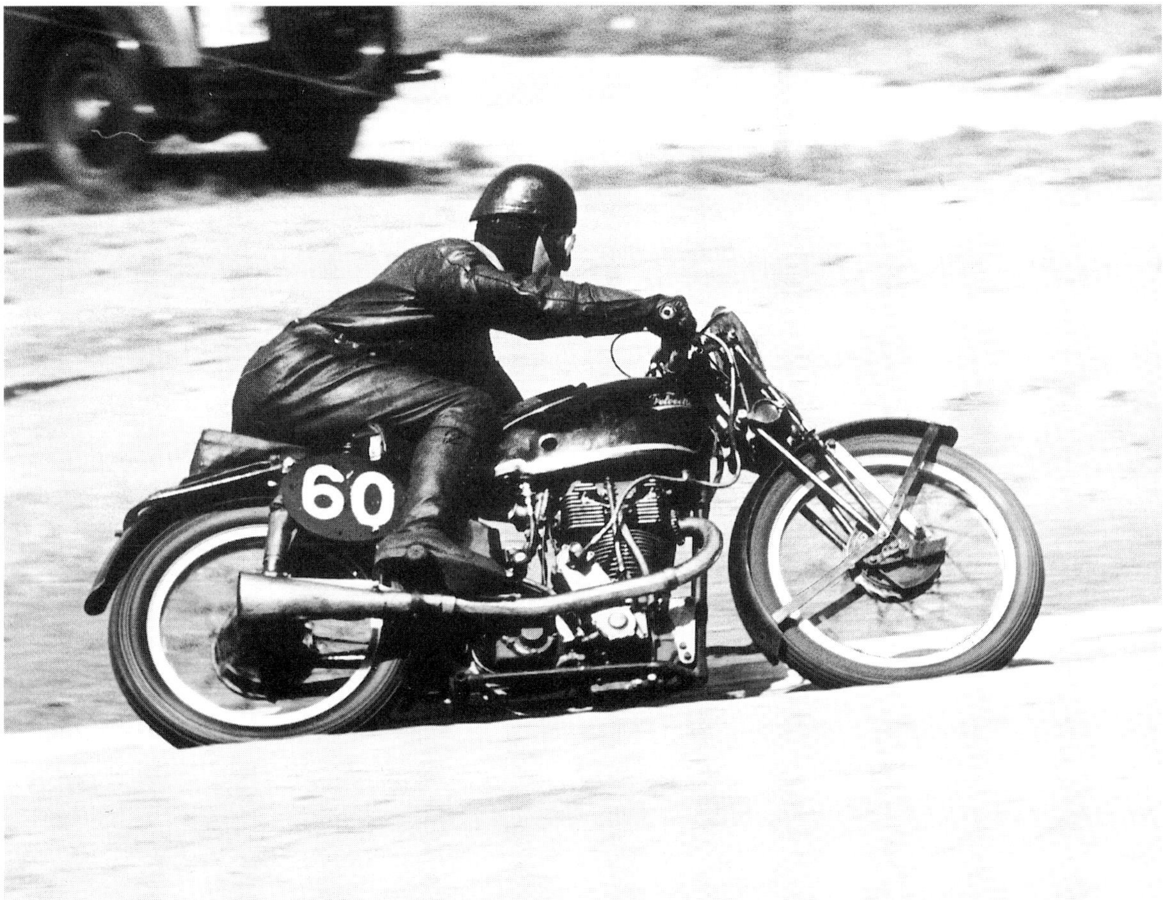
60

Above A famous shot of Woods in full flight down Bray Hill, making up time lost when a faulty rev-counter misled him and dropped him down the field. This was Stanley's tenth and last TT win

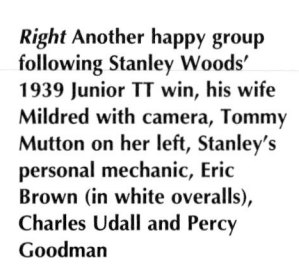

Right Another happy group following Stanley Woods' 1939 Junior TT win, his wife Mildred with camera, Tommy Mutton on her left, Stanley's personal mechanic, Eric Brown (in white overalls), Charles Udall and Percy Goodman

Another view of the first production KTT Mk VIII. It had high-tensile steel rims and black hubs, the front hub being made in two parts—a cast brake drum bolted to a magnesium hub. This was virtually what the works bikes used between 1936 and 1938

plain casting containing a shrunk-in outer ring, a heavy thrust washer and the original bronze-caged roller assembly normally carried within the kickstart mechanism. This bearing, containing eight big-end rollers, complete with its outer ring, was the same as that used to support the camshaft on this and earlier (Mk VI and VII) engines, and the previous works motors with the external camshaft oiling system.

The front fork, like the Mk VII, had the telescopic spring guide, pivoting on silentbloc bushes at each end, double friction dampers on both sides, and a long alloy torque arm to the magnesium-alloy brake plate which incorporated an air scoop. Heavier top and bottom links were introduced post-war.

Hubs, initially, were based on those used on the works machines, both being beautiful magnesium castings. At the rear, a close-grained, centrifugally-spun brake drum cum sprocket, finned for cooling purposes, was fixed to the hub by six special bolts. The same casting, machined with a suitable spoke flange containing 18 holes, plus additional lightening holes, was bolted to the neat, light magnesium front hub. Works hubs introduced in 1936 were basically similar, except that the front was scalloped between the spoke holes on the brake side—a readily identifiable feature. All were dichromate treated prior to assembly and finished in black. The wheel rims, as standard, were chromium-plated high-tensile steel. Following the initial batch, however, the front hub was to become a full magnesium-alloy casting containing a double-flanged, cast-iron liner shrunk in and retained by six $\frac{1}{4}$ in. bolts, while the rims became Dunlop alloy items.

Ignition was provided by a BTH TT magneto—'fit and forget' was their motto. The carburettor was an Amal T-10 TT instrument with a $1\frac{3}{32}$ in. choke and a remote float chamber mounted on the one-gallon capacity oil tank. This was rubber mounted on four points.

The rear fork, made from tapered tubing and extremely rigid, pivoted on phosphor-bronze bushes, lubricated by Tecalemit grease nipples, while the

90 | Velocette

Above Jimmy Garnett from Liverpool following early morning practice, June 1939, with KTT 724, his Mk VI supplied by Archer. The bike and rider are still going strong

Above left Stanley Woods wafting through Union Mills during his tenth TT win, the 1939 Junior

Below left Stanley Woods' 350, similar to Mellors', was a works-development springer. Note the saddle spring mountings and additional megaphone strap mountings effected by the use of clamps

Dowty oleo suspension units required critical setting to the recommended pressure. The works mechanics used a gauge with two connecting pipes which balanced the pressure when fixed to the two valves simultaneously. Wheel bearings, at both ends, were Timken taper rollers, with left-hand threaded adjusting and lock nuts on the offside rear, and right-hand threaded nuts on the nearside front—normal bicycle practice. It was (and still is) important that some slack be apparent in the wheel bearings, particularly the rear one, to allow for expansion as the temperature of the units built up.

For sheer beauty of line, the Mk VIII KTT has few equals. With its long, deep petrol tank, high-level exhaust system and well proportioned power unit, giving a slim frontal appearance, it is both functional and businesslike.

Despite the machine's overall weight of some 325 lb, the distribution is such that handling is precise, making it extremely manoeuvrable. With its sweet, smooth power output combined with the light precision of the gearbox and other controls, it is a delight to ride. If ever there was a 'classic' motorcycle, this is undoubtedly it. Anything produced subsequent to it seemed to lack its fine drawn qualities. One could almost have stopped the clock at that point in Veloce's history.

Commencing at engine number 801, some 49 machines were produced and sold during the 1939 season, despite the inevitability of the war that was looming fast. When it arrived, they were put aside with a fond hope that they would soon be brought out and enjoyed once more.

CHAPTER 13

The Waycott ISDT outfit

When designing Eugene Goodman's everyman's machine, Phil Irving's brief was to make use of obsolete flywheel castings, con-rods and pistons, surplus from the early model K, of which stocks were plentiful. This was the sidevalve Model M that, in prototype form, did not come up to expectations and was discarded in favour of the high-camshaft 250 MOV.

In no way should this be read as a reflection upon his ability as a designer and engineer. On the contrary, that ability is legion and without question; he was merely doing what he was told to do. That initial spell with the company, from August 1930 to March 1931, must have whetted his appetite, particularly since he was instrumental in the birth of 'Whiffling Clara'. Since he and Willis—the only outsiders in an otherwise family concern—worked well together.

Following a period at Stevenage with Phillip Vincent, Irving rejoined Veloce in late 1936 and became involved in detail design. Among other things, he was responsible for the cycle parts of the Stuart Waycott sidecar outfit built for the 1937 ISDT. This had a swing-axle sidecar chassis based on the Australian Goulding design.

Willis prepared the engine, using a TT motor with the

Stuart Waycott's works 596 cc International Six Day Trial machine using a TT motor with an enlarged bore and stroke of 85 × 104 mm. Note the extra scavenge pipe from the timing cover, the swillpot on the carburettor, and the extended front engine plate for the very necessary fourth—or fifth—sidecar fixing point (*Dennis Quinlan*)

big new 'Huntley and Palmer' head and fully enclosed valve gear. He increased the stroke to 105 mm and enlarged the bore to some 85 mm, giving a total capacity of 596 cc, the biggest single-cylinder Velo ever produced at the factory. According to notes in Irving's little black book, the frame was based on an MSS/KSS Mk II with the standard steering head angle of 27 degrees which required the use of top fork links of 3 in. centres, compared with standard links of $3\frac{1}{2}$ in. centres.

In 1938, the front downtube was bent to allow for a reduction in head angle to 23 degrees, therefore reducing the trail to $\frac{13}{16}$ in. and lifting the front end at the same time. In addition, a stronger fork spring was added—of 8 in. free length with a poundage of 225—thus improving the ground clearance and the handling.

A further proposed modification was to change the fork links to those of $3\frac{1}{4}$ in. centres, but there is no record to show whether this was actually carried out or not.

One well recorded feature was the provision for rapid plug changing with the tall motor—a hole through the fuel tank, allowing access for a long tubular spanner. Among the other features was an increased-capacity oil tank—basically that of a Mk V KTT turned through 90 degrees with suitable attachments. An extended front engine plate provided a very necessary

International Six Day Trial competitors for 1936. Left to right: Vic Brittain, Stuart Waycott, Eddie Belstein (passenger) and George Rowley. All were members of the winning team. The outfit was built specially for the job, and on this occasion was fitted with a modified overhead-camshaft 495 cc TT engine. It was apparent, however, that an enlarged engine would soon be required to compete with the BMW 600

fourth sidecar fixing point, and a swill pot arrangement was provided to counteract the possibilities of fuel starvation when keeping the wick turned up on a long, fast right-hander. Note, too, the upswept exhaust system shown in the photograph, the inverted fishtail silencer and 'Loch Ness Monster' seat. The last was the forerunner of the dualseat and was developed by Willis for the TT models to overcome the possibility of the rules being misinterpreted when a saddle and pad could be read as two seats instead of one.

Also note the fold-up prop stand with its over-centre locking arm—to facilitate rapid rear wheel removal—and the additional oil return pipe from the extra scavenge pump in the inner timing cover, a feature of Veloce works racing engines, as mentioned previously.

The kneegrip, you will note, was fitted much further back than usual. This was to align with the grip on the

A rare photo of Harold Willis in discussion with the opposition's chief, Joe Craig. It is said that Craig would have been pumping Harold for information (*Goodman Collection*)

opposite side, which was positioned to allow for that plug changing facility. The front forks were different in that they were basically of TT type with damping on both sides to control the movement, but without the telescopic spring arrangement. Additionally, since it was advantageous for all three wheels to be interchangeable the front wheel was a two-piece device, just like the rear. Therefore, it was necessary to fit a special fork blade on the right-hand side with a flat section to which was attached the brake plate in the manner of the Sunbeams of the 1930s. This allowed the brake to remain in place, while the wheel itself was removed. A spare wheel was attached to the sidecar. Detachable distance pieces, necessary for wheel removal, were secured by Bowden cable to prevent them from being lost.

As was commonplace among Midlands manufacturers in those days, much testing was carried out at Donington Park. Having carried out the development work, and being the competent rider that he was, Irving proceeded to Donington with the young Peter Goodman who, at that time, was making a name for himself in road racing and had offered his services as ballast. However, he may have had second thoughts about sidecar passengering, because Irving was to give the outfit a thorough tousing. Despite the fact that it was a trials outfit, he was pushing it round at speeds that were within a second of the then lap record for the racing sidecar class.

It was as well that the outfit was subjected to such a hammering, however, because three of the front fork tubes snapped. With only a week to go to the six-day event, they had to high tail it back to Hall Green, and rebuild the forks with heavier gauge tubing and more substantial links, which were a fixed fit on the spindles.

A similar pre-trial testing spree took place at Donington the following year, 1938, when the piston broke, the rod damaged the liner and both valves were bent in the process, which necessitated a complete engine strip to clean out the mess. Damaged components were replaced and a new piston was manufactured from a lump of suitable alloy from the ill-fated Aspin experimental stock, which was well worth the effort because Stuart Waycott emerged as a member of the winning team.

According to Phil Irving's notes, the power output was 35 bhp in 1938, the exhaust note was very sharp and the valve gear rather noisy.

Some years later, while Peter Goodman was serving in the RAF during the war, he was posted to Darley Moor, near Ashbourne in Derbyshire, and was using the Waycott outfit for transport to get him about. Having been the only survivor in an aircraft crash, he was somewhat nervous about continuing flying, made worse on one occasion when he was taken up and given a particularly rough ride by a certain pilot. So when the said pilot required a lift into town, Peter took him in the Waycott outfit and proceeded to show him a thing or two about low flying Velocettes!

Stuart Waycott eventually emigrated to Australia where he took up sheepfarming. He died a few years ago.

Post-war, this famous outfit was campaigned by Reg Lewis of Bristol, in whose hands it was invincible, winning just about everything on the grass in the South Western centre, before being put aside and eventually broken up. The massive engine remained in his shop window for many years—to be stolen by an unsuspecting thief, unaware of what it was. It was too hot to handle; and was rescued from a scrap heap where it had been dumped.

More recently, stripped and rebuilt by Andy Savage, it has been installed in a suitable frame and is expected to appear at the occasional Vintage race meeting.

CHAPTER 14

The factory racing 500s

In passing, some mention should be made of the factory racing 500s used by Mellors and Woods pre-war. Frame and cycle parts were standard KTT, modified to accommodate the tall engine in that the underside of the big fuel tank had to be cut away to clear the cambox. The rear tank mounting was changed by cutting off the original brackets on the frame to provide clearance for the carburettor. Instead a bracket was fixed on the frame, between the two tank halves, and threaded to take $\frac{7}{16}$ in. × 26 tpi stepped bolts. These were inserted—one on each side—through a tube welded into the tank, incorporating a rubber mounting in the manner of the early 7R AJS.

Right Dr Helmut Krackowizer always has had a keen eye for detail. He made this drawing of a 1937 factory 500 in 1944. Note the mounting lug for the rear of the fuel tank

Below The then TT Riders' Association president, Bill Lomas, climbing out of the Gooseneck during the 1986 Lap of Honour. He's on 5005/7, one of the works 500 race machines, owned and restored by the author

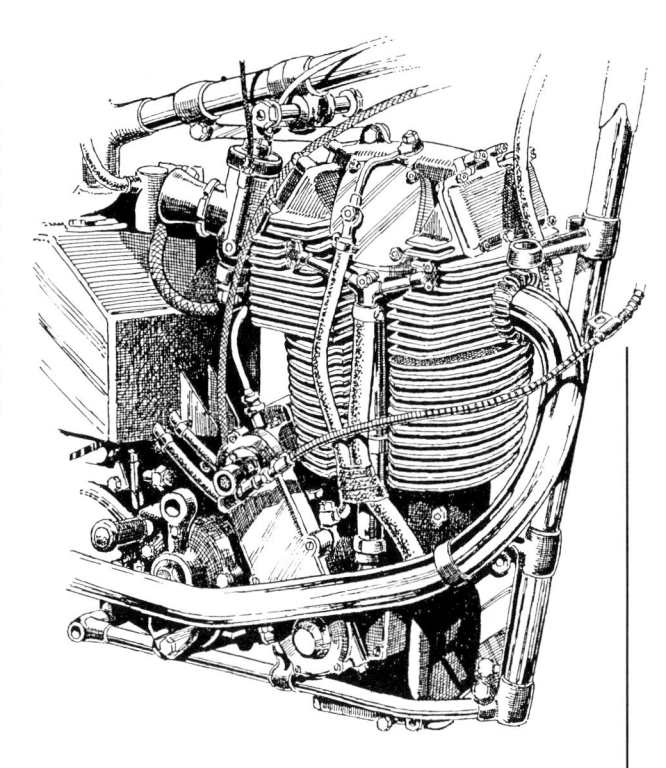

The pride and joy in the Archer camp in 1939 was this 'dog kennel' 500 springer, which Stanley Woods had used in 1936. Here it is at the back of the Falcon Cliffe Hotel being fettled by Les' father. Standing alongside are, left to right, Harry Caldwell, Jim Garnett, Les Archer and Dennis Offord. In 1939, Archers had carried out a policy of supplying and preparing race machines for selected customers and showing them the ropes. Caldwell and Garnett were two such fortunate riders of Mk VII KTT models. They justified their selection by finishing 30th and 31st. The works 500 was eventually sold, post-war, to Rod Coleman. He took it to New Zealand where it remains to this day, in a sorry and dismantled state, the engine having been virtually destroyed in a fire (*Les Archer*)

The rear sprocket/brake drum carried $\frac{5}{8}$ in. × $\frac{1}{4}$ in. chain. The front brake was a two-piece device, like the works 350s. It was produced by machining a rear, finned, brake casting and was scalloped between the spoke holes on the flange to save weight. This casting was bolted to a neat magnesium hub, giving a surprisingly rigid assembly.

The engine was based dimensionally on the MSS, having a bore and stroke of 81 × 96 mm. The con-rod, of MSS length, was made from a KE805 forging and machined all over like a KTT. For a while, pre-war race engines, including the 350s, had a small-bore copper pipe clipped along one side of the rod. With suitably machined tolerances, it passed oil to the small-end and through a jet on to the underside of the piston, in an attempt to keep it cool. This idea was dropped after the war, when it was found that the rivets tended to loosen.

The 1 in. diameter driveside mainshaft was drilled through the centre for crankcase breathing. Initially, the driveside main bearing was a double-row lipped roller, as on the MSS and KSS II. Later, it was replaced by a double-row barrel-shaped roller, while the timing side made use of the normal single-row lipped roller of the standard KTT. Valve sizes were $1\frac{15}{16}$ in. inlet with $\frac{5}{16}$ in. diameter stem, and $1\frac{27}{32}$ in. sodium-filled exhaust with a $\frac{7}{16}$ in. diameter stem.

Cam and valve gear were normal KTT with heavy-duty bottom bevels, Oldham couplings, and top and bottom bevels supported by bearings rather than bushes. The vertical drive shaft was waisted and the additional scavenge pump used.

The slipper-type piston was forged and lightened and gave a compression ration of around 8.5:1. On dope and with careful setting, it could be taken to 10:1 by the

Stanley Woods in full flight on the 500 down Bray in 1938 (*The Motor Cycle*)

The factory racing 500s | 97

Above A try-out at Donington Park in May 1939, prior to the TT. Stanley Woods is pushing off a Senior Race 500, freshly rebuilt by Tommy Mutton, who is also pushing. Others are, left to right, Charles Udall, Ted Mellors and Sid Stevenson. Note the works two-piece front hub with scalloped spoke flange (*Betty Griffin*)

Above Harold Willis, with Austrian rider Franz Binder, congratulating Ted Mellors in 1938. The machine is a factory 500. Particular note should be made of the alloy torque arm on the front brake, which is attached to a lug bolted to the fork blade, not brazed. Also, the megaphone mounting bracket is clipped to the subframe tube. There's an extra oil feed from the timing cover into a jet which helped lubricate the bore. This facility was also there in 1939, but was not used—it was plugged with a bolt

removal of a substantial shim from the base of the barrel.

The carburettor was usually a $1\frac{7}{32}$ in. RN, although one engine was set up with a choke of $1\frac{1}{4}$ in. for Mellors in 1939. Due to the size of the assembled engine, it was almost impossible to install it into a frame without first removing the head.

Power output was in the region of 39–43 bhp at 6500 rpm, 6700 being absolute maximum. Top speed was in the region of 125 mph.

These engines, and some of the works 350s, usually had a special vane-type of engine shock absorber, incorporating rubber blocks similar to that device at the back of a Norton clutch. It was capped by a detachable alloy cover. Presumably, the standard spring type had given trouble at some time. In my experience, this probably meant that the inner spring locating dogs at the back of the so-called splined clutch had broken off, rendering the unit inoperative.

CHAPTER 15

The Roarer

The big prize in the racing game had always been a win in the Senior TT, but for many years Veloce had only contested the Junior class, using the 350 on which they had based their fortunes. Indeed, there was a time during the early 1930s when Percy Goodman was against building a Senior class contender. He felt that it was just not the right thing to do when their 'bread and butter' lay with the Junior model range.

However, circumstances had changed and they were now in at the deep end with full-house works 500s, in addition to the Junior models. The 500s were fully justified, too, since the production MSS roadster was by now well and truly established.

The company had responded to the seasoned advice of the great Stanley Woods and come up with the goods in the form of a competitive springer on which he was to finish second in 1936, with a fastest lap thrown

Above right **In the Island during 1938 and 1939, following a test session. Left to right: Stanley Woods, Percy Goodman and Charles Udall. Sid Stevenson takes care of the machine** (*Veloce publicity*)

Below **The news that Veloce were working on a supercharged twin was given by** *The Motor Cycle* **of 26 January 1939**

T.T. CHALLENGE

In the Velocette factory at the moment a machine is being evolved in accordance with modern racing requirements. The firm is determined to do its utmost to advance motor cycle design, to uphold the prestige of the British industry throughout the world, to keep abreast of subsidised foreign efforts and to blunt the thin end of the wedge by means of which the foreigner is attempting to undermine the popularity of the British motor cycle.

The machine that is being worked upon is a supercharged twin designed to eliminate all the inherent defects and disadvantages that attach to flat-twins, either transverse or otherwise, vee-twins, or multis having a greater number of cylinders. This machine is being considered entirely from the racing angle, it is being built solely for racing, and no detail which is thought necessary in a successful racing machine will be sacrificed on the grounds that its exclusion would, in the future, render it simpler to make a production job.

At the same time, preliminary development has brought to light the fact that the design possesses many features which would be highly desirable in a touring production, and it seems likely that development will not cease with the completion of the racing machine.

From stem to stern this is a new design; the makers have started with a clear piece of paper; they have endeavoured to empty their minds of everything they have done in the past and to bring completely fresh ideas into being. Every part, with the exception of such items as electrical equipment, carburettor, tyres, and so on, is being made in the Velocette factory. Engine, gear box, transmission, and frame are to be of Velocette design and manufacture.

Details of the construction cannot be given at the moment, but it can be said that the arrangement of the crankshaft and camshaft, the method of driving the compressor and magneto, the arrangement of the shaft drive and wheel suspension are points of utmost interest.

It is hoped to have the machine—as Harold Willis puts it—"in good régime" for the T.T. in June. Great efforts will be made to accomplish this, and such is the determination to be represented in the Race that the firm is prepared to concentrate on the preparation of only one machine. They point out that one machine produced thoroughly is likely to perform better than three hurriedly prepared mounts, and they would rather pin their faith to a lone entry than be out of the Race altogether.

They are tackling this job with a keen, enthusiastic, fighting spirit, and their efforts will surely put heart into all branches of the movement. More power to them and may good fortune attend their endeavours.

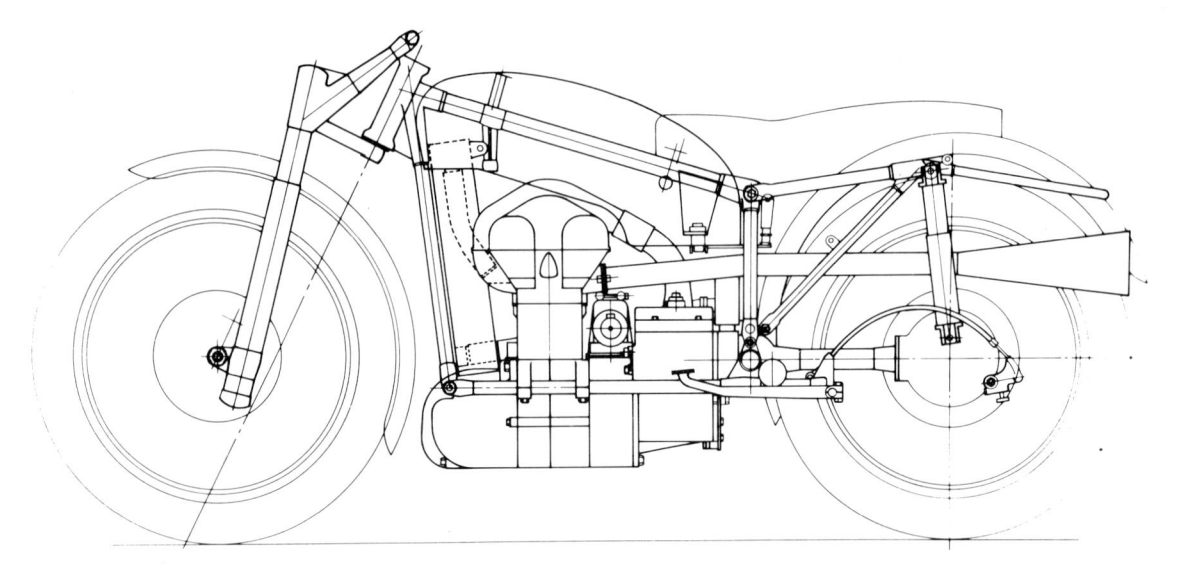

Above **An early general arrangement drawing of the proposed supercharged shaft-driven twin in liquid-cooled form. Note the telescopic forks**

in. In 1937 he was to finish second in the Senior with Mellors fourth. At about this time, Willis in his usual dry way, was heard to remark that it was time they dropped all this '1066' business, referring to the petrol tank transfer which listed the company's victories in the 1926, 1928 and 1929 TTs, adding that 'we shall never win another TT whilst we have that under the name'.

The transfers were duly changed and, lo and behold, Stanley chalked up a Junior first in 1938, ably backed by Mellors in second spot. In a last-ditch attempt to find more power, a bigger inlet valve was introduced the day before the team left for the island. That gave them the edge they required. The pair were to finish second and sixth respectively in the Senior event.

Despite these achievements, however, a Senior TT win eluded them, and it appeared that to retain a chance it would be necessary to look into the possibilities of forced induction allied to multi-cylinders. This was a formula that had been well proven by this time, since both BMW and Gilera were really making the racing world sit up and take notice with respectively a blown aircooled flat twin and a blown liquid-cooled four.

The BMW was light and fast, but didn't handle too well, although one major attraction, above all else, was the fact that, as it was shaft driven, there were no problems with oil being deposited on the back tyre. On Veloce's own, and similar, race machines, the whole of the nearside back end of the bike was usually smothered in lubricant at the end of a long race. That didn't help lap times one iota!

The boffins attributed the poor handling of the BMW to the fact that, being shaft driven, the torque reaction

Percy Goodman tries the Roarer for size in 1939 (*The Motor Cycle*)

caused it to yaw. Willis and his team, however, thought differently, stating that it was more likely due to gyratory problems with the big crankshaft—they were right, as it transpires.

Immediately following the 1938 TT, Veloce began an ambitious design and manufacturing exercise with the aim of producing possibly the most technically interest-

A genuine 1939 photograph of the Roarer, as indicated by the black exhaust pipes

This close-up shows a weld repair on the downtube to rectify a crack caused by hydrogen embrittlement

ing and advanced machine that had been evolved hitherto.

Charles Udall was given the job of designing and producing detailed drawings, based on guidelines resulting from decisions of policy at board level. Percy Goodman, having always maintained that a race machine should be basically similar to a production roadster, therefore laid the foundations for not one, but two machines that were similar in concept. The second machine, to be designed and drawn in detail by Phil Irving, was to be known as the Model O—but more of that one later. This, of course, was Goodman's typical means of justifying to himself the effort being put into the special racing machine project.

First and foremost, it had to be shaft driven, like the BMW, and what better than to enclose the final drive shaft within the left-hand rear fork. The design provided for two cranks which were securely geared together drive to the Lucas magneto, mounted atop the casing between the two shafts. The 5 in. diameter crankshafts, with centres only $5\frac{1}{4}$ in. apart, would keep the overall engine width down to acceptable levels, and offsetting the centre-line of each cylinder by $\frac{1}{4}$ in. would put them well out into the air stream while allowing room for a vertical bevel drive shaft to pass between them to drive the overhead camshafts.

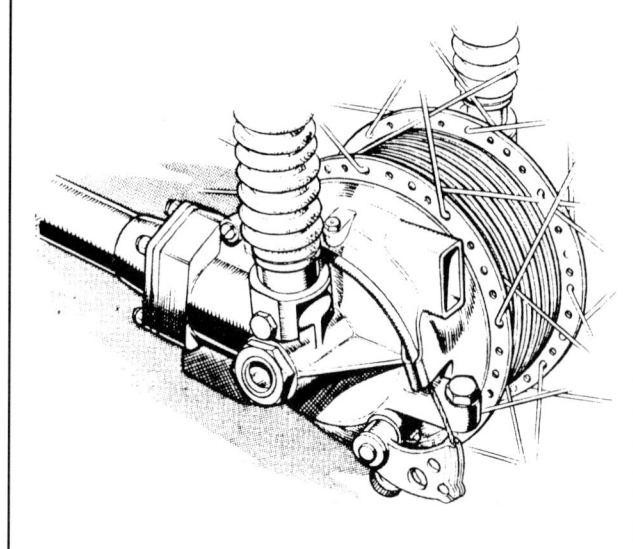

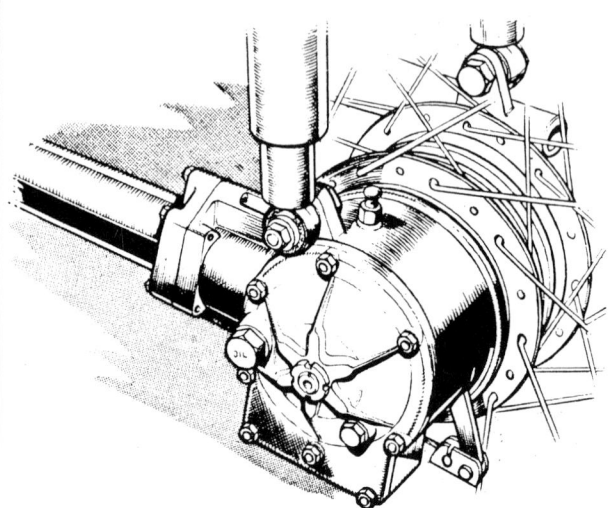

A KTT engine on test with a straight, rather than bent, exhaust pipe had shown a worthwhile increase in power, so with liquid cooling in mind, it was decided to produce the unit with the exhaust ports facing rearwards. This would have the added advantage of extending the bifurcated induction manifold to the extent that the increased length would assist in damping out the pulsations from the rear-mounted blower. A special frame was produced with proven geometry which would allow the whole of the power unit to be installed snugly between the widely-spaced

Above **Proof that racing improves the breed; compare the Roarer's final-drive design (top) with the scaled-down version on the Velocette Valiant of 1957 below it**

Below **Tommy Mutton and Jimmy Owen, having painstakingly built the supercharged twin power unit, trundle it round to the test house on their home-made barrow. This consisted of an old packing case, a couple of lengths of tubing and a pair of old cast-iron flywheels, surplus from the early camshaft production** (*Betty Griffin*)

and located on the usual Velocette taper, but keyed for critical location.

The left-hand crank drove, via the coupling gear, a dry single-plate clutch, later to be changed to a three-plate design. The clutch, in turn, was mated to a four-speed gearbox with indirect ratios containing large-diameter gear wheels. This allowed the main weight of the crankshafts to be suspended low down between the main frame rails, while the gearbox output shaft, some $3\frac{1}{2}$ in. higher to be precise, was bang in line with the rear fork pivot and aligned with the drive shaft through a specially made Bendix Weiss constant-velocity joint. The offside crank, apart from driving the overhead-camshaft drive gear via a couple of spur gears off the front end, would also drive the supercharger (a Centric device) from the rear via a skew-gear

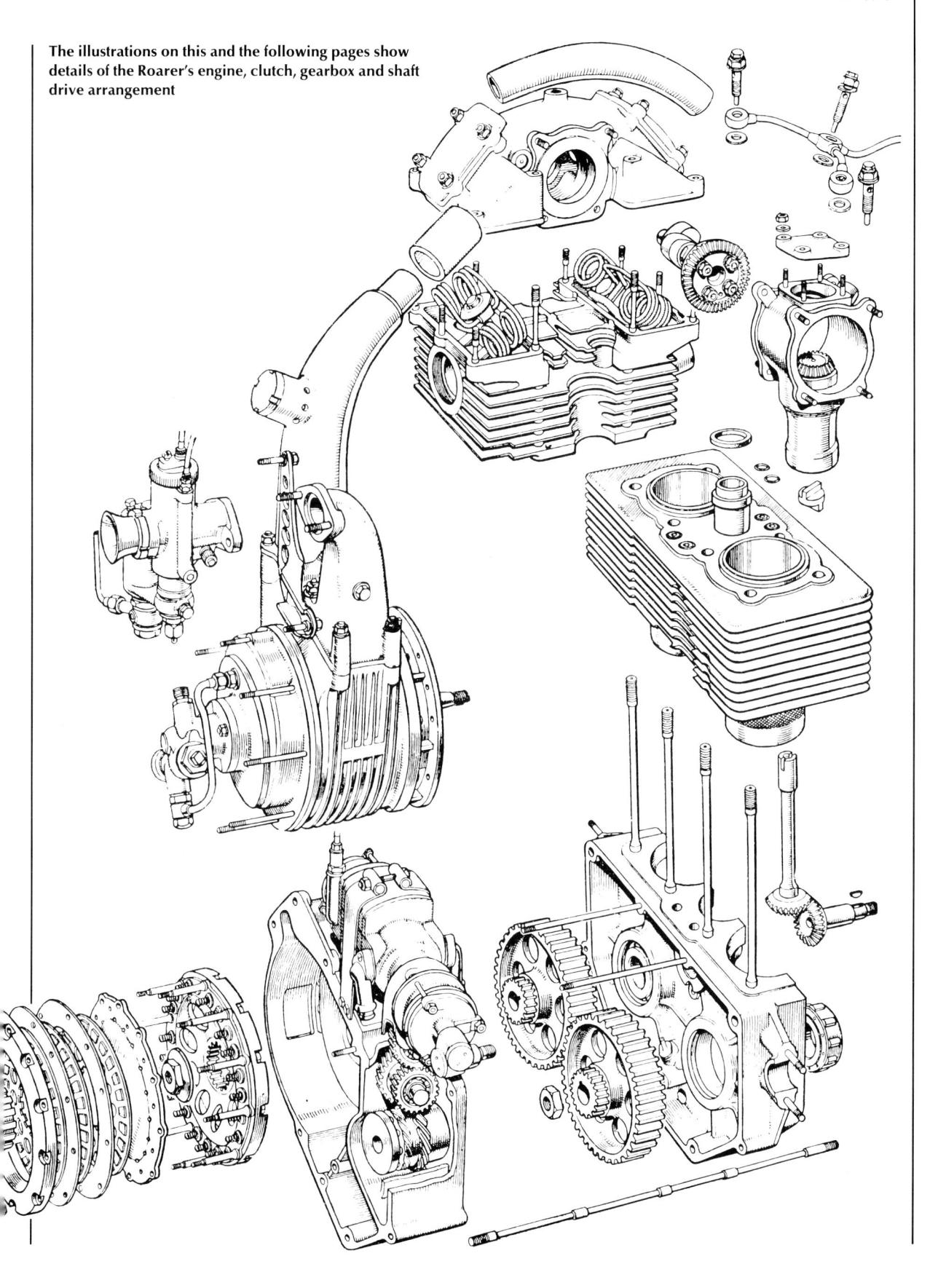

The illustrations on this and the following pages show details of the Roarer's engine, clutch, gearbox and shaft drive arrangement

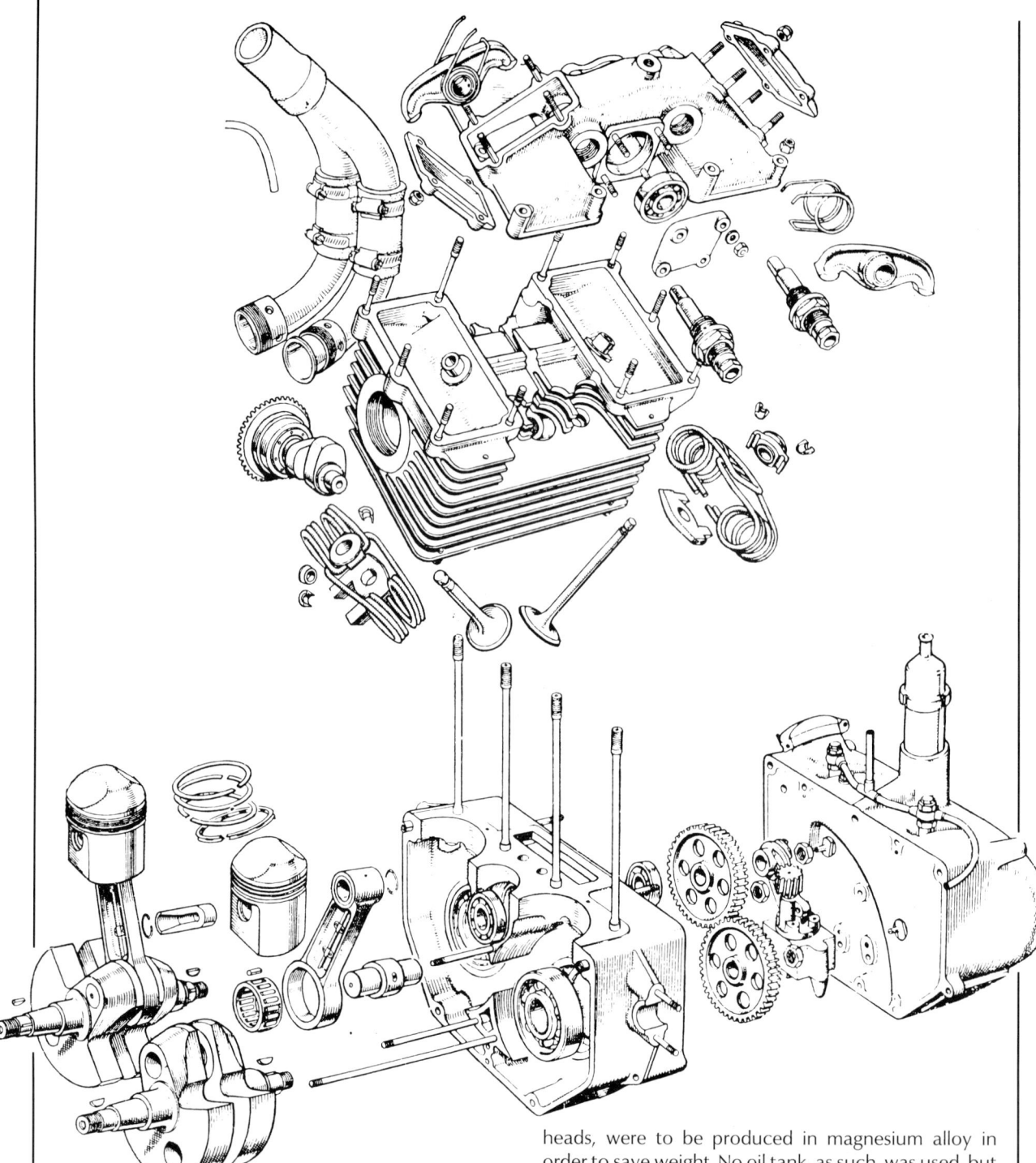

rails, along with the complete transmission system, including the rear wheel, while the top half, including forks and front wheel, could be bolted on later. Front forks, incidentally, were to be of a telescopic design, and both hubs of an advanced full-width type in magnesium alloy with 8 in. diameter brakes.

All castings, with the exception of the cylinder and heads, were to be produced in magnesium alloy in order to save weight. No oil tank, as such, was used, but a bulbous casting right at the front of the engine contained a sufficient quantity of lubricant and provided suitable locations on its machined rear face to accommodate an oil pump skew-driven from the front of the left-hand crank, plus quills and other auxiliary galleries to cope with the job in hand.

It is well known, of course, that the machine was produced in aircooled form only, Percy Goodman's

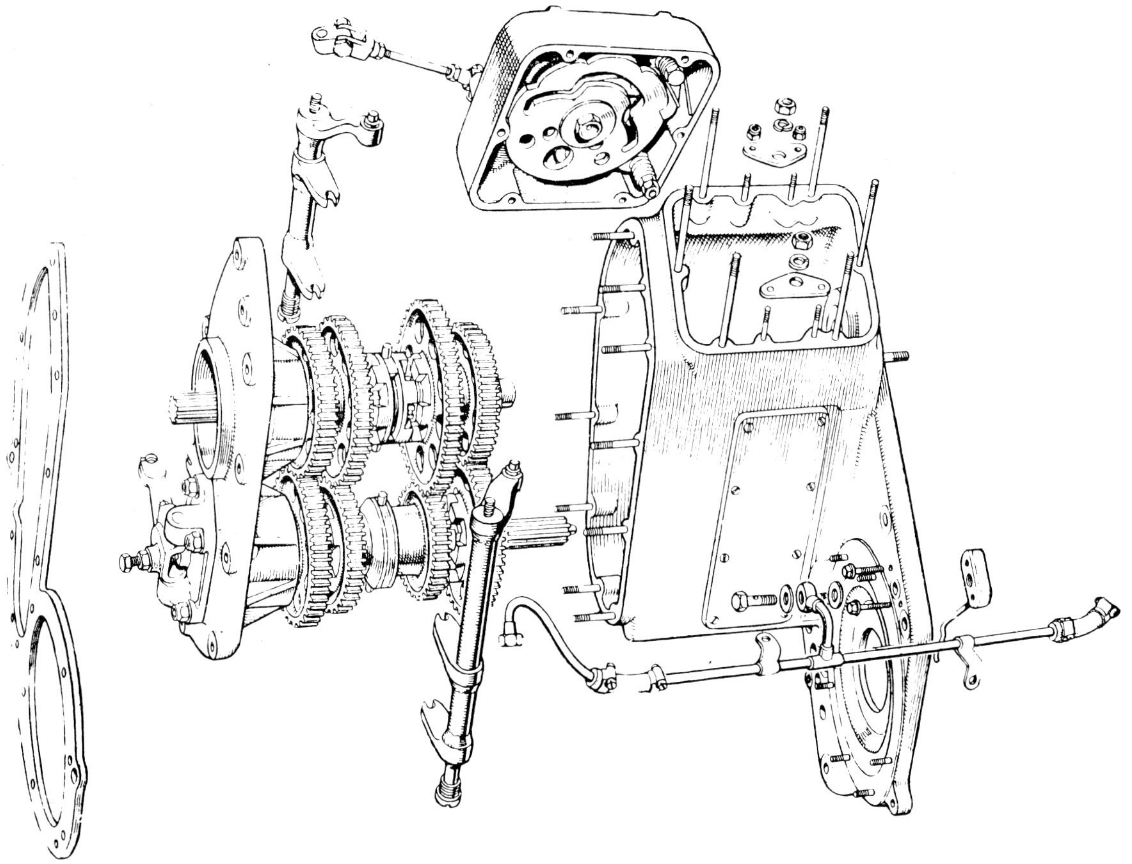

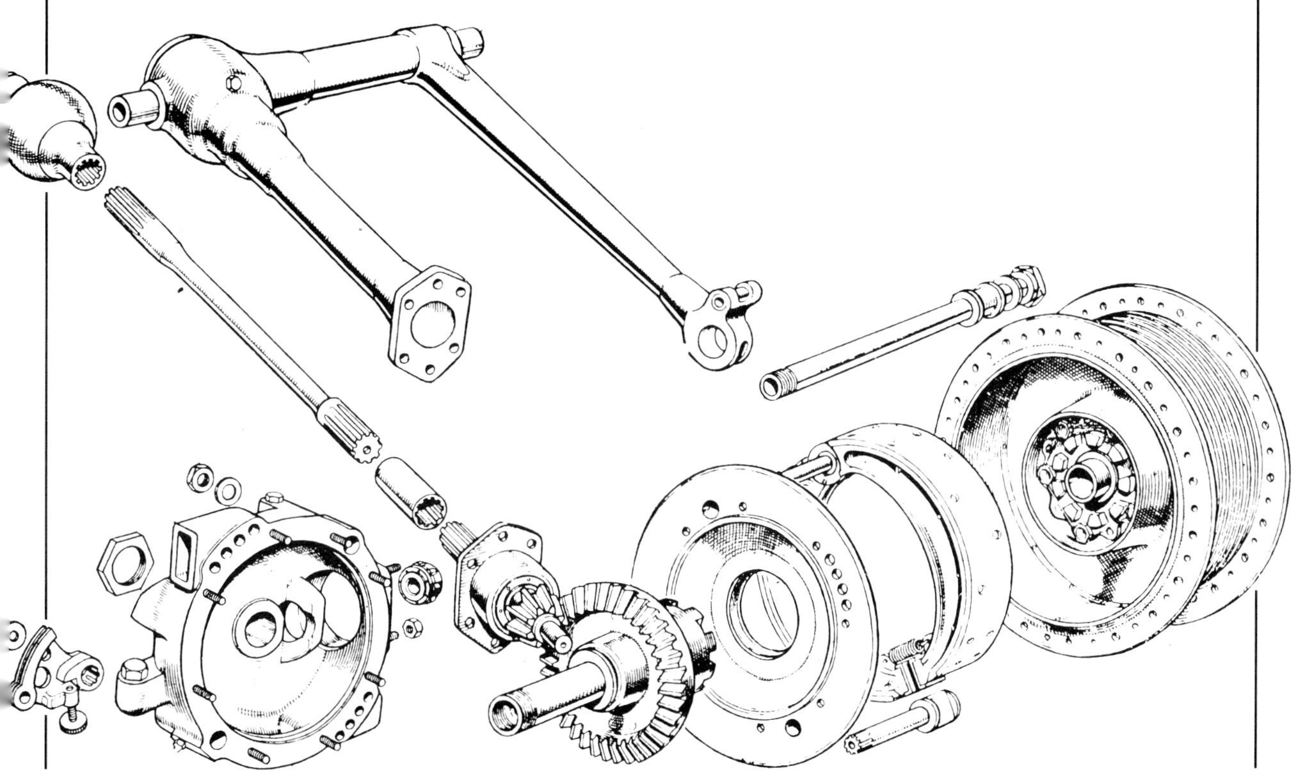

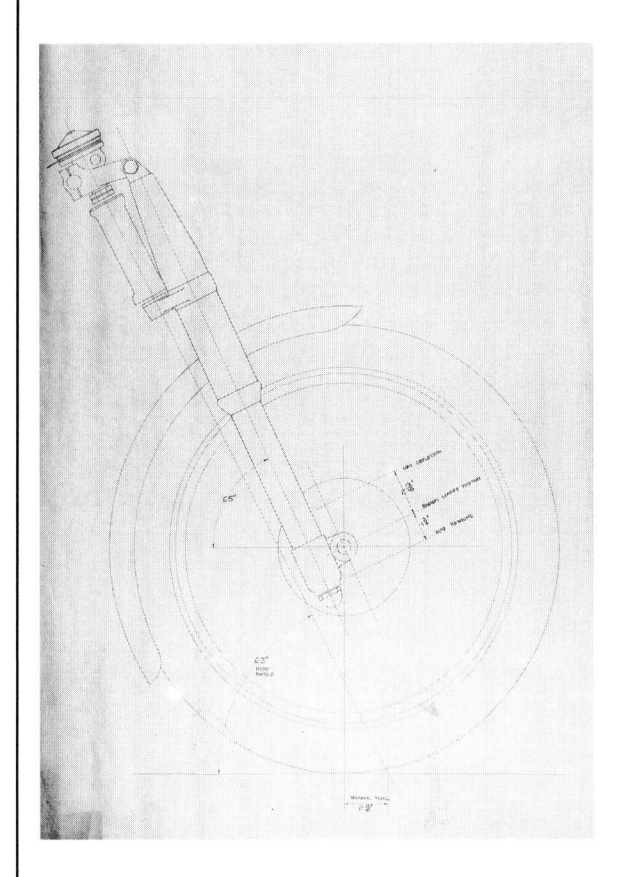

Left **Details of the proposed telescopic forks for the Roarer**

Below **The Roarer power unit, having been built and bench-tested by May 1939, was installed into the as-yet unpainted frame. Time was short! It was necessary to weld a stiffening web in the area of the saddle mounting, and presumably it was worth stiffening up the area around the steering head at the same time. The alloy plate screwed to each side of the bulbous oil tank is merely to blank off the core holes from this casting. It is interesting to note some of the contents of this building, which was part of the repair shop. Inevitably, a number of crash-damaged machines await repair. Three Mk VII KTT petrol tanks are resting among an assortment of wheels, tyres and saddles. On the extreme left stands a discarded cammy racer with 'Loch Ness Monster' seat, a lashed-on tool box and other features that suggest it could have been a Mk VI KTT. The MG Midget against the wall apparently belonged to Harold Willis**

policy dictating the need to stay with established practice, which may also have been the reason why the well proven Webb girder forks were used, although these were specially made to accommodate the $\frac{7}{8}$ in. diameter tubular front wheel spindle. We also know that Stanley was far from convinced that a telescopic fork was as good, let alone superior, to the

Veloce/Webb girders. In fact, when approached on the subject, his words were 'Not on your Nellie!'.

The cylinders were a monobloc casting, like the separate heads, in heat-treated Y alloy with shrunk-in liners that were heavily spigoted for head location. The pistons were forged and meaty to withstand the heat. They were fitted with special wedge-shaped compression rings and aluminium-bronze scrapers. Conrods, by the way, were an H-section forging, machined all over, and carried a small-bore copper pipe referred to previously. Big-ends were 16-roller caged and identical to the KTT, except that the rollers ran directly in the rod, as there was insufficient room to press in an outer ring. This was due to the close proximity of the rods one to another. At the closest point, they were only $\frac{1}{16}$ in. apart.

Above Willis and Udall were friendly with the technical people at Wellworthy, who recommended applying aircraft technology to the pistons and bores of the Roarer. For instance, Bristol Aircraft had suffered from over-oiling of the bores in their Jupiter radial engines. It was cured by using a keystone-section ring to eliminate ring flutter. So the Roarer pistons, machined from forgings supplied by Hughes Johnson of Oldbury, incorporated such rings and included the use of an aluminium-bronze scraper to assist heat dissipation. Note the small-bore oil pipes, clipped and riveted to the connecting rods, the huge main bearings to withstand the load of the 100 per cent balance factor, and the method of securing the engine in the vice—a substantial block, some hefty steel sheets and tubing to the mounting brackets at each side

Left A Jock Leyden cartoon that appeared during wartime, matching the supercharged Roarer as 'truth' against Germany's blown BMW 'propaganda'

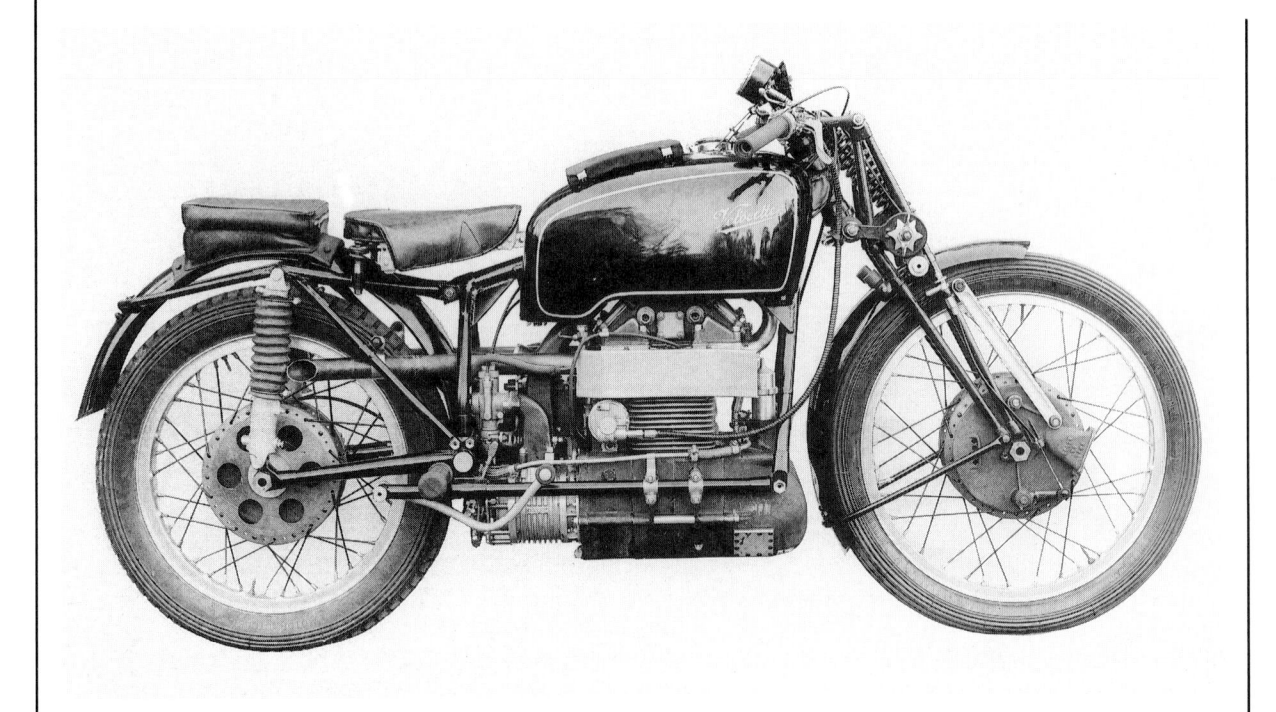

Above Another 1939 photo. The Italian alloy rims were stamped Rudge Whitworth, who were the importers

The separate camboxes were joined together by a double-ended top bevel housing, which contained conventional crown bevels driven by the single vertical driving gear—only one heavy-duty Oldham coupling was used.

The bore and stroke of 68 × 68.25 mm gave a total capacity of 497.7 cc.

The crankshaft rotation was significant in that it threw oil into the centre of the crankcase lower half, allowing for a tapering of the cases which gave adequate cornering clearance. Also, as the oil collected at the base, it could be easily scavenged back to the main tank.

Initially, the engine was set up with a compression ratio of 8.78:1 and a boost pressure of a relatively low 4 psi. A moderate cam timing was used and power output was encouraging. However, time was running short, and it was late in May 1939 that the engine was installed in the unpainted frame, which left much work to be done in order to ready the machine for the forthcoming TT. In fact, final preparation was carried out on the ferry while crossing to the Isle of Man.

There was no question of shelving the project at this late stage, for too much effort and expense had been incurred. Furthermore, it was well known within racing circles that this special machine was on the stocks and expected to be given an airing.

During this time, Willis had told Matt Wright, of AMC, about this machine, in confidence, of course. He stated that they were preparing a special supercharged twin that would either go like the clappers, or be a flop!

There is no doubt that, at the time the TT entries

Above **The Roarer's engine, gearbox and shaft drive assembly**

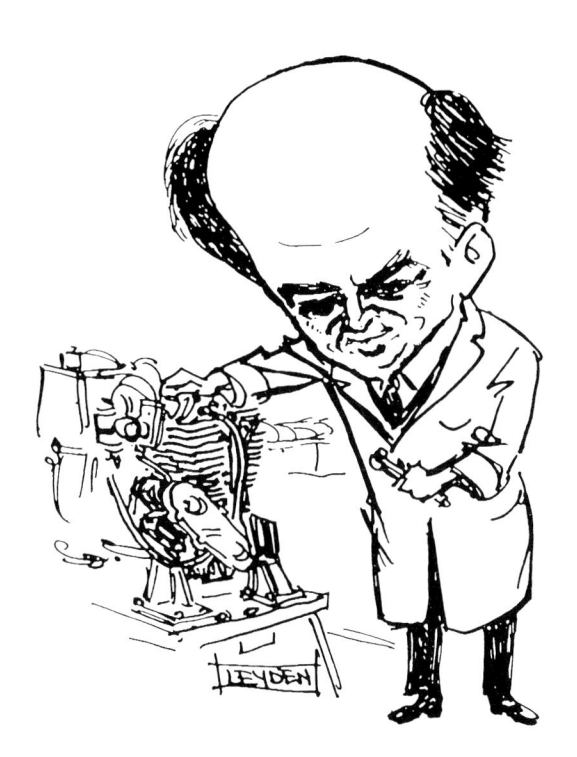

Jock Leyden also drew these two striking caricatures of Willis (on the left) and Percy Goodman (above)

were placed, Veloce had been optimistic in actually racing the machine, because both Mellors and Les Archer—the latter aboard Woods' 1936 Senior machine— were entered on the usual 495 cc capacity models, whereas Stanley was down to ride a machine of 499 cc.

Stanley's sole practice lap on the machine was a lowly 39 minutes, caused by the need to change plugs, as the soft grade would not stand any use at all, while the hard racing plugs suffered from an excess of oil from the blower and wouldn't allow the machine to run properly.

There was no time to mess about, of course, since Stanley, and Mellors for that matter, had to attend to the serious business of practice with the usual Junior and Senior capacity mounts.

Following the TT, further development took place back at the works where, on the test bench, boost pressure was increased to 13 psi, by driving the blower independently. At the same time the compression ratio was reduced to 7.5:1, an extended valve timing (more like that on the KTT) was used and the carburettor choke size was increased to $1\frac{1}{16}$ in. The result was an increase in power output to 54 bhp net. However, this was not considered satisfactory, even at that time, since there was still a tendency for the engine to overheat, and with a war on, it was decided to shelve the whole project.

Regrettably, the idea was never revived because supercharging was banned post-war and much effort was required in other directions, The unique machine was destined never to grace another racing circuit.

Stanley Woods poses with the Roarer shortly before taking it out for the solitary practice lap during the 1939 TT series (*Stanley Woods*)

It is interesting to note that in a letter to Stanley Woods, dated 11 January 1939, Percy Goodman reminded him of the great expense incurred in producing the new 500 racing machine, and told him of the company's need to economize. Because of this, he asked Stanley to accept a lower retaining fee—£300 instead of the usual £400. Goodman went on to say 'an important point to bear in mind, should the special machine prove to be satisfactory in the TT races, we propose to enter you in some Continental races so that we can gain full value in publicity and prestige'.

Stanley's reply, in accepting the lower fee 'under the circumstances' was that he hoped the great expense of the special machine would not be a recurring charge in 1940 and that 'you will see your way to increasing the amount of the retainer once more when the time comes.'

A Senior or Junior TT win in 1938 was worth £250 from Veloce, while £100 was awarded for second place. The ACU paid £100 and £70 respectively.

The only record, to date, of the Roarer ever having been ridden—on this occasion, on test at Cadwell Park, May 1989, and ridden by the author's younger son, Adrian

Stanley Woods always preferred to ride on a Terry saddle which, unlike the Dunlop rubber variety, allowed him to jam his feet firmly on to the footrests with the calves of his legs firmly dug into the rigid saddle frame. Although I don't know the figure, I believe he collected a relatively tidy fee from Terry for doing so.

The Lancashire representative for Terry Saddles was an Irishman, popular among riders and trade alike, who, just prior to the 1923 TT, invited Stanley Woods to use one of their superior saddles. Having had a particularly hard ride on a leaf-sprung saddle in the previous year, Stanley eagerly took up the offer and promptly gave Terry their first TT win, which they never forgot.

When the special 500 was built between those last two TTs pre-war, one could not obtain a constant-velocity joint in Britain, but they were made in America, and a couple were imported specially for the new machine. One was fitted, while the other was put on the shelf as a spare. During the war, Veloce were approached by the Air Ministry who said that they urgently needed such a joint. I understand that it had been required for a new type of bomb sight. It was willingly handed over.

Post-war, the machine was taken into the workshop, dismantled and refurbished, but assembled minus the internals, since it was required for use as a show piece. It was to spend much of its time being moved around the various Velocette dealerships, and this was made so much easier without the heavy internals— all-up weight was some 375 lb.

At one time post-war, when Peter Goodman had finished a good third and shared the fastest lap with Artie Bell in the 1947 Senior TT on Stanley's old mount, there was much jubilation in the camp and his father, Eugene, remarked that 'we must get out the Roarer, convert it to atmospheric induction and we could then perhaps win a Senior TT'. It was no idle speculation, he meant it.

However, it was not to be because, within a few weeks, Peter had been brought down by a marshall attempting to remove a bottle from the track, when in the lead at a Strasbourg race meeting. His injuries were the cause of much concern although, thankfully, he recovered and is well to this day, but Eugene turned against racing from then on and was supported by his sister, Ethel. With two against one, racing was to be on a shoe-string budget from then on.

The internals for the blown twin remained in a box under a bench for many a long year, during which time a family of rats made their nest in the box. They ate all the protective grease and wrapping paper from the

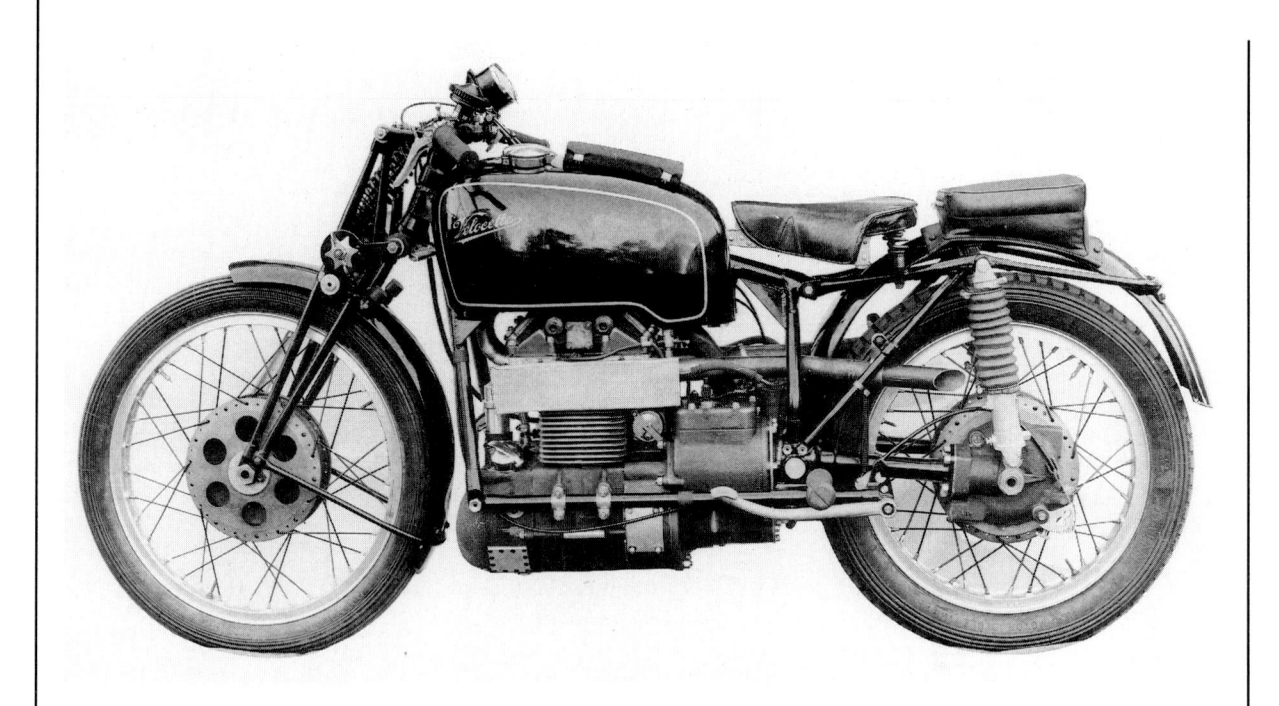

Below The Roarer's engine being assembled

Above and right Further contemporary photos of the Roarer

parts, while their urine was most corrosive, the contents becoming a solid mass of rust. As recently as 1970 one of the works mechanics, with nothing much to occupy his time, requested that he be allowed to build the components back into the bike, which then lay forlorn in the old race shop. He was told not to bother, as it was all too far gone. So when the factory closed, early in 1971, the bike had gone and those internals were converted to scrap by C. C. Cooper & Company, the scrap metal merchants who had bought the site and most of the contents.

Ram-air ducts assist cooling

CHAPTER 16
The Model O

Company policy being that a race machine should be based on a production model dictated the need to lay down foundations for the design and production of a prototype road machine, similar in concept to the blown, shaft-driven twin, the Roarer. As mentioned, Charles Udall was responsible for the detail design drawings of this unique Grand Prix contender, while Phil Irving's task was to design and build the roadgoing version known as the Model O.

Being the practical motorcyclist that he was, Irving had proved his worth at Vincent HRD and was now applying his skills within the Veloce camp, having designed and built an MSS with swinging rear fork. The fork was a substantial fabrication with fixed wheel location and eccentric pivot spindle for chain adjustment. The telescopic friction dampers located at their upper ends within a curved slot to give a quick and simple means of adjustment for load variations. This was to become a standard feature on subsequent roadgoing Velocette springers.

The MSS also enjoyed the benefit of generous enclosure of the wheel, a hand-beaten and welded mild-steel skin having been produced. This reduced the need for additional lugs and tubes and contributed to a certain amount of weight reduction.

The machine was put to a variety of uses by works personnel, including Franz Binder, the Austrian rider who was occasionally to be seen riding it around as a hack.

The O was a much more ambitious project, however. With certain guidelines and under the watchful eye of Percy Goodman, Irving was given a free hand. He and Charles Udall sat at adjacent drawing boards to design their respective models, and one cannot help but conject that a certain amount of rivalry must have existed between them.

The plan was to produce a machine of soft, smooth power characteristics, with good low-down torque and exceptional flexibility, the sort of characteristics produced by a Rolls-Royce motor car of the period, for instance. An output of 30 bhp at something less than 6000 rpm, with easy starting, were the maxims aimed for.

Assembled, like the racing machine, with a balance factor of 100 per cent, the interconnecting gearing allowed the centrifugal forces at mid-stroke to cancel out each other, resulting in dynamically smooth power delivery. The two crankshafts, set side by side transversely with centre-lines 5.1 in. apart, were geared together at the front. They had additional bolt-on flywheels, since the built-up crank webs, made from 4 per cent carbon-steel plate, heat treated and with pressed-in hardened shafts, gave insufficient inertia on their own. Crank rotation was in the opposite direction to the racing machine. Helical timing gears, using the M tooth form, were driven from the rear of the left-hand crank through an intermediate idler gear to the high camshaft—two pairs of cams were keyed to a common shaft—situated between the lower extremities of the two cylinders. Drive to the clutch and gearbox was from the right-hand, or starboard, crank—the terms 'port' and 'starboard' were used by both Willis and Irving in connection with these machines, components being marked 'P' or 'S', rather than 'L' or 'R' for left or right respectively.

Irving chose a single-plate clutch initially, only to find that it would not stand the multiple torque of a twin, so it was changed to a three-plate design. While drawings exist showing a car-type three-speed gearbox, the design chosen was one incorporating what amounts to an MOV/MAC type cluster, turned through 90 degrees, which allowed the use of a normal Veloce camplate.

The eccentric pivot spindle for chain adjustment on the Irving-built MSS

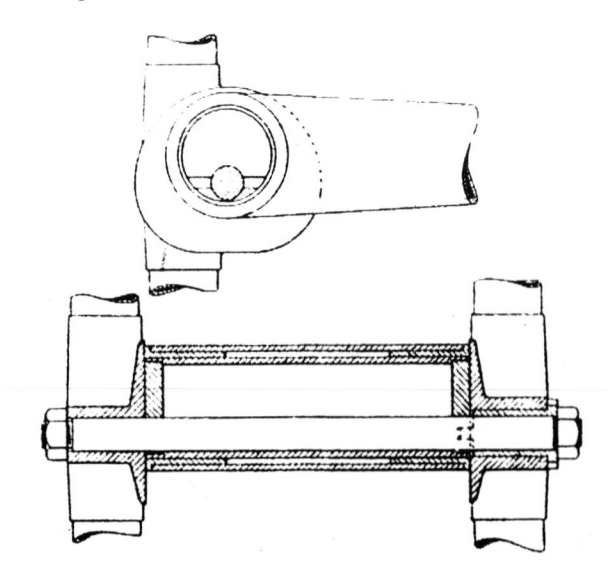

The Model O twin photographed at Fellside, Borrowash, in recent years (*Jeff Whitworth*)

This was conveniently placed to accept the standard right-hand gearchange mechanism with the additional facility of a gear position indicator. Final transmission was by shaft via a Layrub rubber-bushed universal joint at the gearbox end, plus a simple Metalastic universal joint at the rear which connected to the straight-toothed bevel box bolted to the swinging rear fork. When drawn initially, provision was made to accommodate an optional BTH magneto, but a car-type distributor and coil ignition were chosen in the interests of easy starting.

The Miller dynamo was driven directly from the crankshaft through a dog location and retained on the prototype by a flat steel plate encircling the dynamo body. This located on a large wire circlip and was pulled into position by two $\frac{5}{16}$ in. diameter studs, although drawings exist showing an extended housing, which was to be machined to accommodate part of the dynamo body and be retained by a clamp bolt. A further gear, driven from the port-side crankshaft and mounted below it, was to drive a gear-type oil pump, with a long suction pipe extending into the sump. Alongside the pump was a detachable cartridge filter, but this was not considered necessary on the prototype.

The back of the oil pump gear formed part of the outboard kickstart ratchet mechanism, which was driven by a shaft that was mounted independently across the underside of the box at the rear. The shaft was connected to a neat bevel box and supported on each side by bearings contained in frame lugs adjacent to the swinging-arm pivot. Provision was made in this mechanism to allow for the movement of the power unit on its flexible mountings while maintaining correct operation. The spring-loaded ratchet tube was disengaged from its location by the use of a hardened $\frac{1}{4}$ in. diameter pin on a face cam, in normal Velocette fashion.

The kickstart lever itself was designed to fold in its entirety out of harm's way in the event of a fall. It was subsequently used on WD and post-war rigid MAC machines.

The top half of the engine was designed with a monobloc cast-iron block, a 1 in. core between the bores being provided to accommodate the pushrods, which were splayed out from a four-in-line arrangement to the rockers. The bore and stroke, at 68 × 68.25 mm, would be the same as the MOV, total capacity being 496 cc. In fact, the prototype machine used an alloy block with shrunk-in liners and a bore of 74 mm, giving a total capacity of 688 cc. It made use of a pair of KSS piston blanks, suitably machined to a slight convex with small cutaways for the valves—reminiscent of the crown of a piston from an iron MSS.

The head, another monobloc casting, incorporated rocker shaft support pillars, and it is interesting to note that when this is removed, one has to take the pushrods with it. These cannot be extracted unless either the

The Model O photographed in the summer of 1985 at Fellside, the author's home (*Jeff Whitworth*)

rockers have been taken out or the valves removed. Unusual for Velocette, the cylinder head joint of two machined flat faces incorporating a copper/asbestos gasket has proved to be not quite up to the usual standard and has tended to leak from time to time.

Valves, all with $\frac{5}{16}$ in. diameter stems and identical head diameters, were standard MAC, while the guides in aluminium-bronze and knife-edged to wipe surplus oil from the stems, are located into the head by simply fitting a wire circlip into a suitably machined groove. Springs, collars and collets were also standard MAC/KSS with close-fitting coils. Two no. 6 Amal carburettors were fitted downdraught and side by side, sharing a single float chamber with two banjo feeds produced specially by Amal in brass.

The rocker cover, a one-piece casting, was initially secured by two large thumb screws, which proved inadequate. It was soon modified to a four-pin fixing—a subsequent drawing, produced in August 1939, showed additional stiffening webs plus an abundance of finning at the front, but as far as can be ascertained this component was never produced.

Engine oil was contained in a finned sump bolted to the underside of the crankcase. This was later enlarged in capacity, as the original gave rise to some starvation and subsequent failure of the plain bearings that were used throughout.

The whole engine/gearbox assembly was rubber-mounted fore and aft, the rear being supported on a rubber-enclosed crosstube and retained by clamps in similar fashion to the gearbox mounting of a rigid MOV/MAC. Understandably, the frame was different from anything produced hitherto by Veloce. It employed a bifurcated steering head lug, incorporating fuel tank mounting ears, that was very similar to a Scott head lug. Widely spaced duplex tubes ran down and under the outer corners of the engine unit, turning sharply upwards and terminating at a crosstube mounted to the rear of the single top tube. There was provision for a roll-on centre stand, although the stand itself was discarded long ago, possibly when a sidecar was fitted. Some fittings remain on the frame to this day.

An abbreviated subframe incorporated the mounting for adjustable rear suspension loading slots, notched for four positive locations, and like the Irving MSS was covered by a mild steel skin with provision for a seat pan, a separate rear pad and lifting handles on each side. The tail portion was hinged to facilitate rear wheel removal and incorporated a very neat over-centre catch to keep the tail up, much like that found on a gramaphone lid.

The rear fork, of lugged and tubular construction, was designed to allow the direct drive shaft an uninterrupted run. The rear brake torque arm completed a narrow triangle on the starboard side, while an additional mild steel strut completed the triangle port side. WM 2 × 19 in. wheels with cast-iron brake drums and dust extraction holes—like a KTT—were fully interchangeable. Both had a dog location to suit the rear drive and internal speedo-drive gear. The QD spindles were of substantial tubular construction, locating on a left-hand threaded fixed point within each hub.

Brake shoes, too, were peculiar to this machine, being of fabricated steel. The outer spoke flange was typically Veloce with six 1 in. diameter holes. It was bolted directly to the drum with alloy spacers between in true Vincent HRD (Irving) fashion. The front fork was basically a standard MSS/KSS Webb pattern with an offset leg on the left—like an ICI Sunbeam—to allow for wheel removal while leaving the unique alloy front brake plate in situ.

According to Eugene Goodman, the machine didn't handle too well initially, so he cut an inch out of the top tube, pulled the ends together with a hawser and welded it up! The fork ends were lengthened by $\frac{1}{2}$ in. and the machine then handled perfectly.

Today there is ample evidence of the fork extension, but nothing to prove that the top tube was shortened. In 1984 Bertie Goodman confirmed that he had been there when the tube shortening took place, but said that the frame would have gone back into the frame shop to be correctly set up to the new geometry. However, when checking the copy for this book in 1989, Peter Goodman remarked that, in fact, the Irving-designed, rear-sprung MSS had required the top tube to

Nearside of the Model O. Note forward tank mounting lugs and dynamo location, plus the offset fork leg allowing for the removal of the QD wheel (*Jeff Whitworth*)

be cut, not the Model O.

Bertie Goodman took over the machine in late 1939 and used it as daily transport for a couple of years, finding it extremely reliable, fast and pleasant to ride.

However, on one occasion, it stopped abruptly and he found part of a conrod protruding by his right boot. The engine was subsequently dismantled and new suitably strengthened rods were produced. The main bearings were also pegged at the same time, since they had been found to have moved. As far as can be ascertained, it remained sound after this and was intact when Bertie joined the Fleet Air Arm during the war. However, in the late 1940s, an employee dug it out and ran it without checking the oil with the inevitable calamitous result. It was acquired from the works in the early 1970s by the late John Griffith. Now it is owned by Titch Allen. The engine has since been rebuilt with new bearings and, apart from a tendency for the head joint to leak, it is in good working order.

Having been privileged to road test the machine, I found it delightfully smooth and docile with the extreme flexibility that had been envisaged at its inception. Careful running in was necessary at the time, precluding any thoughts of taking it beyond 40–45 mph, but it handled as if on rails. Had Veloce developed it further and put it into production instead of the LE during those austere post-war years, one wonders whether the outcome may have been different.

CHAPTER 17

The Velocette clutch

The Velocette clutch has always been a source of mystery to the uninitiated, to the extent that it has been scorned by many ignorant of its finer qualities. Its strength lies in the rigidity of the main inner and outer bodies which must not be weakened by drilling for lightening purposes. Provided all parts are clean, flat, in good general condition, and correctly assembled and maintained, it will give reliable service for a very long time. One must, however, be aware of the workings and adjustment procedure, and be sure that adjustment is correct in order that it remains trouble free.

Veloce, being aware that the mystique existed, even among the racing fraternity, would take pains to ensure that private owners' machines were correctly set up in that department whenever the works mechanics were in attendance. Therefore, it was not uncommon at the TT, for instance, to find a couple of mechanics walking down the line of riders and machines preparing to start, carrying quite a sizable lump of wood. They would pick out each Velocette, drop the lump of wood under the bike, lift the rear wheel off the ground, and comment to the rider, 'Just want to check your clutch.'

This didn't necessarily mean that the adjustment would be changed, but by inserting a $\frac{1}{4}$ in. diameter peg into the hole in the final drive sprocket, nudging the wheel first one way then the other, and checking the cable by feel at the same time, it was possible to quickly establish whether or not the critical thrust-race clearance was present. Any slight adjustment felt desirable was made in the process and saved the day on many an occasion.

Incidentally, on early Velocette final drive sprockets, there were no such holes for adjustment purposes. Instead, this was done by the use of a C-spanner provided in the toolkit, until one day, someone had the bright idea of doing it by the now time honoured method.

That the Velocette clutch lift operation is by the use of a bell-crank arrangement, thus lifting only half of the clutch and causing it to tilt so that it relies on the rotation of the clutch to lift the remaining portion, renders it of servo type. A full complement of springs would make it much too heavy to lift fully and squarely without such assistance. It is typical of Percy Goodman's thinking following the original design in 1922, when the scissor arrangement then in use proved rather too heavy when beefed up to suit the power characteristics of the new overhead-camshaft 350.

It is important that this bell-crank—or gate as it is sometimes called—is correctly shimmed and parallel to the casing at half-lift to ensure its correct function.

Doubtless, those who have witnessed Velocettes preparing for a push start to a race will have noticed that, in addition to pulling the engine back on compression, it is necessary, having lifted the clutch, to pull the machine back still further to allow it to square up and thus be free to push start.

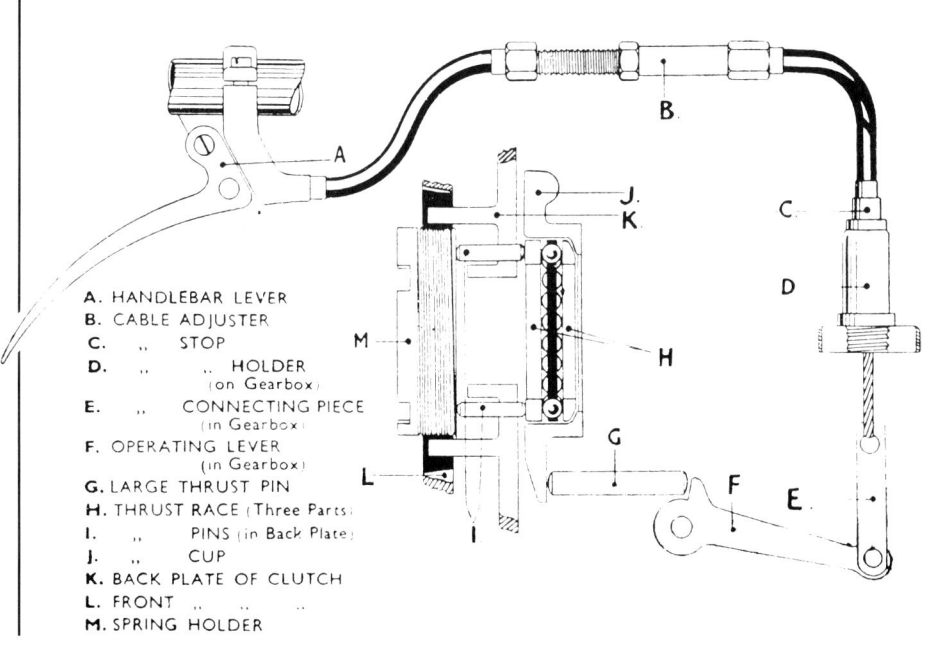

A. HANDLEBAR LEVER
B. CABLE ADJUSTER
C. ,, ,, STOP
D. ,, ,, HOLDER (on Gearbox)
E. ,, ,, CONNECTING PIECE (in Gearbox)
F. OPERATING LEVER (in Gearbox)
G. LARGE THRUST PIN
H. THRUST RACE (Three Parts)
I. ,, PINS (in Back Plate)
J. ,, CUP
K. BACK PLATE OF CLUTCH
L. FRONT ,, ,, ,,
M. SPRING HOLDER

Details of the Velocette clutch operating mechanism

CHAPTER 18
WD models and post-war production

Veloce had supplied an MSS to the Ministry of Defence for evaluation towards the end of 1939, but when eventually the MoD responded with a request to tender, it was the MAC which was selected as a more suitable machine. However, the precise specification was such that quite a number of modifications were required to deal with the sort of terrain envisaged.

Obvious requirements were a lower compression ratio and lower bottom gear ratio with a reduced overall gearing, plus a crankcase undershield, a tubular-pattern silencer, and a multi-plate clutch instead of the standard single-plate design. All were features of a machine set up for Six Days competition.

Kneegrips, too, were redesigned in the form of rubber moulded around a soft iron core, screwed to the tank where they couldn't fall off.

An initial order for some 500 machines was received under the heading 'French Military Mission', of which the first 25 were despatched and promptly lost at sea.

The KSS Mk II in its final form to 1948 specification, introduced gradually during 1947 and all sold by the end of the same year. Wheel sizes remained 20 in. rear and 21 in. front right to the end

By that time France had fallen, so alternative outlets were sought. The MoD sent a further batch to depots throughout the UK. Tidworth, Hilsea, York, Catterick, Overton-on-Sea, Preston, East Boldon, Holmes Chapel, Llanelley, Corsham, Newquay, Oswestry, Burscough, Marston Bigot and Chilwell were among their destinations—in all some 11,000 machines were supplied.

The infantry Driving and Maintenance school at Harrogate took several, which were used by Freddie Frith and 'Crasher' White who were instructors there before moving to the D&M school at Keswick. Additionally, spare engines from 12201 to 12321 were supplied to the Royal Ordnance Depot, Chilwell.

Phil Irving was given the job of uprating these WD models from the original MDD spec. to what we now know as the MAF specification. The prime requirement was to ensure that as little as possible would suffer damage in the event of the machine being laid to earth.

Since despatch riders were taught the act of dropping the model quickly to the ground in the event of a sudden attack, such a requirement, of course, was paramount. As a result a substantial rear brake pedal was fitted with a stronger pivot point, and on the other side there was a kickstart lever that folded in its

The WD version of the MAC, known as the MDD, which was a slightly modified version of the standard model (*Goodman Collection*)

entirety, plus the redesigned gearchange mechanism previously referred to.

Material shortages determined the need to employ cast iron for the one-piece gearbox end cover and kickstart housing, plus the timing cover, both being produced by the Birmingham Gas Stove Company.

The timing cover produced a few problems in that as the casting cooled, it invariably became bent, so the pattern was changed to give a bend in the opposite direction. Thus, when cooled, the cover remained relatively straight and square ready for machining.

Other changes were introduced, such as a malleable cast crankcase shield which was part of the frame, snubbers added to the fork legs à la KTT, a cast-iron front hub, and a long torque arm added to the rear brake. The last located on the prop stand mounting lug and removed the tendency to snatch from the braking system.

At the end of the war, many of these machines were reprocessed through the factory to emerge in black and gold livery with standard ratios and alloy covers. As such, the new post-war MAC was introduced, the rebuilt models being sold at a price fixed by the government.

Initial post-war civilian production, therefore, commenced with the MAC invoiced from the factory in March 1946, and without exception all sold overseas. Materials were in short supply, particularly the $\frac{7}{8}$ in. 8-gauge tubing for the frame cradle. Surplus WD frame components were used, and for a time there was an MAC which was virtually without a cradle. However, it suffered from so much vibration that a malleable cast cradle was instituted before resorting to the normal tubed type.

The reintroduction of the MOV was a natural progression since, as we know, many of the parts were interchangeable. Production of these was to commence in May 1946, also for export. From June onwards, the MAC appeared spasmodically on the home market, home sales of the MOV commencing in August of the same year.

Government regulations concerning the supply of raw materials were a major factor here, for there was only a limited amount available and export market sales were to take priority. Gradually, however, as the supply situation eased, the company was to reintroduce the MSS in September 1946, to be followed by the camshaft models in November. The first eight of the latter machines off the line were to touring specification and, therefore, designated as KTS. After these the remaining overhead-camshaft models were all of the

Velocette

sporting KSS variety plus, of course, a limited number of production KTT machines, which were purely for racing.

August 1947 saw the introduction of the Dowty Oleomatic front fork on some, but not all, KSS machines. This became standard equipment the following year on all the roadgoing models, since Webb had ceased production of the girder fork. I must hasten to add that while the 1947 show model KSS was presented with Dowtys, according to the record book, KSS production had ceased by the end of 1947, when all the machines had been sold.

Assembly of the overhead-camshaft engine had always been a specialist's job—it couldn't just be

Above right **The WD MAF Velocette (M, Armed Forces) to the revised specification, having had the Phil Irving treatment. Note folding footrests and kickstart lever together with additional snubbers on the fork blades** (*Velocette Owners' Club*)

this direction that when an engine was assembled, it was marked with 'M' for Moss or 'H' for Herbert. Thus, if any problems arose and assistance needed to be sought outside the factory, the right supplier could be notified in advance and invited to advise. Such difficulties, at a time when effort and expense were aimed in the direction of the watercooled LE, which was being

An example of a 1947 KSS Mk II (Engine no. 10671) (*Philip Tooth*)

thrown together, but needed meticulous and systematic attention to detail if it was to run with the quiet precision for which it had been designed.

No doubt some of the machine tools at the factory were showing signs of age, while new personnel, unused to such irregularities, would have had difficulty in obtaining the desired results from such equipment.

Post-war, Velocette took bevels from two manufacturers. By tradition, one was Alfred Herbert, while the alternative supplier was Moss Gears.

Normal weekly production at that time was around 100 machines, of which a fair percentage were KSS, the maximum being some 116 machines in one week when 99 of the rejects were camshaft models with noisy bevels. So many problems had been encountered in

tooled up, obviously had some bearing on the decision to cease production of the KSS for good.

However, while it lasted, the KSS was to differ only in detail from its pre-war guise, as indeed was the MSS. Gone were the push-pull twistgrip and the pressed-steel front hub, the latter being replaced by a cast-iron component, which improved the efficiency of the front brake. The front brake adjustment, formerly part way up the fork blade, was simply located, from 1939 on, in the stop on the brake plate itself.

Kneegrips had changed from a rubber pulled over a steel plate to a soft iron plate bonded into the rubber and secured by a couple of $\frac{1}{4}$ in. BSF screws. This was

Below right **Post-war MSS production ceased for a while in June 1947. It began again with this updated model in February 1948, using engine no. 7477, and ended at 8304 that June**

much neater and had been taken from the WD model. The gearbox had already received the change of camplate, thus reversing the pedal operation, and now the pedal itself gained an improved range of adjustment by making use of serrated mating faces on a two-diameter pivot shaft. Other detail changes of lesser note included the fitting of a piston with a slightly offset gudgeon pin, which was designed to overcome a tendency for the piston to slap, and a bigger inlet valve taken from the KTT Mk VII.

The Dowty fork model did require additional modifications, such as a change of front wheel (although still of 21 in. diameter), complete with alloy brake plate designed specifically to suit the fork and used on subsequent telescopic-fork Velocettes, a fuel tank much narrowed at the forward end to allow fork leg clearance on full lock, and a rear-wheel-driven speedometer. The last necessitated the use of a narrower rear hub with slotted drive sleeve threaded left-hand to prevent the possibility of it unscrewing itself from the hub when in use. Such details applied also to the MSS, since that, too, was to be turned out both in girder fork and finally in Dowty fork form, until production ceased in June 1948.

It must be said that despite the austerity of the early post-war years, chromium plating, which at that time

Above Engine no. MAC 16754 confirms this to be a late 1951 model following the introduction of the all-alloy engine

Below The first springer MAC introduced for the 1953 season. Apart from the tubular silencer, take particular note of the black handlebars and wheel spokes which were phased out the following year

didn't amount to very much on a Velocette but nevertheless included such major items as wheel rims and exhaust system, was of exceptional quality. Even after many years of hard use and neglect, it could be cleaned up and would continue to shine without blemish while affording real protection. The production run was short-lived for both the KSS and MSS model, however. Post-war, some 2303 of the latter models were produced, against 1299 of the camshaft machine, while only 499 MOV 250s were made before they, too, were taken off the menu in September 1948. This left only the MAC as the well established 'bread-and-butter' product continuing to sell well. By the end of 1950, 7214 of these had run off the production line.

Eugene Goodman. Much effort and expense had been expended in developing and tooling up for production of this unique machine; some were to marvel at it, many were to scoff. It proved successful to a degree, but at a price! Consider that through its lifespan, just about every item on it was modified or redesigned—the words of the works director, not mine—and he went on to say that the LE killed the company, aided by the Valiant, Vogue and, finally, the Viceroy. However, they thought it was the right thing to do at the time.

The loyal followers of the breed were to mourn the passing of the MOV and the MSS. So were those discerning riders who had continued to buy the KSS. The only representative model to remain was the MAC,

An improved MAC for 1954 with a fishtail silencer and later Woodhead Munro dampers. The frame still has no sidecar lugs, but the kneegrips have been moved further back

By this time of course, the LE had been launched, but a necessary breathing space had been allowed for some development to take place on the MAC. The first move was, understandably, to design a new front fork that was all Veloce. Based on that of the LE, it made use of the simple, yet effective, spring locating clips designed by Phil Irving pre-war for the experimental stressed-skin, rear-sprung MSS and Model O.

The MAC fork, unlike that of the LE, did benefit from the provision of oil damping. Malleable iron steering head crowns made it a direct geometric replacement for the Dowty fork, employing the front hub and alloy brake plate already in use.

The light-engined machine (LE to all) had arrived to the cost of the well established, traditional models on which the company had built its fortune. The underlying theme had always been to produce an 'everyman's motorcycle', at least this was primarily the dream of

which was to enjoy the benefit of a gradual facelift. There was the emergence of the Velocette telescopic fork in 1950, and for the following year a new all-alloy barrel and head were added to a crankcase which had also been tidied up. The new timing cover lost its cast-in name, the gearbox end cover was cleaned up, and the oil tank capacity was increased along with the provision for a detachable felt filter, the same type as that fitted to the LE. A modified primary chaincase with a single strap replaced the traditional screwed-up type—a retrograde step, as it turned out.

The MAC was again updated for the 1953 season with the introduction of a new swinging-arm type

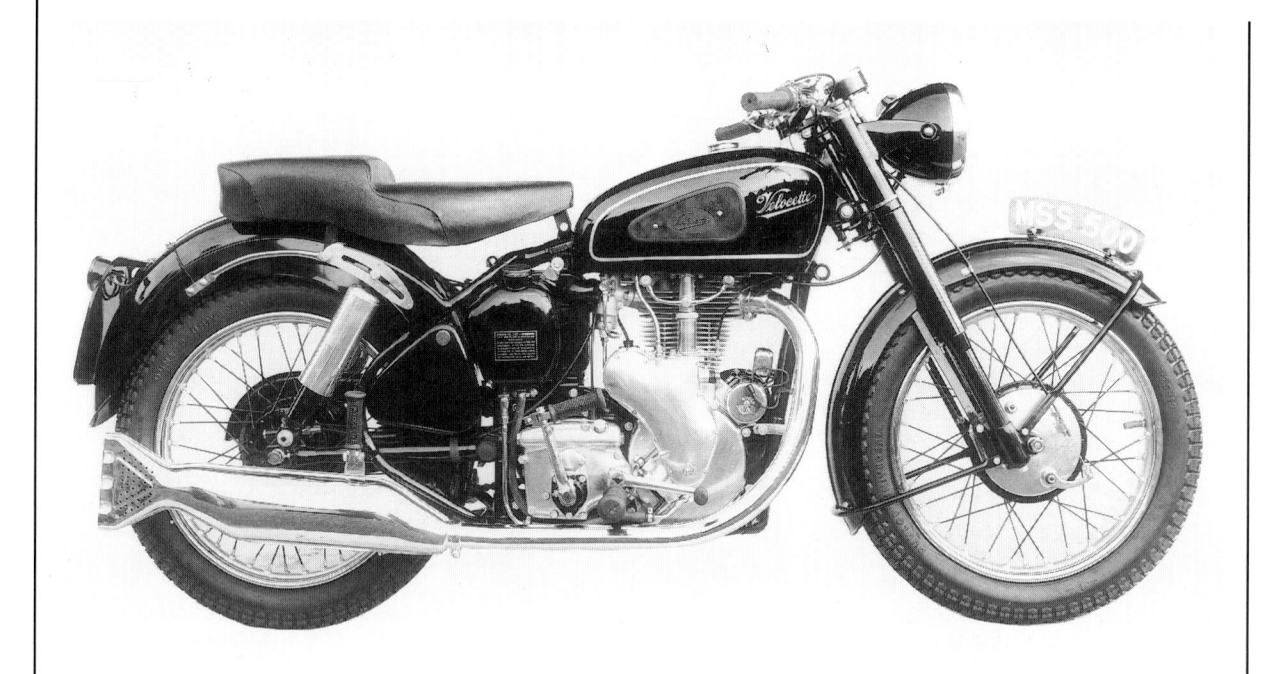

The first production MSS Springer no. 10001 was invoiced to Bill White, of New Zealand, in December 1953. It was probably the Show model

sprung frame and a redesigned gearbox, which incorporated the complete enclosure of the hitherto 'open to the elements' gearchange linkage, plus a few other niceties. These included yet another fuel tank shaped to allow steering lock clearance, since the new form of telescopic forks required a fresh pair of crowns to match the geometry of the new sprung frame.

The all-alloy engine, tidied up in 1951, had proved eminently satisfactory. Despite the usage of an alloy cylinder, and no doubt because a split-skirt piston was used with closer running tolerances, it was to prove mechanically very quiet, and oil tight. The new gearbox was based on the previous MOV/MAC design with narrow gears, but the casing and end cover were to accommodate a rather neat linkage arrangement which eliminated the external links and knuckles that were prone to rapid wear. The camplate and selector mechanism, formerly situated at the front end of the box, were now placed at the rear as in the case of the overhead-camshaft models. The magneto for 1953 was a Lucas instrument, although some machines were produced with the old BTH unit while stocks lasted. Other detail modifications continued to improve the machine mechanically.

It may seem somewhat surprising, since Veloce were the first to design effective rear springing of the swinging-fork variety on their full-blooded works racing machines way back in 1936, that it had taken them so long to put it on to the drawing board for their production machines. Undoubtedly, one major factor, quite apart from time and finance (bearing in mind their effort towards the LE) must have been the lack of availability of suitable spring units.

Dowty air-and-oil legs were out of the question on account of cost, nor were they considered reliable enough to foister on to the general public. Woodhead came to the rescue with a new line in spring dampers specially designed in conjunction with Veloce who, in drawing up a new frame based on that of the KTT, made good use of the slotted arc principle which allowed for a simple and effective means of accommodating varying load conditions. This clever arrangement had been designed by Irving pre-war and patented jointly by him and Veloce at that time.

In common with KTT practice, the pivot lug was mounted on a heavy-duty 10-gauge vertical saddle tube and the rear forks were similarly of the taper tube type. The KTT had a one-piece unit joined at the forward end, just behind the pivot bearing, by a $1\frac{1}{4}$ in. diameter bracing tube. It pivoted on bushes within the fork on a shaft secured in the frame lug. However, the separate fork legs of the new arrangement were clamped to a spindle that was allowed to pivot within bushes mounted in the main lug.

In fact, the very first racing sprung frame with rudimentary air-and-oil suspension struts produced by George Dowty—three were made for the 1936 TT—used a system not unlike this new MAC. The rear forks, being separate, were clamped to a pivot shaft which was supported on cup-and-cone steering head bearings mounted within the main frame lug, but unlike the

MAC, which used a plain shaft, on that first racing springer both the fork and the pivot spindle were splined for additional rigidity.

The new MAC springer, introduced at the 1952 show for the 1953 season, sported a rather nice alloy rear brake plate to match the front, a heavily valanced rear mudguard with detachable tailpiece to facilitate rear wheel removal and new chainguards. A long brake pedal was also provided and its pedal-to-rod pivot point was cleverly arranged in the same plane as the swinging-arm pivot itself, thus eliminating that annoying fluctuation on the rear brake pedal that one experiences on some machines when braking on undulating surfaces. This was nothing new to Veloce, however, since it was a feature of the Mk VIII KTT, which had a two-piece pedal, albeit a little more complex, to achieve the same result.

A simple spring-up centre stand, initially in alloy, was fitted and a nice long prop stand continued from the previous year's introduction. The latter was quite cleverly designed in that it was almost impossible to ride off with it down, simply because when starting the machine with the right foot, the stand was conveniently placed where it would foul the rider's left leg.

Dualseats being the vogue during the 1950s, a one-piece double seat with two levels was supplied as standard. Veloce had found, through experience with the LE, that two-level seating offered advantages for the pillion passenger. The raised rear portion gave added support to the solo rider, too.

A retrograde step was the continuation of the strap primary chaincase, introduced in 1950, which, unlike on previous Velocettes, used a neoprene fillet moulded to fit around and between the two faces of the pressings and retained by a one-piece steel band joined by a long 2BA screw. It proved to be a nuisance, although those owners who had previously ridden AJS and Matchless machines were better placed to cope with the new arrangement, since AMC had been using such a seal since the early 1930s.

Lighting equipment, as usual, was by Miller. A new oil tank and toolbox were designed to suit the new frame, and a neat wire mesh gauze oil filter element was sandwiched between the back of the oil tank and the same old battery mounting arrangement. Handlebars remained black enamel, as did the wheel spokes, but chrome rims were reintroduced with cadmium-plated nipples and other fittings, plus chromium-plated accessories. These included the Clearhooters horn rim, control levers, brake rod and other usual fittings.

One other item that was changed was the silencer, for this was of a tubular pattern, without a fishtail, and reminiscent of that used on the WD series.

The ride was typically Velocette: firm, comfortable and predictable. Now any owner wishing to add panniers and other equipment conducive to creating a heavily-laden machine (with passenger for distance touring, for instance), had only to move the rear damper units to the back of their adjustment slots—

Sales director Bertie Goodman was the manager of the former works racing team, so it's not surprising that he should pursue a policy of developing competition machines—hence this Scrambler version of the MSS which was introduced experimentally during 1955

On the introduction of the sprung frame for 'domestic' use in 1953, Bertie fitted a KTT engine and gave it a high-speed test in the Island to satisfy himself that it was up to scratch (*Veloce publicity*)

done in a matter of minutes—and the machine was adequately set up for the purpose.

Performance was lively and gave a good useful range of power with a top speed in excess of 70 mph, Braking was firm and progressive—with the lining material then available, combined with the cast-iron drums front and rear, the brakes were no longer prone to fading. On the whole, it was a very good, sound machine.

However, owners taking delivery of a new machine had to put up with a tendency for the clutch to drag, until the newness had worn off. This was overcome by merely selecting neutral on approaching a stop. Velocette riders invariably develop this technique. Usually, it was necessary to put up with this until the 500 mile service, by which time the high spots had been removed and then the clutch could be finally set up for trouble-free riding.

The new springer MAC had arrived and was selling well. Petrol rationing, so very necessary during and immediately after the war, had ceased in 1952, motorcyclists had been clamouring for new and good used machines, and dealers handling refurbished ex-WD machines of all makes had been making a lot of money. Veloce Ltd had only the LE and the revamped MAC to offer, and there was a demand for at least one more in the range. American agents Branch had promised a firm order for at least 500 machines if a 500 was added to the range. The simple answer was to reconsider the MSS. The new frame, based on the KTT which, in turn, had been developed from the full-cradle KSS and MSS frame and despite the fact that it was slightly lower overall, could accommodate the bigger power unit quite readily.

However, the old, tall cast-iron MSS engine was now outdated, having been discontinued in 1948. Although it would fit, it was redesigned, incorporating all the new features of the MAC with its clean lines and all-alloy top half. It was thought desirable to shorten the stroke and reduce the length of the rod to that of the MAC, while increasing the bore size to produce a square engine of 86 mm bore and stroke dimensions. The result would fit readily as an assembled engine/gearbox unit into the new frame.

The flywheels were dimensionally identical to the old long-stroke wheels, but incorporated a relatively new method of assembly in that the hefty crankpin was a heavy press-fit into the flywheels. This arrangement dispensed with the use of retaining nuts, since these would have been in close proximity to the main bearing housings and, particularly with the shortened stroke, would have caused serious problems.

This method of crankshaft assembly was not new to Veloce, however, since the works racing twin-cam engines of 1951–2 used such a method as, indeed, did the experimental one-off twin-cylinder machines produced pre-war.

Main bearings on this new MSS were a hefty Timken taper-roller type, which necessitated careful assembly and shimming to give a 0.004 in. load when cold to

Above **Compare this 1955 MSS with the 1954 MAC. The tank lining has changed, as has the seat and the rear number plate. Cadmium-plated spokes are in evidence**

Below **A Willow green 1955 MAC, similar in specification to the MSS, but showing only one sidecar lug on the rear frame loop!**

allow for correct tolerances at normal operating temperatures. This method was well proven, since the change from lipped rollers had taken place in 1947 on the old MSS when difficulties arose with the supply of the special, and expensive, L462 bearing used on the driveside. The Timken replacement was readily available off-the-shelf and relatively inexpensive.

Unlike that of the MAC, the 500 head housed hairpin valve springs, crossed over for ease of accommodation and identical to those used pre-war on the blown shaft-driven twin. Additionally, the valve guides were designed to give knife-edge contact uppermost to wipe excess oil from the valve stem, another direct result of racing practice, since the twin-cam racing engines used such guides.

A separate rocker box accommodated pre-assembled rockers and bearing caps. It was sealed to the top of the head with a reinforced Hallite gasket, being pulled down by a multitude of $\frac{5}{16}$ in. BSF bolts.

The MAC gearbox, with its narrow train of gears, was obviously not up to the sort of power produced by the bigger engine, so a new gearbox, based on the same design, was produced. This was $1\frac{3}{16}$ in. wider to accommodate the gear cluster of the previous KSS/MSS models. A new clutch with a pair of extra plates had been added. The final drive chain dimension was increased to $\frac{5}{8} \times \frac{3}{8}$ in. and the overall gear ratio raised. The result was probably one of the nicest machines to come out of Hall Green.

Since it was expected that this beefy, yet tractable, mount would appeal to the sidecar fraternity, additional lugs were incorporated in the frame from its inception for the 1954 season. From then on, such lugs and, indeed, the heavyweight gearbox and new clutch were to become standard wear on all subsequent models (MAC included). However, the narrow type II box was continued on the smaller machine during 1954 while stocks lasted.

Meanwhile, the Woodhead WM1 dampers had changed from initial all-black units with spring covers, retained by a $\frac{7}{16}$ in. diameter nut and a screwed-on eye, to a type with welded eye and alloy covers, later to be replaced by plated ones, retained by split collets. The fishtail silencer had also returned, albeit redesigned and more bulbous, but in keeping with the excellence of presentability of the new mount.

Performance-wise, the square MSS was undoubtedly beefy and solid with a top speed of 85 plus that was to prove to be the underlying basis of future development along the same theme. One problem had arisen on the MAC, however, as a result of the crankcase redesign back in 1952, when more meat had been added to the cases. This resulted in intermittent failure of the timing

Bertie Goodman proudly presents the 1958 ISDT model to the press (*Roger Maughling*)

side main ballrace and, in consequence, this was changed for the lipped roller, as used on the drive side, in common with what had been standard practice on the KTT. No further problems were encountered.

In my opinion, the new heavyweight gearbox, though excellent, was lacking in one respect—that the support for the mainshaft, at the kickstart end, relied upon the relatively small ball bearing that had been adequate on the early three-speed, and rigid MOV/MAC four-speed units, but was prone to failure on the sprung-frame models. This was particularly true when an owner tended to over-tighten the rear chain, which was not uncommon. The rider was not usually aware of this failure until something drastic occurred, and on occasion the shell split as a result of incorrectly meshed gears, caused by the bearing failure.

The later clutch, incorporating a pair of additional plates, was also likely to suffer more from abuse, since in order that all the plates could be accommodated, they were somewhat slimmer. This resulted in a readiness to distort when they were incorrectly adjusted and was only rectifiable by replacing the majority of the components. It is not surprising, therefore, that some of the rider/agents and others involved in the preparation of race machinery reverted to the earlier clutch with the lower number of thick plates, in conjunction with a full set of long springs and their respective ancillary parts. This arrangement gave satisfactory results when correctly set up, and after all this was the assembly used on the factory ohc 500s for a good many seasons.

CHAPTER 19

The post-war works 350s

Peter Goodman was to take charge of KTT production following his demob from the RAF in 1946. Commencing at engine no. 901, these machines were quickly earmarked for their respective agents from the end of the year on. The first of the batch, as was normal practice, went to overseas agents, at first in Czechoslovakia, Switzerland and Hungary.

Peter himself, who, incidentally, was christened Clifford Eugene—although his father chose to call him Peter—was to continue in competition using pre-war works machines. Meanwhile, cousin Bertram, having also been demobbed, from the Fleet Air Arm, married Maureen and selected a new model KTT 911 for only his second ever road race—the 1947 Ulster Grand Prix.

Petrol, which at this time was still on ration and of the low-octane pool grade, was a bit of a headache to some manufacturers, particularly Veloce's main opposition, Norton. Their engines, with big-finned alloy heads cast around bronze skulls, could not readily dissipate the excessive heat without seriously lowering the compression ratio. Veloce, on the other hand, enjoyed the benefits of a good quality, all-alloy cylinder head which could cope with the situation so much better. In fact, by making use of the old Mk VII piston with its lower crown, and slightly increasing the depth of the valve pockets, the resultant combustion chamber shape allowed for a compression ratio of just under 8:1 to be attained with quite beneficial results.

The specification post-war was basically as pre-war, except that heftier fork links were introduced top and bottom, the valance on the rear mudguard was discontinued, and the rear Dowty oleo suspension struts were produced in steel, instead of the alloy used in 1939.

Certain selected riders were given a big-inlet-valve head and later a new type 11 cam. One such machine, it transpires, was quietly borrowed by AMC during the early stages of design and development of the post-war 7R.

Tooling up for the LE and maintaining the production of the other models—most of which were soon to be dropped—were limiting factors as far as the racing budget was concerned, and following Peter's heavy prang at Strasbourg the budget was to become somewhat leaner. Only by the good offices of such stalwarts as Dick Wilkins, who sponsored Bob Foster, and Nigel Spring, the Lincolnshire marmalade manufacturer, could Veloce continue to contest the Grand Prix scene to the extent that they did.

Spring had been in the thick of record-attempt sponsorship before the war and, in particular, was responsible for campaigning Nortons and later the overhead-camshaft Ajays from Wolverhampton with Bert Denly as jockey.

Foster's 1947 Junior-winning machine, in fact, was Les Archer's pre-war model, uprated to works spec.

Quite apart from all his other successes, Freddie Frith along with Kenneth Bills (and eventually Charlie Salt and Ernie Lyons) rode under the Spring banner as the number one works runner, and was to win the 1948

Les Archer and his mechanic, Dennis Offord, making final adjustments to the carburettor of this works KTT, assisted by C. B. (Amal) Smith (*EMAP*)

Junior TT with Bob Foster, the previous year's winner, in second place.

Seven special engines were produced for 1948, all with big alloy cylinders, the big inlet valve and extra scavenge pump. Bertie Goodman used no. 911, Frith 954 and Ken Bills, 956. Quite often, several engines carried the same number, for instance when a potentially quicker unit was built up as a replacement. It eliminated the need to alter documents when travelling abroad.

For 1949 Veloce produced a new breed of double overhead-camshaft engines based on the old bore and stroke of 74 × 81 mm, in addition to which a couple of 500s were also produced. However, it is arguable as to whether or not the potential advantage of the double-cam device on this long-stroke motor—still 81 × 96 mm—was outweighed by the extra top hamper and relative lack of low-down torque.

The special 350s, however, were eventually to gain a new lease of life, although much development work was necessary before they became fast and reliable. This was to become Freddie's crowning year, for he won every Junior race in the calendar including, of course, the TT. Thus, he retired as the first world champion in the 350 class, later to be honoured with an OBE for his fine achievement. It must be added, however, that he did not use the double-cam engine in every race. While it was capable of being run continuously at 7600–8000 rpm, as against the 7200 rpm top whack of the rocker engine, the latter was chosen on occasions because of the greater torque low-down.

The new twin-cam engine was designed by Bertie Goodman in conjunction with his father, Percy, who, it transpires, had asked Charles Udall if he would give the lad a hand along the way. Udall, however, declined with the suggestion that Bertie should learn to stand on his own two feet!

Nothing was taken from the pre-war design, which was merely a twin-cam arrangement mounted atop the cylinder head of the old 'dog kennel' engine and prefixed MTT.

As usual, crankcases were in magnesium alloy, although the cylinder and head retaining studs were spaced $\frac{1}{8}$ in. further apart from standard—that is 3 in. square instead of $2\frac{7}{8}$ in. square. The 500's dimensions were $3\frac{3}{32}$ in.

Tommy Mutton (*left*) and Charles Udall testing a works engine that was earmarked for Freddie Frith's use in the 1947 Junior TT. This engine is a pre-war unit with the 10 in. square head and long con-rod, depicted by the size of the cylinder. Note that the test oil tank is from a 1933 'dog kennel' machine and incorporates a filter chamber on the return side

Above Peter Goodman was a brilliant rider who entered the TT once only, in 1947. He finished fourth in the Junior and third in the Senior on this pre-war works machine, sharing the fastest lap with Artie Bell (*Keig*)

Left At first glance, this rather dark photograph has the style and appearance of the immortal Freddie Frith. However, the dashing rider is none other than Peter Goodman, with the wick turned well up as he comes out of Braddan Bridge in the 1947 Junior TT. The front brake air scoop, seemingly poking out of the front tyre, suggests that he is using a pre-war works bike. Compare this with Stanley Woods' 1939 TT winner

Overleaf The KTT endeared itself to professionals and privateers alike. Here we have Continental circus regulars, Sid Mason from Cookham leading Leicester's Phil Heath (Norton) round city curve in an International meeting at Schotten on St Swithun's day!

Crank assembly was initially standard KTT, but due to the occasional failure of the roller cage at prolonged higher engine speeds, plus flexure of the bolted-up crankshaft, it was necessary to beef-up the whole assembly, using a larger-diameter pin. This was a heavy press-fit into the flywheel, with an 18-roller cage and ring from the 500.

What emerged was what we now recognise as the standard big-end for subsequent MSS/Venom/Viper models.

Some said that it was a pity that the drive side mainshaft wasn't increased in size to that of the 500, which was carried on a special double-row roller bearing with barrel-shaped rollers, or the double-row lipped roller bearing (no. L462), as used in the KSS MkII. However, by narrowing the width of the con-rod at the small-end and reducing the size of the gudgeon pin to $\frac{3}{4}$ in., some weight was saved here, too. A special forged piston was also used which, if nothing else, contributed to safety at the higher revs envisaged.

A lovely big cast-aluminium cylinder, fully enclosing the vertical drive shaft tube, in the manner of the 500s, gave it an impressive business-like appearance. Veloce always believed in putting the fins well into the airstream. The thick wall liner with a double spigot location was the usual interference fit in the muff. Mahle chromed bores, direct on to the alloy, were tried at one stage, but proved unsuccessful on account of cylinder distortion, so the well proven method was reverted to.

The additional scavenge pump in the lower end of the inner timing cover—normal on works machines—was incorporated with a special two-piece, pressed-up and keyed driving gear. This necessitated shortening the drive shaft and supporting boss on the oil pump to accommodate it.

Larger than standard Oldham couplings and a wasted drive shaft, allowing for that torsional flexibility were special modifications deemed necessary, although it may be argued that continued bottom driving bevel failure on particularly the 500 version may have been attributable to such flexing, causing the cam train to lag momentarily prior to maximum loading. I believe the technical term is cyclic irregularity.

Vertical bevels were special .001 up on standard size and supported by a combination of Timken taper and journal bearings within a large alloy housing. The bevels themselves were readily identifiable by the deep radius at the base of the coupling slots.

The cylinder head was produced by modifying the patterns of a single-cam head, some 9 in. square—not as big as the pre-war works heads, but this casting, suitably machined, was ready to accommodate the flat

Below Bob Foster finished second to Freddie Frith in the 1948 Junior TT on this machine with a special engine. Among the group are entrant Dick Wilkins, Jimmy Simpson, Kenneth Bills (always in the picture!) and Bertie Goodman (*The Motor Cycle*)

Left Freddie Frith receives congratulations after winning the 1948 Junior TT. The machine was basically a standard Mk VIII frame, no. 114, with a special single ohc engine with the big-finned cylinder, a special cam and a $1\frac{5}{32}$ in. RN carburettor. An additional works scavenge pump was used, as were special internal gear ratios to assist the climb up the Mountain. Alongside Freddie stand Nigel Spring, Kenneth Bills and Bill Mewis, who could be relied upon to ensure that every nut and bolt on the bike was secure. Mewis was in charge of the transport department at AKD, from where his boss, Dennis Mansell, worked closely with Spring as joint sponsors

Below This is Ernie Lyons, second only to Freddie Frith in the 1949 Junior TT, plus an equally fine third place behind a brace of works Nortons in the Senior later in the week. On both occasions he rode Nigel Spring-entered 'works' double-overhead-cam machines. Ernie's exemplary performance was probably never fully appreciated on this occasion. He is shown rounding Ramsey Hairpin on the Junior model, which he says was the best bike he has ever ridden (*The Motor Cycle*)

underside of the new long cambox. This same head casting was used for 350, 500 and, indeed, the 250 that was to come later. However, the 500 was a bit short of material to the extent that one head was to break into two pieces following a Continental blow up with Bill Lomas on board.

Rapid cam wear became apparent at an early stage of development and was only overcome by making provision for a constant flow of oil to pass through a small hole at the base of the hollow valve pusher. This was formed by blowing air through a tube while the stellite face was red hot, before grinding the contour.

The stylish Freddie Frith at Waterworks in the course of winning the 1949 Junior TT. The bike is a works double-overhead-cam machine, entered by Nigel Spring. The footrests have no rubbers, but there are plates welded on the ends which were essential to keep the rider's feet on them over bumpy surfaces. The front hub is a standard production type, but the fuel tank is of slightly increased capacity

These engines were very difficult to set up, and this was usually done one valve at a time, the cambox being held by a multitude of $\frac{1}{4}$ in. studs and nuts trapped close to adjacent fins. Each cam had its own range of adjustment for fine setting and, of course, the tappets had to be set before assembly. After checking, the whole lot had to be removed for further adjustment, while taking into account the settling of the joint gasket in the process.

Nevertheless, as a 350, it was undoubtedly successful, although compared with a 7R AJS in particular, it remained rather heavy with the old lugged frame, and, of course, the girder forks. Despite such disadvantages, Bob Foster became World Champion in the class for 1950 — a most creditable performance.

At one stage, Bertie had considered revamping the old pre-war blown twin by dispensing with the blower, since this was no longer allowed, and reversing the heads to allow forward-facing exhausts. No doubt, the valve gear would have come in for some juggling, too! However, since Charles Udall (under whose control the design had rested following the demise of Willis in 1939) was dead against it, and his pull at board level was not inconsiderable (I believe he threatened to resign), the idea was dropped.

A small band of highly skilled fitters, having served their time on KSS production, were selected to produce the racing machines. Charlie Almond and Albert Partridge specialized in building up the crankshaft assemblies and completing the bottom half, while Les Leach and Jimmy Gibbard were responsible for preparing the cylinder heads and valve gear. Arthur Moseley and an assistant would assemble the engines and gearboxes and build the complete machines.

Len Udall (brother of Charles) and Tommy Mutton, both pre-war race mechanics, were charged with running the experimental department, the whole outfit being contained in a Nissen hut shared with the repair department.

Additionally, race mechanics, Frank Panes and Hedley Cox, were required to attend to any of their work necessitating the drawing of unfinished parts from the stores or preparing them from scratch. Quite apart from the need to finish off the main bearing housings, by means of a hand-operated cutter to a matched pair of cases, more often than not, the cases were porous, which was overcome by forcing waterglass into the lower bevel housing to prevent leakage of lubricant. Oil pumps had to be carefully assembled, clamped into a special jig and run in with turkey oil before thoroughly washing out prior to final assembly.

Cylinder heads were taken from the stores complete with seats and fully machined, but the porting required much hand work with rotary cutters and finishing mops. Valve springs needed to be carefully set to a predetermined load, rockers also to be in line, square with the cam and assembled with their respective return

Bertie Goodman congratulates Cyril Julian on his fine third place in the 1950 Junior Manx Grand Prix, riding KTT 999 (*Goodman Collection*)

This is one of the twin ohc engines of 1949, designed and developed by Bertie Goodman and his team. It was thought that there were seven of these special engines, and much midnight oil was spent on them. Using these, along with the occasional single ohc engine, Veloce won the World Championships in 1949 and 1950 (*The Motor Cycle*)

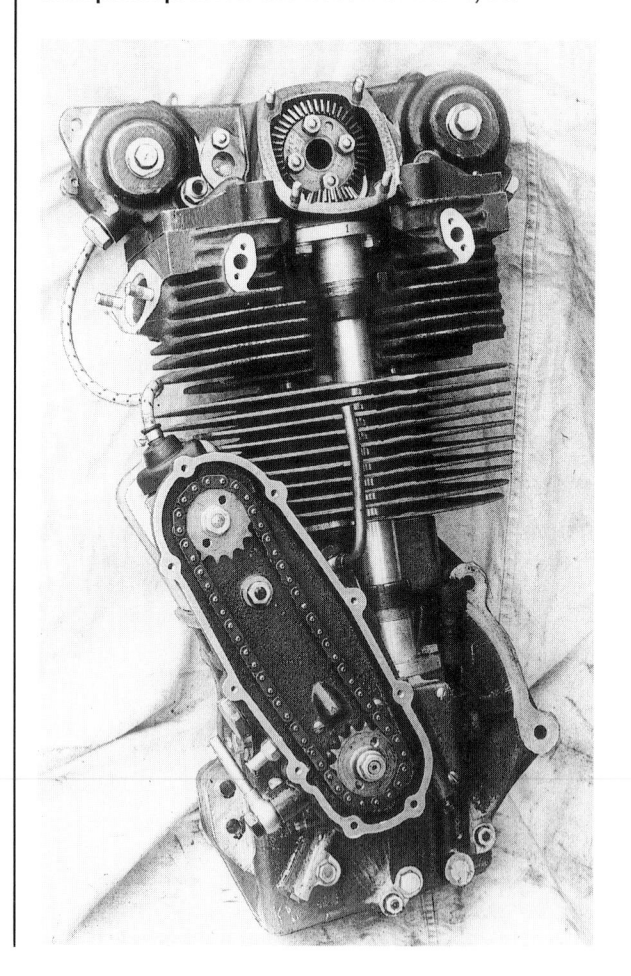

springs to keep them in constant contact with the cam.

The whole process of engine assembly was painstaking and methodical with meticulous attention to every detail—it became quite an art. The finally assembled unit was taken to the test house, set up on one of the test-beds and run lightly for an hour and a half. Then, having had the oil pressure and the flow checked, it was put under load and the power output checked. It would only be passed off when a specific output—usually 28 bhp—had been achieved.

Any modification or rectification was carried out, and all details of assembly and performance were noted against the engine number in the fitter/mechanic's notebook for future reference.

The rest of the machine received the same meticulous attention before being handed over to one of the testers—Les Thomas, Frank Webb or Don Harrison—who would attach a silencer, reduce the main jet size and take it for a spin on trade plates. Finally, apart from carrying out any rectification required, each machine would be visually checked from stem to stern and all nuts and bolts double checked for tightness, prior to passing it over to the despatch department and thence to the selected owner or his agent.

An occasion worthy of note took place in 1950 when John Jones of New Zealand, apprenticed to Bill White, the Auckland Velocette distributor, was over for a 12 month spell at Hall Green to learn the ropes first hand. Many years before, Bill White had been presented with one of the earliest ex-works 500 racing machines (no. MT 5001) reputed to have been the machine used by Walter Rusk to win the 1934 Ulster Grand Prix. This machine had been updated to 1936 specification with an all-alloy top half, retaining its 'dog kennel' magnesium cambox. John had brought the engine back to the works to be fettled and, having completed the work, set it up on the Heenan and Froude dynamometer in the test house.

It was found that the ignition and air control cables did not match up with the controls on the test rig and only by reversing the connections could the test be carried out. The motor had been running for a little while with the magneto connected to what looked like a closed air lever and the air looking like a retarded ignition lever. Bertie Goodman, who was never far away on such occasions, suddenly walked through the door, enquiring how long the engine had been running like this, and took to the controls.

Meanwhile, amidst the din, Jones was trying to tell Bertie about the changing over of the controls, but Bertie didn't hear. He was, in the meantime, pushing the controls into what would normally have been their respective operating positions, at the same time opening the throttle hard. This caused a huge explosion, as a result of a rich mixture and fully retarded ignition, which shook the test house. Everyone took cover, and before the dust had settled Bertie had already begun to work out how much it would cost to put the damage right!

Much lightening took place in 1950, including the use of big alloy tanks for the TT and alloy brake pedal parts, handlebars and clamps. An alloy oil tank on Bob Foster's machine split at one Continental outing and had to be welded up by Ted Frend of AMC. On another occasion, a start line mêlée allowed Les Graham to get well away on the 7R and when Bob Foster eventually got away, he was not aware that Les was out in front. So when Frank Panes put the board out to Bob '2nd less 1 min', Bob's eyes popped out like chapel hat pegs, but despite putting up the fastest lap, he couldn't make up the deficit.

During this race, while Frank kept Bob informed of his position from the pits area, the AJS boys were keeping him informed on the other side of the course. The Veloce crew had a good working relationship with the AJS opposition, but in no way could they get help from the Craig boys who didn't want to know. Nortons were unapproachable in more ways than one!

On a Manx Grand Prix occasion during the late 1940s, the various factories were on hand as usual with workshop facilities and mechanics to assist their respective clients. As normal, the Veloce race shop was very busy when in came Gordon Wilson (of Gordon Tools) with his KTT, requesting that his front forks be attended to. They showed signs of having been bent slightly sideways, and it was obvious to Bertie that the machine had been brought over to the Island in this state, which somewhat abused the facilities available— this was not uncommon. The machine was left, to be collected later in the day. A quick and economical remedy was to place the forks over on full lock, lift the front of the machine into the air and drop it firmly to the ground, twice, which had the effect of pulling them back into line. While not being quite the correct method, this satisfactorily overcame the problem under the circumstances. The machine was taken out for practice, after which the satisfied owner was so pleased that he returned with a full set of Whitworth spanners which he presented to Bertie for his trouble.

KTT production ceased in 1950, no. 1086 being the last machine sold in the UK, with three others being invoiced to overseas agents early in 1951. An odd final machine was produced to special order and sold to an Algerian agent in 1953.

Total Mk VIII production, therefore, was a total of 238 machines, of which 49 were pre-war models. Today, they are rare and increasingly desirable. While only marginally competitive in Vintage and Classic events, nevertheless, they are a joy to be seen, heard and ridden whenever one turns out for an occasion.

Overleaf **This report of the 348 cc ohc KTT engine appeared in an Iliffe book,** *Motor Cycle Engines***, published in 1951**

The 348 c.c. Overhead camshaft KTT VELOCETTE

The Whys and Wherefores of a Famous Engine Designed Specifically for Road Racing

By "UBIQUE"

EVERYONE knows that, for years, the KTT Velocette was unique in being the nearest possible thing to a genuine T.T. model which was available to the public. It was, in fact, designed and intended for road racing, and this must be remembered when considering the following notes.

Looking at all the parts neatly laid out on sheets of brown paper, I was at a loss to know where to begin. Finally, after discussing the point with Messrs. Percy Goodman and Harold Willis—now, unhappily the late Harold Willis—I decided to start at the top and work down, yet in actual practice my first question dealt with the cylinder barrel. What are the materials, and how are they mated?

Rather to my surprise I learned that the silicon-aluminum-alloy jacket, with its very deep radiating ribs, was "cast on," the nickel cast-iron barrel, with its corrugated outer wall, being heated and placed in the mould before the alloy was poured.

Mr. Willis did not think there was much to choose between this practice and that of pressing-in a liner or shrinking-on a jacket, but actually Velocettes, he said, had had slightly better results with the practice outlined; it prevents the possibility of the liner "creeping."

The head, I gathered, was of heat-treated "Y"-alloy, a metal chosen for its light weight, strength and high thermal conductivity. The head ribs of the KTT are roughly 9in square in plan view, and the camshaft casing and the boxes for the enclosure of both valves and their double hairpin valve springs are cast with the head, so you can judge the importance of a lightweight material.

Of course, I asked why these huge cooling fins were employed, suggesting that it must be almost impossible for a considerable draught of air to reach the rib roots.

In this matter Mr. Willis told me I was correct, but that careful tests showed that it was of greater importance to get a big cooling surface right out into the draught than to rely on such air as might possibly pass the front wheel, mudguard, fork, frame, etc., reaching the roots of the fins. That explains the importance of high conductivity, does it not?

Again, he pointed out that the joint between the head and barrel, at the top of the spigot, consisted of a laminated copper washer. Each of the four laminations is about 0.009in thick, and this arrangement makes a very satisfactory job with direct metal-to-metal contacts throughout.

Internally, the head is approximately hemispherical, the long-reach 14mm plug being placed high up and screwed directly into the head.

"My next question was, "Why do you employ different materials for exhaust and inlet valve seatings?" I then asked.

"The head is heated in an electrical furnace to a temperature of 200 degrees C., and the seatings previously mounted on special jigs, are pushed home very quickly. Speed is essential in this process, for as soon as the seatings come in contact with the hot head, they also expand and lock in position."

"For the inlet valve, the seat of which is apt to be damaged by grit, a nickel cast-iron is employed on account of its hardness.

Pressed-in Seatings

"How are the seatings held in position?" I then asked.

"A hard aluminium-bronze alloy is used for the exhaust seat, because the high conductivity of this metal helps to keep the exhaust valve cool and, incidentally, its high coefficient of expansion helps to maintain good contact with the head casting at high temperatures.

The pale gold of aluminium-bronze valve guides next caught my eye. The high heat conductivity and high coefficient of expansion, plus the fact that this material is an excellent bearing metal, make it very suitable for the purpose. Add to this, ample lubrication from the cam-box and the very high finish of the valve

Boxes for the enclosure of the valves and their double hairpin valve springs, as well as the camshaft casing, are cast in one with the massive "Y"-alloy cylinder head. The drawing also shows complete details of the camshaft assembly

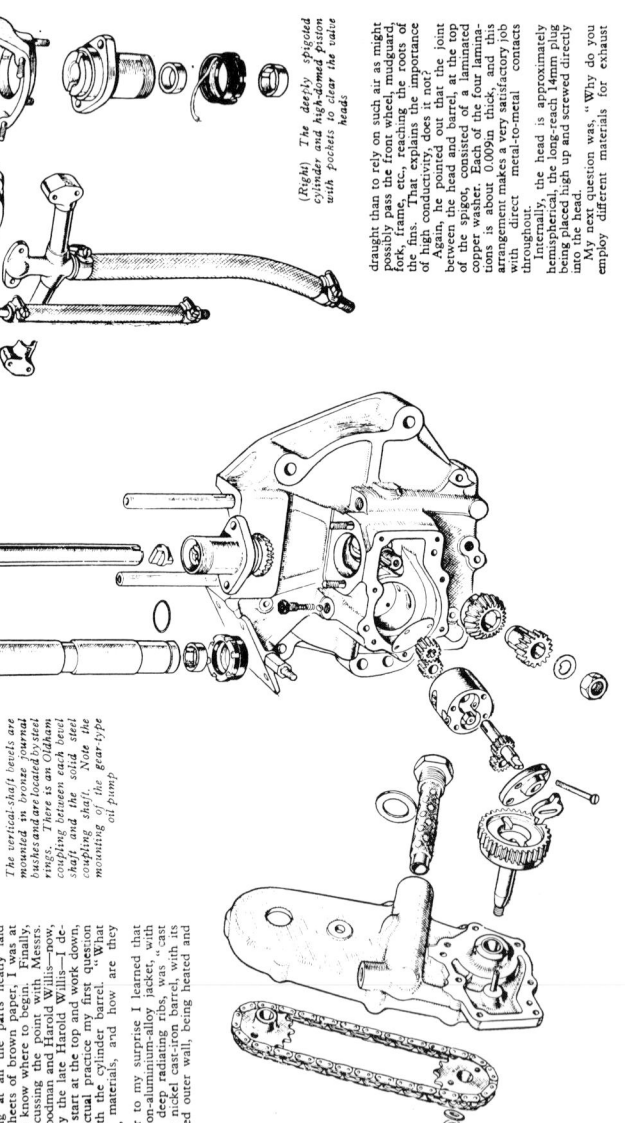

(Right) The deeply spigoted cylinder and high-domed piston with pockets to clear the valve heads

The vertical-shaft bevels are mounted in bronze journal bushes and are located by steel rings. There is an Oldham coupling between each bevel shaft and the solid steel coupling shaft. Note the mounting of the gear-type oil pump

A diagrammatic view of the lubrication system of the KTT engine, showing the feeds to the big-end bearing and to the overhead camshaft and rocker gear. The oil is pumped at the rate of 1/16th gallon a minute to a check valve, the object of which is to prevent oil seepage from the tank to the crankcase when the engine is stationary.

stems and guides, and I was not surprised to hear that wear at this point is negligible over long periods.

Incidentally, the valve stems work with quite close clearance limits, the actual figures being 0.0015in for the inlet and 0.003in for the exhaust.

"Why is the inlet valve of larger diameter than the exhaust?" Both my mentors answered this question. Perhaps I may summarize their remarks by saying that it is not difficult to fill a cylinder by atmospheric pressure than to empty it when the piston pushes behind and there is help at certain vital speeds from a specially designed exhaust pipe.

"The valves themselves? Well, the inlet is made of a cobalt-chrome steel having high tensile strength and hard-wearing surfaces. It has a throat diameter of 1 5/16in., and its stem is reduced to the smallest possible diameter consistent with safety, so as to reduce port obstruction. K.E.965 steel was chosen for the exhaust valve because it retains great strength at the very high temperatures at which it is called upon to work."

Valve Timing

The port diameter of the exhaust valve is 1 7/16in, of both valves is 5/8in. Both have moderately recessed heads, but whereas the material of the inlet stem is hardened for this purpose, so a hardened end-cap is used.

I asked if the valve timing were a secret, but it was given me without the slightest hesitation. Checked with a tappet clearance of 0.020in. in each case, the timing is as follows: inlet opens 55 degrees before top dead centre, and closes 65 degrees past b.d.c.; exhaust opens 75 degrees before b.d.c. and closes 45 degrees after t.d.c.

One hundred degrees of overlap. Think of it! That ought to get the inlet gas column moving and ensure that the valves are well open when they will do most good!

The correct running tappet clearances are: inlet 0.015in., exhaust 0.025in.

Even the details of the valve spring cup

and roller are of unusual interest. It was pointed out that the groove in the top of the valve stem is extremely shallow in order to reduce the strength of the split collet is so designed as to grip the stem, and under the wedging action of the spring cup this grip is almost sufficient without the groove.

Free to Rotate

The item which corresponds to the usual spring cup (and is described as such above) does not, in fact, form a direct thrust face for the hairpin springs, the looped ends of which are hooked on to a separate steel spring abutment, loosely mounted round the "spring cup." Thus, at the expense of a little extra reciprocating weight, the valve is free to rotate, which is a desirable feature.

At their lower ends the valve springs are tucked into longitudinal holes drilled in a steel plate which surrounds the upper part of the valve guides, and these plates have, at each end, a tapped hole to carry the fulcrum of a spring removing tool.

"What spring pressures are necessary for this engine?" I asked.

"Measured with the valve closed, a pressure of 110lb, plus another 25lb for the return spring on the rocker, the latter an important point which we will discuss when we get there."

"Does the total enclosure of the valve gear cause any kind of trouble in the way of overheating?"

"No, the interior is cooled by a liberal circulation of oil."

"Some years ago you used a two-cam-shaft racing engine," I said. "Why, in this engine, have you reverted to the single-camshaft type?"

"It was about to mention that very point," said Mr. Percy, "as it is a matter of some historical interest. The twin-camshaft job, in spite of its theoretical advantages, presented certain practical

difficulties. [Since overcome as recent Velocette racing engines have demonstrated.—Ed.] It was difficult to provide reasonably accessible tappet adjustment, and to enclose the mechanism—a point which, as you know, we consider to be important. Further, for the first time we had trouble with the vertical shaft drive, which could be traced indirectly to the upper works of the valve gear."

"After much experiment we found that the best all-round results could be obtained from a single-camshaft engine if the rockers could be held in constant contact with the cam. At first this spring caused scoring and rapid wear of the rocker heels only to provide a jet of oil directly on to the point of contact between cam and rocker, but also to face the heel of the rocker with Stellite. These precautions have been completely successful.

Floating Bushes

On inquiry, I found that these rockers are made from stampings of air-harden-ing, nickel-chrome steel of 100-ton tensile test. Between each rocker and its massive eccentrically mounted pivot-pin is a bronze floating bush.

"Why are the cams made separate from their shaft?"

"Well, the cams, which are designed to give constant acceleration and deceleration both at a straight carbon-steel, deeply cased, and have 1 per cent carbon in the case. The shaft is of 3 per cent nickel steel, case-hardened to form a track for the driving-side roller bearing. The cams are pressed and keyed on to the shaft. The rollers on the drive side are caged and a ball-bearing on the other end of the shaft takes the end-thrust from the bevel gears."

"What about the vertical-shaft drive?"

"Most of it is standard, including the upper pair of bevels. The crown bevel is bolted to its back plate by four bolts, and the bolt holes are elongated to provide a half tooth adjustment for timing. The lower bevels have been strengthened to withstand the extra strains imposed by high speed and heavy valve springs."

"Why the lower bevels and not the upper ones?"

"Because the shape of the small-diameter bevels of approximately equal size is more favourable to tooth strength."

(Left) Immense rigidity is a feature of the crankshaft assembly end of the unusually narrow crankcase. The flywheels are made of heat-treated carbon steel, while the big-end pin has a diameter of no less than 1 3/8in. Big-end rollers measuring 9/16in x 3/16in are located in a Duralumin cage

"I note you retain the hunting tooth."

"Yes, the odd teeth in the vertical-shaft drive distribute the loading as evenly as possible. The vertical-shaft bevels are mounted in bronze journal bushes, the thrust being taken on the end faces. Steel rings are lightly pressed on to the shafts to take the bevels length-wise in their bearings. There is an Oldham coupling of oil-hardened nickel-chrome steel between each bevel shaft and the solid steel coupling shaft. This coupling shaft is mounted in plain bearings in its enclosing tube, and the tube is held at each end by asbestos-packed glands, and although it appears to be quite rigid, there is just a trace of intentional flexibility in the mounting."

The unusually narrow aluminium-alloy crankcase is noticeable without need of questions, and the single-row caged roller bearings on each side are supported directly under the massive walls in which the main strength of the crankcase lies. The only additional stiffening is provided by shallow webs on the outside of the drive side. As in other Velocette models, the primary drive lies inside the final drive, and therefore the engine sprocket is close up to the main bearing. Thus, there is a very little overhang and no need for a multiplicity of crank bearings.

Immense Rigidity

A glance at the compact and immensely rigid crank unit with its single-row big-end and comparatively narrow flywheels, also at the smooth, web-less interior of the crankcase, shows how that effect of slimness is attained, but here more questions were necessary.

"What are the flywheels made of?"

"Heat-treated carbon steel."

"Why heat-treated?"

"How are the crank axles fixed in the flywheels?"

"Just pressed in, and located by a pin. The pin is really a screw lying parallel with the shaft, partly in the shaft and partly in the flywheel boss. These shafts, of 3 per cent nickel steel, are very slightly tapered so that the inner races of the main bearings are securely locked when pushed home. The outer races are shrunk into the crankcase, so that they also are firmly held."

Then I asked about that massive crank-pin, which adds so materially to the rigidity of the crank unit. It is made of nickel-chrome steel, case-hardened to form the inner race of the big-end bearing. The main diameter is 1 3/8in, and the ends are very slightly tapered to pull the ends into the flywheels against wide shoulders. The nuts which fix it are of heat-treated nickel steel.

Rollers of 5/8in x 7/8in are employed in the big-end bearing. These rollers are located in a Duralumin cage, the bars of the cage being relieved on their inner surface so that only the outer ends of the rollers touch the cage.

The reason for this is that the Dura-lumin cage is apt to wear the hardened crankpin, and the relief of the bars prevents damage to the roller track. That, of course, is a fact, though it may seem hard to believe that more wear is caused by the light-alloy cage than the heavily

pression ratio of approximately 10.9 to 1, the piston head must be steeply domed. It is! So much so, indeed, that circular pockets are formed in the sides of the crown to clear the valve heads. The skirt is of slipper form, and the whole is made of heat-treated "Y"-alloy, sand-cast.

"Why sand-cast?" I asked.

"Because it has given us better results that way," was the reply.

There are small, vertical ribs from the gudgeon-pin bosses upwards, and there is a circular rib at the level of the bosses for maintaining the shape of the slippers. Two narrow pressure rings of Wellworthy "Thermocrom" (heat-formed, not hammered) and a slotted scraper ring are fitted.

"Each engine, individually, is adjusted by shims under the cylinder base so that the cylinder head capacity is 35 c.c.," said Mr. Willis.

This 348 c.c. engine develops 27 b.h.p. at 6,500 r.p.m. It may be run at 7,000 r.p.m. in the normal course of events, and may be run with safety up to 7,500 r.p.m. for short periods, and will run up to 8,000, though this is considered to be beyond the limits of reasonable safety.

loaded rollers. The outer race of the bearing is pressed into the connecting rod big-end and a bronze bush into the small-end.

The massive forged connecting rod is made from an oil-hardening nickel-chrome steel, heat-treated to about 80 tons tensile strength.

"Of course," said Mr. Willis, "we could use a steel with higher tensile strength, but tensile strength is not the only necessity for great toughness is also required. The rod is machined all over and polished on the outside. This is not only useful for removing surface scale and weight, but also tends to reveal surface cracks or flaws."

The outer race of the connecting rod bearing is pressed into the connecting rod big-end, and a bronze bush into the small end.

Of case-hardened nickel-chrome steel, the gudgeon pin is no less than 7/8in diameter; it is hollow and is taper bored at the ends to reduce weight. It floats in the little-end of the connecting rod, and is retained in the piston bosses by spring-wire circlips. As was pointed out, the outer extremities of the gudgeon pin are so chamfered that any tendency for the pin to move endways tends also to jamb the circlips in their grooves, rather than to displace them.

In order to provide the standard com-

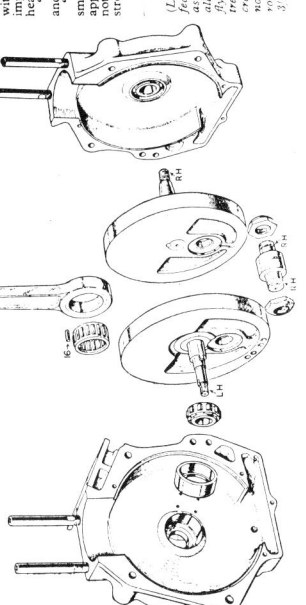

CHAPTER 20

A new dohc 250

Rex McCandless had produced the Featherbed Manx Norton in 1950 which set a new standard of comfort and roadholding never before encountered. This had not gone unnoticed at Hall Green, for Bertie Goodman, as race chief, had decided to make a batch of three new 250s. Apart from being a new venture into the smaller class (for the first time, at least, since the two-stroke effort of the 1920s), and with double ohc at that, it was also to incorporate a redesigned frame layout which made use of twin tank support rails in the manner of the McCandless Norton design.

However, to accomplish this, the KTT lugged frame was used as a basis. Indeed, the initial frame was one of those discarded 1936 sprung frames that was cut and modified, the overall height being reduced, a new fabricated steering head lug produced and the two top rails welded up. This left it with the inherent Featherbed weakness requiring additional support (in the case of Norton, this took the form of a hefty steering head to cylinder head support), overcome on the Velo by the use of a long tube between the steering head and the crosstube in front of the seat. It was secured by taper-headed bolts and incorporated a threaded adjuster for tensioning purposes. This tube, incidentally, passed through a hole in the large alloy fuel tank, and the bolts through the eyes at both ends had to be extracted to remove the tank.

A new pair of oil-damped telescopic forks were made. These had fabricated crowns and a pair of main tubes with brazed-on spring locating lugs that were threaded and retained in the lower crown with ring nuts, as used on the LE. The lower fork sliders, while being basically those in use on the MAC, nevertheless used much heavier lugs for the location of the large-diameter wheel spindle nuts and a substantial brake anchor.

The front wheel, with a 19 in. rim and a special magnesium brake plate, made use of a pre-war-design two-piece brake drum and hub in cast-iron and magnesium. This gave a marginally stiffer assembly, but it is debatable whether or not such gains may have been lost by the reversed operation of the actuating arm that was so placed for convenience rather than design.

Wheel bearings of the journal variety on a non-detachable spindle presented problems with removal of the wheel, despite the detachability of the large diameter nuts around which the left hand side of the leg was cramped for alignment purposes. The rest of the frame and rear wheel were virtually standard KTT, except that the subframe was modified to accommodate a mattress-type racing seat reminiscent of an early 7R, and the top of the Dowty oleo leg located within an arc of alternative mounting holes for adjustment in the manner of the Irving Veloce patent taken out pre-war and used on the model O.

The engine, with 68 × 68.25 mm bore and stroke, was of the double ohc type with a cambox that was actually interchangeable with that of the other models, while the cylinder, a die-cast Alfin, was the basis from which

Cecil Sandford all ready to start in the 1951 Swiss Grand Prix aboard a dohc 250 with a four-speed gearbox. The rubber band across the front downtube secures a plug and spanner (*Dr Helmut Krackowizer*)

Hindquarters of the 1951–2 works 250 and 350 machines, showing the range of adjustment for the top of the oleo dampers, plus the additional footrest which allowed for some variation in riding position (*Dr Helmut Krackowizer*)

subsequent MAC alloy barrels were produced during the following year.

Crankcases, in magnesium and identical, indeed interchangeable, with the works 350, housed a pair of flywheels from standard KTT forgings, but with a pressed-up big-end—like the Roarer and subsequently the Venom, etc. The pin shanks were of $1\frac{3}{8}$ in. diameter and hollow, but plugged after assembly in the manner of Villiers engines of the period. The con-rod, machined from a KTT forging, also carried an 18-roller caged big-end, as used on the 500s, while the dural cage, fluted to allow the passage of oil, was located on the outer ring, rather than the pin. The last was also extended in width some 50 thou. beyond the rod width, locating within a counterbore in the flywheel.

A duralumin-bushed small-end with $\frac{3}{4}$ in. pin, and a piston produced from the same forging as that used for the Roarer pre-war, completed the set.

The inlet valve used was that of a pre-war KSS at $1\frac{9}{16}$ in., although there was scope for improvement, despite the limitations of a relatively small combustion chamber. The exhaust valve head measured $1\frac{3}{8}$ in. and was sodium-filled, as on all works Velocettes since pre-war days. Willis, I believe, was instrumental in the introduction of such a valve in the motorcycle field.

Rushed to the Island for the TT practice, they proved not to be very quick; the limited power was at the top end. An increase in compression ratio and some other detail mods improved matters, but it became obvious that much development work was required before the model would be competitive. The new telescopic forks marginally improved comfort at the front end, mainly due to the hydraulic damping, as opposed to the stiff friction dampers of the original girder forks.

Development during the winter of 1951–2 included the fitting of a special short Webb girder fork with needle-roller pivot bearings and a hydraulic spring damper in place of the old spring with telescopic guide, which, according to the late Les Graham (who was to ride the machine into fourth place in the TT of 1952) made it the best handling machine he had ever ridden.

One other aspect of development worthy of note was the toolroom production of six five-speed gearboxes in magnesium alloy casings that were deemed necessary to keep the motor on the powerband, also to be used on the 350s, although there is insufficient evidence that this was done. These were beautifully made units with floating sleeve gear bushes and big mainshafts that were splined to accept the special final drive sprocket, as on the pre-war works models. However, they suffered the disadvantage of being some $1\frac{1}{2}$ in. wider to accommodate the extra ratio. Certain boxes enclosed an oil pump which sprayed oil on to the gears, thus rendering them dry-sump units and saving a few horsepower in the process.

Unfortunately, this extra bulge on the right-hand side presented cornering problems, which had to be hurriedly rectified by making new engine/gearbox mounting plates, thus lifting the assembly $1\frac{1}{4}$ in. out of harm's way.

The five-speed gearbox fitted to the 250 cc machine ridden by R. L. Graham in the Lightweight TT

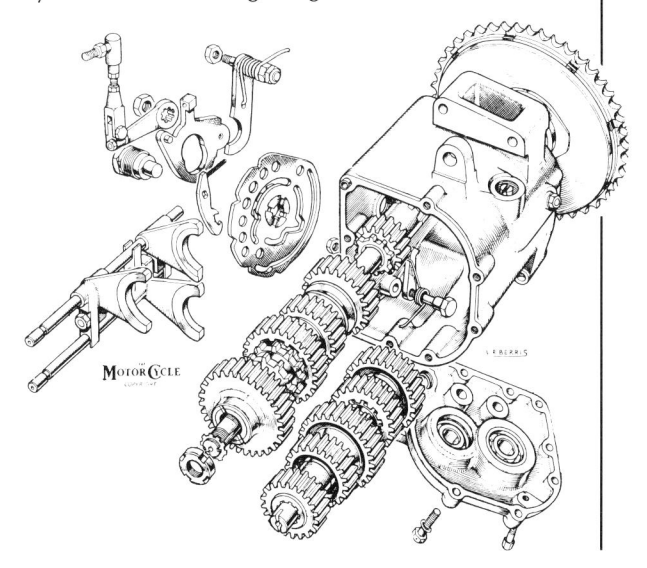

Above A factory publicity shot of the 1951 works dohc 350

Below Les Graham took this dohc five-speed 250 into a fine fourth place behind three works Moto Guzzis in the 1952 Lightweight TT. It had a special pair of forks with needle-roller bearings and a hydraulic spring/damper unit. It handled superbly (*Joe Dainty*)

Invariably, a rather nice family relationship existed between riders and manufacturer, and very often the Goodmans would be called upon to accommodate riders at short notice, prior to an early start to some event or other next morning. Mrs Maureen Goodman regularly supplied sandwiches and flasks of tea for riders and mechanics and other staff involved in preparation of race machines—often late into the night.

Bill Lomas related the story of his approach to Bertie for a 250 for a meeting at Silverstone, to learn that there was no spare machine available. Persistent phone calls necessitated the urgent assembly of a dismantled twin-cam 250 for the event, and the machine was handed over to Bill in Leicester, en route to Silverstone, suitably geared for the circuit.

On arrival, Bill set about putting in some practice, only to find that it would readily rev to the 9000 rpm maximum and beyond, and still need another gear. However, he then found that he had bent the valves in the process. Eventually, having geared it up a couple of teeth, he had no option but to get the machine running by towing it behind a car and then allowing it to rev, while stationary, long enough to straighten the valves in order to regain the lost compression. This was sufficient to give him a start in the race, which he won.

Only when the results were announced in the national motorcycling press, the following week, did Bertie learn of the result. When he requested the engine be taken out of the frame and put on the brake, it was discovered that one of the mechanics had already dismantled the machine to its former state, so the evidence was lost, which was a pity.

In addition to the twin-cam 250s with their lowered frames and five-speed gearboxes, three 350s were also produced on similar lines. Unfortunately, persistent bottom bevel breakages and a lack of sufficient horsepower rendered them uncompetitive, while the 500s had been put aside for good. There was talk of a multi-cylinder machine for the Senior Class, but such rumours were rife at this period.

Bertie and his father had been quietly working towards such a machine, however, based on the classic design used by Gilera and MV Agusta. Drawings had been produced and patterns, indeed the castings, for a slave 125 cc engine had been made to evaluate the

The ultimate KTT of 1952. No longer a production model, but a special works racing machine with a lowered frame, big alloy tank and the dohc engine used to win World Championships in 1949 and 1950. The big front brake was one of two made for the proposed four-cylinder racer which didn't get beyond the stage of an experimental 125 cc test engine due to the death of Percy Goodman. This 350, with its girder forks on needle-roller bearings and a hydraulic spring damper, remained heavy compared to the new technology of the opposition. The Veloce shoestring budget ceased to exist beyond the demise of Percy Goodman. In two days flat, the whole racing operation was closed down and Bertie was given the job of sales director

Above **Arthur Wheeler on a 1952 works double-knocker during the Ulster Grand Prix. The machine had a huge eight-gallon tank that proved a considerable disadvantage at the end of Dundrod's seven-mile straight** (*A. F. Wheeler*)

idea. This was for test-bench purposes only; it was specifically intended not to be possible to fit it into a machine. Alas, Percy Goodman died during 1953, before it was completed, and the whole project, indeed the Grand Prix contention, died with him.

One may be puzzled why Veloce should have found it necessary to use rocker return springs to keep the rocker in contact with the cam at the higher engine revolution range. It seemed to be an admission of defeat to have to do this. Vic Willoughby was obviously aware of the need to look closer at the prospect of eliminating the need for such return springs and found the answer by altering the radius on the rocker from the standard $\frac{13}{32}$ in. to $\frac{5}{8}$ in. Veloce had been embarrassed by rapid cam wear and had recourse to have the later type 17/11 cams hard chrome-plated in an endeavour to maintain a reasonable cam life. Yet, when the chrome eventually gave way, flakes of it would pass into the oil pump and only add to the problems.

Other private riders overcame the problem by considerably lightening the rockers and increasing the rocker radius to $\frac{1}{2}$ in. with satisfactory results, or by

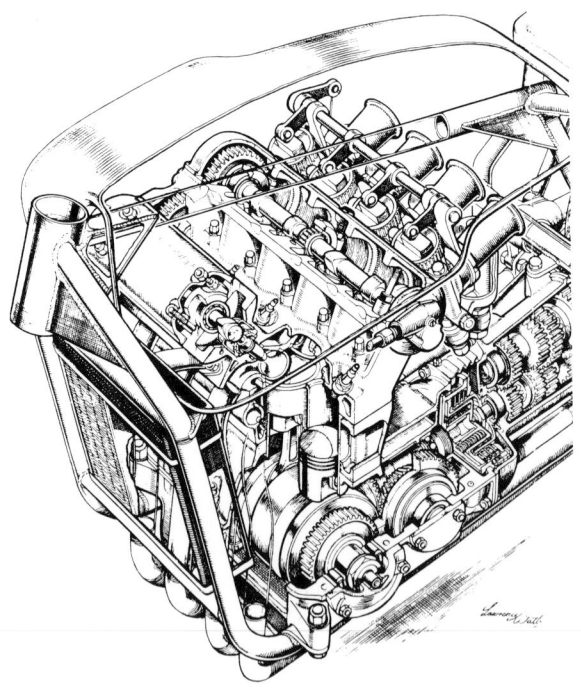

The proposed four-cylinder design that didn't get beyond the building of a single-cylinder test unit (*The Motor Cycle*)

combining these two remedies with a new cam form which, when applied particularly to single-cam 250 specials, would allow an engine to run satisfactorily to 8000 rpm and beyond. A modern cam form with an extended overlap period, used in conjunction with standard unlightened rockers, has proved perfectly satisfactory over many racing miles. With a relatively light pre-set loading on the springs, it allows a standard KTT engine to rev in excess of the normal 7000 rpm. Proof enough that the basic design was right, and such technology applied way back in 1949, for instance, could perhaps have assisted in extending the competitiveness of these superb machines.

Although it was not intended to include Velocette-based specials in this book, this superb shot of Australian Les Denier, riding his 250 Eldee Velo, is most interesting. Apart from being an excellent rider, Les produced the patterns and castings and made the whole machine by hand. The engine was based on an MOV and was fitted to a home-made frame that used BSA front forks (*Dennis Quinlan*)

CHAPTER 21

Viper, Venom and Thruxton

Following the introduction of the MSS springer in 1954, a scrambler version based on it was produced and sold in limited numbers. The motor responded readily to a gradual amount of development, along with other alterations in keeping with the new role of the basic model, so it was not surprising to be told by the company rep, the late Tommy Mutton, in 1955 that a couple of new sports models were being prepared. These were to be known as the Venom and Viper, and were of 500 and 350 cc respectively.

In line with Veloce practice, both models were to share many common components, even to the extent of using bottom ends which, while being stamped individually VM or VR to denote Venom or Viper, were completely interchangeable. The stroke remained at 86 mm, and the Viper used an MSS cam initially. However, to maintain a consistent balance factor, the piston of the smaller engine was sufficiently beefed-up to match that of the 500, while the slimmer 350 barrel (machined from an MAC Alfin casting) was located on a stout spigoted compression plate which satisfactorily effected the conversion. Eventually, the Alfin component was replaced by an iron cylinder that dispensed with the plate.

Undoubtedly, the success of the BSA Gold Star in the Clubmans TT events had to some extent influenced the introduction of the new sports machines. Like the BSAs, they enjoyed the sparkle of a pair of chromed mudguards and fittings, in addition to a chromium-plated petrol tank, relieved in black and with a redesigned gold line and plastic tank motif. The headlamp area, was tidied up by the fitting of a neat nacelle which housed the lighting switch, speedometer and ammeter, while the oil tank not only had a shorter neck, but also sported a breather down to the rear chain.

Unlike the 500, however, the Viper used a $\frac{1}{2} \times \frac{5}{16}$ in. rear chain and the sprockets of the MAC.

New full-width front and rear hubs were designed, similar to those produced pre-war for the supercharged racing twin. Both were in high-duty alloy, the front housing a $7\frac{1}{2}$ in. brake, and having 40 spokes for the first time. The brake drum was in close-grained cast iron and based on the works racing machines of 1952.

The 500 Endurance model—to US specification—in 1956 (*Veloce publicity*)

This is the prototype Venom based on a production MSS and showing slightly more chrome on the tank than the production models (*Velocette Owners' Club*)

The Venom and Viper, soon became popular with the discerning rider, appealing in particular to those who had previously chosen the KSS. Their gradual development in competition underlined the sound features of the redesign that had taken place, and the streamlining of the range had economic and commercial advantages.

However, although the number of machine types made by Veloce was reduced, commercial competition forced them to offer varying specifications on the machines that were left, thus representing enormous production problems.

In my opinion, quality suffered at the expense of quantity, since the range must have been difficult to manage with essentially handbuilt machines in such variety of guises. There were green Vipers and beige Venoms, some in Clubman form with four-gallon tanks based on the KTT pressing introduced in 1961, and some Endurance models—largely a softer scrambler for the American market. Venom and Viper specials were made, some in black and red at a reduced price, with MSS hubs concealed by full-width corrugated covers— no doubt to use up some of the standard fittings at the expense of the more costly alloy components. These, too, among others, were to see the addition of fibreglass covers over engine and gearbox, which eliminated the need to polish the main cases and dispensed with the dynamo drive and final drive front covers, but hid a nasty mix of grit and oil.

The basic MAC was discontinued in 1959–60, while the MSS, standard and Clubman Venoms remained as good solid traditional machines until, and beyond, the advent of a super-tuned sports model, based on production racing development, that was made available to the public in 1964. This was the Thruxton.

Bertie Goodman and Reg Orpin, of London dealers L. Stevens Ltd, developed the idea of the Thruxton, following successes in 24-hour and other events with the Clubman models. Orpin thought of altering the valve angle, but couldn't make his ideas work. He was not an engineer, but a good salesman, so he could see the merit in marketing a special production racing machine.

Orpin asked John Tickle to produce a twin-leading-shoe front brake, before Veloce made their own via Blumfield. No doubt, Blumfield being a shareholder in Veloce had some effect on the decision.

Bertie kept Orpin in the picture whilst Veloce carried out the development work themselves, seeking his opinion from time to time.

The first official Veloce entry in the Thruxton nine-hour race was in the second of these annual events. The riders were Bertie himself and Vic Willoughby. The latter had been talked into taking part and approached Veloce for a suitable machine. Bertie, being an ex-racer too, jumped at the idea, so they formed a team. Valuable experience was gained and, of course, the Clubman model was evolved from this exercise.

This was not a single team effort, however, because other well-established agents had much to offer— people like Geoff Dodkin, Mead and Tomkinson and Arthur Taylor of Shipston-on-Stour. All fielded their own teams and shared in the successes—and

A driveside shot of the pre-production Venom, based on a 1955 MSS

failures—that resulted from such keen competition.

Inevitably, development was carried out around the world by private owners and agents, not directly connected with the long-distance events. For instance, according to one source of information, backed by correspondence with Geoff Dodkin, an American was playing about with cylinder heads and achieving some success on the US east coast.

At the same time, according to information gained from an article in the Velocette Owners' Club magazine, *Fishtail*, an engine builder named Dick Brown in Southern California was commissioned by American rider Bob Beasley to prepare an engine for competition, based on the new scrambler imported into the USA by agent Lou Branch. Branch sponsored Beasley in TT-type scrambles throughout California.

Unknown to Branch, Beasley had approached Dick Brown who, despite having no experience with the marque, was impressed with the general design and decided he could do much to improve its performance. He decided to tackle the job by applying proven principles which, because of his lack of previous Velocette experience, probably had certain advantages. Brown, however, had considerable experience with the Gold Star BSA and immediately chose to reduce the length of the con-rod by some $\frac{3}{8}$ in., to the length of the Gold Star rod, and also that of the Velocette KTT. He machined the replacement to accommodate the standard big-end assembly. To retain the required bore size of 86 mm. an oversize Gold Star piston was used, this being much lighter than the Velocette component, and the flywheels were reduced in diameter. They were re-balanced accordingly.

Since it was well known that Venom valves tangled at anything in excess of the 6500 rpm ceiling, Brown modified the standard head by welding and re-machining to allow for a reduced included valve angle of some 67 degrees. At the same time, he increased the downdraught angle of the induction tract, while allowing for a bigger inlet valve and $1\frac{1}{2}$ in. bore carburettor. Meanwhile, the head diameter of the exhaust valve was reduced to that of the Viper.

Brown carried out the usual lightening of the valve gear, i.e. paring surplus metal from top and bottom rockers and pushrods, and using dural valve spring collars with S&W valve springs. A special cam allowed an increase in engine revolutions beyond 7500 rpm. The result was a beneficial increase in power output on a compression ratio of 10:1.

When Lou Branch eventually learned of the work that had been carried out on this engine, he requested that Brown produce a cylinder head to similar specification, to be sent back to Hall Green for analysis. However, by all accounts, it was not a good example and it never actually arrived at Hall Green, but was sent elsewhere.

Meanwhile, Veloce had begun working on the idea themselves through Bertie Goodman and Jack Passant, their resident mechanic. They produced a head modified to accept a full 2 in. diameter inlet valve. It had a reduced included angle to allow for an increase in revs without fear of it touching the exhaust valve.

I have no proof that what was written in *Fishtail* of the work done in California is correct, although it is quite

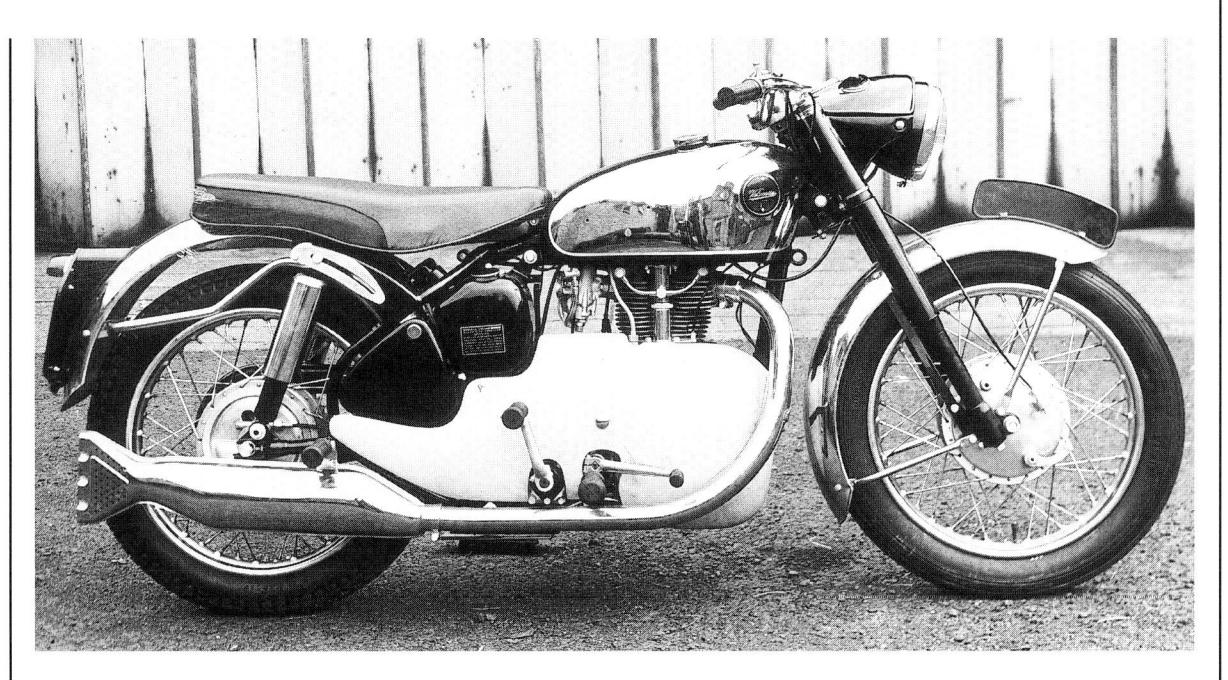

Above Doug Mitchenall, of Avons, and Bertie Goodman were responsible for the introduction of the fibreglass engine covers in 1958. They were also responsible for the Veeline fairings that followed the success of the 24-hour record stint at Montlhèry in 1961. Here we see a standard Venom with engine covers prior to painting (*The Motor Cycle*)

Left A Veloce publicity picture said to be of a 1966 Venom. It's suggested that it is the lower-priced Venom Special with the alternative hubs, based on the old standard components

Below A 1961 Velocette Viper Clubman

A Veloce publicity photo of a 1967 MSS. A good solid single, whether as a solo or with sidecar

feasible. However, letters do exist between the factory and a well-known Velocette correspondent in New South Wales, Australia, where further development work was carried out in the 1960s.

There, special attention was paid to the cylinder head design, since they also knew that valves tangling had been the limiting factor with the standard Venom head. The work was taken a stage further in Australia in that a squish band was developed, allowing for an increase in compression ratio and improved combustion. An inlet valve with a 2 in. head was produced from the exhaust valve of a Lycoming aircraft engine. This was made of austenitic steel, a material that was considered safer at elevated temperatures.

The inlet port was opened out to $1\frac{7}{16}$ in. at the flange, but was tapered to avoid breaking into the rocker box area above. The port was ground and shaped by Sid Willis, a highly competent rider-tuner who finished fifth in the 1953 Lightweight TT on his home-brewed double ohc Velocette, based on a 1936 dohc 350 engine!

Three of these squish-head engines were used in NSW during 1965. Two were campaigned by Sid Lawrence and the late Keith Smith—the latter died whilst riding a 7R AJS in practice at Oran Park in 1966.

As far as is known, there was no trouble with valves tangling in these engines, and they were frequently run up to 7500 rpm in the gears.

Quite independently of this work, similar develop-

A Veloce publicity picture of the Venom Clubman Mk II

ment had been taking place near Pretoria, South Africa, where Allan Harris and a colleague modified to good effect an existing engine with a squish-band head. Since Harris had spent some time in the UK and had ridden production Venoms with some success for Stevens of London, it is not surprising that he should go home and follow this line of development. Geoff Dodkin had also carried out some careful work on the original Venom head to improve the swirl characteristics.

In fact, all the leading Velocette agents were involved in doing their bit towards development and flying the flag in competition wherever possible. As part of the 'happy family' relationship that existed between the Veloce factory (which meant the Goodman family and their workforce) and their agents, such development information was usually fed back to the factory where it was assessed. If commercially viable, such improvements were incorporated in subsequent models.

For instance, independent development work around the world showed that it was beneficial to reduce both the width and the diameter of the flywheel assembly, dimensions which were based on the pre-war MSS, and possibly even the first of the 'dog kennel' 500s of 1934.

Such modifications introduced to the standard Venom and Viper continued into the Thruxton and on to the end.

During the 1960s, L. Stevens, in particular, had produced and catalogued a range of so called 'bolt-on goodies' for sale to the aspiring racer. Such items included an extended induction tract, in the form of a finned spacer to which was added a $1\frac{3}{8}$ in. GP Amal carburettor. To accommodate this long extension, it was necessary to move the oil tank further back and to cut away a fair portion of the lower rear of the Clubman-style fuel tank to boot. A twin-leading-shoe front brake conversion and special racing combined footrest/brake pedal/gearchange set, was also available, plus a two-way damping modification for the front fork, and a few other tiddly bits consistent with combining strength and safety with high-speed lappery—the basis of a new model had been laid.

Above After many successes in production races at home and overseas, the Thruxton was evolved as a readily-available machine for all to buy and carry on the tradition (*Veloce publicity*)

Left Floyd Clymer, of America, produced a batch of Indian Velos based on Thruxton engine and gearbox units, half of which were sold by Geoff Dodkin of London (*Velocette Owners' Club*)

This Viper was produced to special order and supplied by Freddie Frith Ltd of Grimsby in late 1965 (*Veloce publicity*)

Orpin, on behalf of L. Stevens, went the whole hog and built his version of what he felt was potentially a sellable machine, fully prepared for production machine racing. It was based on a Clubman engine and gearbox with a set of TT close ratios.

The completed prototype was taken to Birmingham and the idea sold to the Veloce board of directors, and at Earls Court Show time, in 1964, the new Thruxton Velocette was launched. However, it was a good six months before the first production model came off the line, and it was immediately taken over to the Island for TT week. The first model, with engine No. VMT101, was kept at the factory for development purposes. VMT102 was despatched to Whittakers of Blackpool in June (was this the model seen in the Island?), before being passed on to its eager new owner.

These production Thruxtons, while being based on the Stevens prototype with the improved cylinder head and, in my opinion, a rather too heavy 2 in. inlet valve, along with all the other customising equipment, also benefited from a new, heavier pair of crankcases. These had been further strengthened by heat treatment and, because of machining considerations, they used dowels for location, instead of the usual spigot joint.

Modifications relating to lubrication and breathing were carried out, and a redesigned pair of bottom rockers were installed. These were no longer interchangeable with one another, but improved the lift and closing characteristics of the standard cam.

The outcome was a splendid piece of machinery, producing some 41 sturdy horsepower with a silencer fitted. To some extent, it was to revive interest in the marque, although marginally, since it was at a time in motorcycle history when little, if anything, British was to prove saleable in sufficient numbers to be commercially viable.

Veloce eventually produced at least three special

A 1950s picture of the entrance to the TT workshops at the Nursery Hotel, Onchan, carrying on the tradition set pre-war by Willis, when a visitor had to make contact initially by phone! (*Classic Motorcycle*)

Neil Kelly during his superb winning ride in the Production TT of 1967

engines using the squish-head arrangement, based on the New South Wales development, which included forged pistons machined closely to that of the short-stroke Manx Norton specification. They had modified crankcases and, I believe, in at least one case, needle rollers in the intermediate timing pinion.

Meanwhile, Velocette's last Island fling was a win in the 500 class of the 1967 Production TT. Victory came their way through Manxman Neil Kelly, who took over the factory machine after the original entrant, Dennis Craine, had broken a leg scrambling.

Kelly's practice mount, a poorly-prepared MSS, gave him little experience of the hallowed starting procedure. The clutch slipped, but an old man came out from behind a hedge, took a nail from his pocket, and adjusted it!

Only because of his past record did the stewards allow Kelly to start the race, because he hadn't finished a practice lap. The race Velo, unlike the practice model, was well-prepared, but Kelly was left on the line when it failed to fire up.

Keith Heckles, on the Dodkin Velo, was also in trouble starting but got away. By this time Kelly was exhausted.

Right Ralph Seymour's Thruxton in action and piloted by Danny Shimmin in the 1976 Production TT. He was credited with third fastest time during practice—approximately 93.5 mph

Below One of three squish-band cylinder heads developed in Australia during the mid 1960s (*Dennis Quinlan*)

'Reg produced an aerosol, and squirted it in the carb. I summoned the strength for one last kick and it fired,' said Neil. 'I saw nothing but red for half a lap, I was so angry.'

His first lap was at 87 mph because of the abysmal start, but during it he passed Heckles and quite a few of the 750s.

He said the race was no problem. The bike ran faultlessly, handling well, and had good brakes—particularly the front one. There was bags of engine braking. The most difficult thing was getting it round the Gooseneck and the Hairpin because of the big bottom gear. He was clocked at the Highlander at 129 mph, his race average being 89.89 and fastest lap 91.01 mph. This speed would have given him third place in the 750 class.

Orpin, in close co-operation with Bertie Goodman, took the theme a step further by producing a small number of specials with frames designed and built by Jim Lee of Batley, one using a substantial alloy rear fork on taper bearings. One also had one of the works engines fitted which was to benefit from the squish-type cylinder head, giving a compression ratio of 11:1 with, as a basis, the piston from a 500 Manx Norton, power output being in the region of 47 bhp. Mick Grant, who was working closely with Jim Lee at this time, campaigned such a bike to good effect.

In an endeavour to update the marque still further, American Floyd Clymer purchased 100 engine/gearbox units from the factory and inspired the production of what is known as the Indian Velocette. This was assembled by Italjet of Italy, Clymer died before the

Viper, Venom and Thruxton | 157

project was completed, and it was left to Geoff Dodkin of London to rescue the operation and sell off the surplus.

There are several reasons why there is some confusion about who did what in the Thruxton project. Many years have passed, memories are less sharp, and the Thruxton was only one of many things going on at the time.

However, it is worth recording what several of the parties who were involved have to say now. There are obvious cross references and confirmations in their observations.

Geoff Dodkin: 'The special cylinder head was received by Stevens from Branch, but it wasn't used. However, the factory altered the downdraught angle and squish characteristics themselves to produce their own new head for use in the Thruxton.

'In the 24-hour events, Reg Orpin had one of these heads fitted, but I didn't. I thought it was of doubtful value at the time. I developed my own cylinder head, quite effectively, I feel.

'I think, Jack Passant was in charge of Neil Kelly's TT winner.'

Jack Passant says: 'Fuel tanks split at a Bol d'Or 24-hour event, so I hacked off the rear mounting lug and sat the tank down on a lump of rubber and there was no further trouble with fuel tanks.

'We had problems with frame flexure once we were producing some useful horses with the special engines. To overcome this, a tube was welded between the swinging-arm pivot lug and the lower rails. A special jig was made to measure the amount of distortion that had taken place.

'Experience gained with the works bikes and various ideas received from Veloce agents were incorporated in our development programme.

'There was very little difference in the speed of the Venom or Viper.

'The special engines had carefully radiussed valve seats and flanged valve guides—as on the KTT. We also used flanged mainshafts and the squish-type cylinder head, tappetless rockers and titanium pushrods, plus a needle-roller bearing on the intermediate timing wheel.

'John Tickle provided the early 2LS front brake, which subsequently was produced to Veloce design by Tommy Blumfield of Birmingham.

'Reg Orpin provided the prototype Thruxton from parts supplied from the factory.

'I was not in charge of the TT winner in the Island, Reg looked after that one, but I was over for the Manx later on when Stevens paid my wages for the the fortnight.'

Peter Goodman says: 'Orpin was anxious that Veloce produce a special machine, based on the Clubman models and developed by the agents in the Thruxton and other long-distance events.

'Bertie responded by providing all the special bits, but Veloce would produce engines themselves, including some special ones, all with squish heads based on the NSW development, but modified to our own requirements.

'These engines also used flanged mainshafts, needle bearings on the intermediate timing gears, adjusterless rockers and special pushrods.

'As for the 24-hour record-breaker, as far as I am aware, it was in one piece, as it completed the record, when the factory closed in 1971.'

Reg Orpin says: 'If it hadn't been for Bertie Goodman, myself, Jack Passant and John Tickle, I doubt very much whether the Thruxton would have been made. Bertie was very enthusiastic and a clever engineer, Jack a very capable engineer (mechanic), John very able to produce small batches of cycle parts for me overnight.

'Parallel with this project, Bertie and I planned to produce 12 racers with special engines, five-speed boxes and duplex-type frames. I ordered these engines and agreed a price, but I called a halt after seven were made, as they did not give enough bhp, and Bertie could not obtain the tooling for the large finned squish head and cylinder barrel, which we felt were essential for power and appearance. Five of these engines were sold off to Ken Swallow, Geoff Dodkin, Ralph Seymour, Robert Le Conte—I retained the rest to develop.

'My cylinder head was based on the Manx Norton, which was good and reliable, but it was also influenced by the one made by Branch and had some of our ideas as well.

'I had 12 or 14 different frames made. Two were made in Australia. All of these frames were mobile test-beds.

'We set out to beat the BSA Gold Star and it really was a great shame that Velocette ran out of money. They had lots of problems, so perhaps it wasn't surprising that Bertie was in a minority of one in being really enthusiastic about the project. We meant to race the bikes and sell them to the public also.'

CHAPTER 22

The 24-hour record

It is well known that Veloce Ltd, having traditionally taken an active interest in long-distance record attempts, did pull off the magic 100+ mph record over a period of 24 hours at Montlhéry in France during March 1961. This figure, as far as I am aware, has never been beaten, other than with a larger-capacity machine.

A standard production Venom was the basis of the machine carefully built for the job in hand, developed and track tested at the Motor Industry Research Association's test facility near Nuneaton, where some 1400 miles were covered at over 100 mph. The machine was to use the prototype fairing produced for the Venom Clubman Veeline model by Mitchenall Brothers. This was cut into four pieces and rejoined, making it narrower and shorter.

The engine breathed through a $1\frac{3}{16}$ in. Amal GP carburettor with a $\frac{3}{4}$ in. wide packing piece between carb and head, which had been found beneficial under test-bench conditions, while jetting was over-rich for safety reasons. The exhaust system terminated in a megaphone of KTT dimensions, while sparks were supplied via a BTH TT magneto with manual advance.

The power characteristics were good, with excellent torque through the range to deliver a maximum of 39.8 bhp at 5900 rpm, and were very smooth.

A historical picture of the Venom ridden so successfully at Montlhéry in March 1961 at an average speed in excess of 100 mph for 24 hours. The five-lobe shock absorber is quite clearly visible (*EMAP*)

Georges Monneret congratulating Bertie Goodman on the success of their joint venture in capturing the 24-hour record of over 100 mph with the Venom in March 1961—it still stands

A further breather pipe was carried flexibly to a copper pipe brazed to the rear brake torque arm and turned inwards towards the brake drum where it could help lubricate the chain to good effect.

In true competition fashion, spare cables were taped alongside those in use. The clutch cable passed through a threaded adjuster into the gearbox where it was readily to hand if required. This adjuster was another KTT feature. The clutch itself, having been allowed to settle and finally adjusted, was then spragged to prevent any creepage.

The fuel tank had been produced specially, using a standard pressing, but spread at the base with a new bottom added. This increased its capacity slightly and gave it a somewhat bulbous appearance. Frame and cycle parts were standard items, except for an additional rear mudguard support bracket, plus a strap brazed across the two damper mounting brackets which also served to give additional anchorage for the rear guard. No front mudguard was fitted in the interests of safety and cooling.

Alternative rider's footrests were provided in the form of fixed pillion rests to which were welded hefty wire brackets, turned upwards, to retain the rider's feet. Additional strengthening struts between front and rear footrest mountings helped stiffen the subframe under the arduous conditions anticipated. The clip-on type

Unusually, a five-lobe engine shock absorber assembly was chosen, possibly in the interests of reducing the tug on the mainshaft, since it is not unknown for such shafts to creep out of the flywheel with the standard three-lobe arrangement.

The gearbox, too, with its set of Clubman ratios, was given the full KTT treatment, including the radiussing of the camplate indexing slots to facilitate positive engagement allied to a sweeter gearchange.

As one would expect, attention to detail was all important. A special primary chainguard of U-section, with a large-bore drain, carried a length of foam rubber to soak up excess oil. It was also rubber mounted, while a carefully set double chain oiler delivered the vital lubricant from a tap on the front of an extension to the standard oil tank, which increased its capacity. The tank was also rubber mounted and carried the mounting for the remote TT float chamber, in the manner of the KTT. On the right-hand side was an overflow pipe that terminated in a rubber hose somewhere down below and out of harm's way. Also on the right was welded a heat shield to protect the rider's leg from the hot contents.

Every picture tells a story

Above A later 24-hour record attempt with a Viper at Montlhèry was thwarted by various problems. Sales director Bertie Goodman is seen here during one of his many stints

Below The ill-fated 24-hour record attempt 350 during a routine pit stop. Left to right: works mechanic Jack Passant, Bertie Goodman, Robert Laconte, Georges Monneret, Reg Orpin and Ted Pink

handlebars required critical setting, since they all but fouled the tank and fairing on the limited lock available. Dunlop alloy rims were shod with racing tyres, and spare sets were available for quick changing when required. Ferodo racing lining material was fitted to the brakes.

With a top gear ratio of 3.92:1, a speed of 110–112 mph was readily attainable, so the machine with a spare engine and wheels, etc, was taken over to France where further testing took place on the day before the event.

Some organizational problems were encountered in France, however, not least of which was the appalling condition of the track—large gaps were to be found between the 25 yard slabs of concrete. Some form of lighting was deemed necessary, too, for the overnight stint and was hurriedly rigged, using 50 Marchal headlamps set up around the circuit. The riders chosen were Veloce sales director Bertie Goodman, *Motor Cycling* staffman Bruce Main-Smith, plus Andrew Jacquiers-Brett, Alain Sagan, Pierre Cherrier, father and son Georges and Pierre Moneret, and Robert Leconte.

With their vast experience of the track, the Monnerets monopolized the riding, usually in one-hour stints. The need to remove the gearbox end cover to straighten out the internal link rod (a twisted piece of metal which Charles Udall had insisted be tried instead of the traditional yokes and clevis assembly) damaged

Bruce Main-Smith in full flight during the successful record attempt with Venom VM3412

by over-enthusiastic use of the gearchange pedal—the French regularly changed gear with their heels I am told—plus the expected wheel changing and the single replacement of the back chain dropped the average speed somewhat. However, no other trouble was experienced with the machine. The motor ran like a train, yet despite the tremendous hammering taken by the riders, most of whom were suffering from blurred vision, the deficit was reclaimed and the records eventually taken for 12 and 24 hours for 500, 750 and unlimited solo motorcycles. The 12-hour average was 104.66 mph, and for the 24-hour period, it was 100.05 mph.

The oil tank had been topped up at 4–5 hour intervals, and fuel consumption at a maintained 107 mph worked out at 35–6 mpg—maximum speed was just under 115 mph.

A year or so later, a Viper was prepared and taken over for a similar attempt. This used a dry-sump gearbox, oil being fed by jets over the gears and pumped back to the main supply, thus saving a few horsepower. Despite suffering a consistent misfire (later found to be caused by arcing in the HT pickup of the Lucas racing magneto), it maintained the required average. Had the attempt been successful, it would have been an added bonus to the successful Venom spree, but alas the top of the sandcast piston parted company with its lower half and that was that. Later, it transpired that a number of factors were responsible, quite apart from the arcing HT pickup. An additional section had been placed across the fairing to stiffen it, just in front of the cylinder, which caused overheating, and since the track had been extensively resurfaced, much sand was in evidence, which showed itself when the engine was dismantled.

The historic 24-hour record-holding Venom is now on permanent display at the National Motor Cycle Museum in Birmingham.

CHAPTER 23

A new roadgoing 250

It was in the early 1960s when the author learned of a proposed new 250 roadster Velocette which immediately whetted the appetite and conjured thoughts of a revival of the MOV. It seemed feasible, too, since the MAC had been phased out in favour of the Viper and one could see the possibility of using existing surplus components from the alloy MAC which, with the lighter 1953 frame and gearbox, could well have produced a modern version of the famous pushrod 250.

At this time, too, a new law had been introduced, limiting provisional licence holders to riding nothing bigger than a 250, so the timing was right and the market was wide open. Other than Royal Enfields and the new Ariel two-stroke twins, there was not much else in competition, unless one considers the AMC 250s that occasionally broke their crankpins.

The excitement was highlighted further when, on investigation, it was learned that the new engine was to have a chain-driven overhead camshaft. One could foresee the possibility of a simple, yet effective, design which would be based on the traditional Veloce narrow crank assembly, an all-alloy top half with single camshaft, driven by a tensioned chain encased in the manner of the famous cammy Ajay. Alas, nothing more was heard of it, no doubt the works being too involved with the problems of the LE, the tooling for the Viceroy scooter and trying to make ends meet.

It was disappointing, to say the least, although now I must admit that I am pleased it didn't come off. When I saw the prototype engine, following the closure of the company, I was horrified to find that it was a monobloc engine/gearbox design with conventional (unconventional for Velocette) flywheel assembly with outboard primary drive, using Burman lightweight gearbox internals—as used on the Ariel Leader. Its head was obviously based on that of the Royal Enfield 250, and the chain drive for the overhead camshaft was intended to pass through tubes, as on the Norton prototype P10 designed by Charles Udall.

Mock-up of the proposed chain-driven, overhead-cam 250 planned during the early 1960s. It was based on Royal Enfield basic components, such as cylinder head and crankshaft (*Temple Press*)

At this time, Veloce had come to an arrangement with the Enfield Cycle Company, of Redditch, to service and sell the Royal Enfield spares range which, no doubt, had some bearing on the decision to look at the possibility of producing a saleable machine at minimal cost. To my mind, however, and the minds of others who followed the thoroughbred Velocette breed, it would have been quite unacceptable.

VELOCE LIMITED *(in liquidation)* P.O. Box No. 275. Hall Green Works, York Road, Hall Green, Birmingham B28 8LN

Telephone: 021-777 1145
Private Branch Exchange
Telegrams: Veloce, Birmingham
Codes, Bentley's

VELOCETTE MOTOR CYCLES

Royal Enfield Spares & Service Division
General Engineers & Suppliers of Petrol Engines

Your Reference   Our Reference

4th February, 1971.

N O T I C E

With effect from Friday, February 5th 1971, the main gates to the works will be locked, and all employees should enter and leave via the office entrance.

No vehicles will be allowed past the gates, and the car park should be used.

....
Liquidator

The actual notice which was pinned to the notice board by the liquidator, rescued by the late John Griffith. It was typed by Desne Dodkin

CHAPTER 24

The demise

There was a period during the late 1960s and early 1970s when interest in motorcycling was at a relatively low ebb, in fact one rarely saw a motorcycle on the road. Despite, or because of, their range of models, Veloce were finding difficulty in maintaining a steady sale of machines, along with many others. The increasing overheads and the problem of rising labour costs were taking their toll and, in consequence, any margin of profit was diminishing rapidly.

Gone were the days of hiring dedicated personnel, keenly interested in the marque and prepared to work for a reasonable wage. No sooner had a new recruit been trained and settled into machining or assembly work at Hall Green, than he moved up the road to the Longbridge motor works for double the wage!

Regrettably, during the scooter boom of the 1960s, Veloce decided to produce such a machine (the Viceroy) that would perhaps fulfil the category of the 'everyman's' machine that Eugene had envisaged. Though there were those on the board of directors who were prepared to start with a clean sheet of paper and lay down the design and tooling for a simple device to match the Vespa or Lambretta, for instance, there were others who could not forget the company's proud ancestry. The result was that they chose to produce yet another technically advanced machine that, being typically Veloce, was far superior to anything produced hitherto — a reed-valved, two-stroke flat-twin with shaft drive.

The tooling for the scooter was so costly and the sale price such that there was no chance of reclaiming the tooling costs, let alone making a profit. Eventually, a fresh outlet was found for the efficient power unit — for

The original factory by the corner of Cateswell Road and York Road, Hall Green. If the building could talk, it would tell quite a tale! (*Veloce*)

powering small hovercraft, which were all the vogue at the time.

Meanwhile, the overall sales of machines were such that in order to satisfy the company's bankers, in continuing the existing overdraft situation, Sir Alfred Owen was appointed to the board of directors. Nevertheless, it soon became apparent that trading could not continue, so while various options were investigated — the possibility of a consortium of dealers taking it over being one — the company went into liquidation on 4 February 1971.

Production rights, surplus machines, spares and some tooling were sold to Matt Holder, of the Airco Jig and Tool Company, who had acquired similar rights to the old Shipley Scott design some years before. Other spares and machines were sold to various dealers and interested individuals, while the $3\frac{1}{2}$ – acre site, much tooling and steel stock, and the soul of this historic company, was taken over by C. C. Cooper, a local scrap merchant.

The sight of the huge press tools for the LE being craned on to one of Cooper's lorries, along with boxed sets of new bevel gears for the ill-fated Viceroy scooter was an indication of what was happening — and quickly, for soon it was gone, factory and all.

Some of the tooling for the KTT was saved, along with the only Bendix Weiss constant velocity coupling that was left, which had been specially produced for the blown shaft-driven racing twin, the Roarer. All creditors were paid out 17 shillings in the pound.

Not surprisingly, some of the directors were to suffer from sleepless nights for quite a long time following the closure, since it must have been an almost impossible situation to have lived with, having had a lifetime's involvement with the most respected family concern in the industry.

One might ponder the possibility of whether it may have been worthwhile selling off the surplus machines and spares, selling what must have been a valuable site in the centre of Birmingham, and moving out into the backwoods with a skeleton staff and continuing with a single model, rebuilding from there. However, with hindsight, it is often easier to see what should have been done. Who can blame Bertie and Peter and the rest, at their age, for deciding that enough was enough.

Conjecture

One may like to guess at what may have developed but for a number of factors. What might have occurred if, for instance, there had not been a war, if Harold Willis had not died when he did, if Veloce had chosen not to have produced the LE? Inevitably, we would have continued along the road of sprung frames, and since Veloce were in the forefront, we could well have seen the stressed-skin theme developed and almost full-enclosure, too. That Model O prototype twin, designed and built with full-scale production in mind by the talented Phil Irving, who was a practical and experienced motorcyclist, might have had a good chance, particularly in the light of the popularity of the vertical twin that ensued. We know that following initial development teething troubles, it was to prove fast, reliable and very smooth.

Had road racing continued unchecked with continued use of forced induction, and particularly if Willis had remained at the helm, the Roarer would undoubtedly have been further developed on the lines of its initial conception with liquid cooling and telescopic forks, and could well have been a winner. I would like to think, too, that we could have seen both a springer MOV and KSS, examples of which exist, built by private individuals around the world. Having ridden a 500 version of the KSS and the one and only Vulcan V-twin, who knows? As for the 'everyman's' machine, that too was a pipe dream!

The author with his elder son, Grahame, and the Roarer following a long and painstaking rebuild, back in Douglas after 50 years' absence on 2 June 1989. Note that the black exhaust pipes indicate a complete, *running* machine; chromed pipes were fitted when the machine had no internals. The ratting cap covers a BMW sticker, applied to the racing number plate to show that the machine had been passed by the scrutineers! (*Jim Davies*)

APPENDIX 1

Specifications

Model	MOV 1933–48	MAC 1933–52
Bore (mm)	68	68
Stroke (mm)	68.25	96
Capacity (cc)	248	349
Compression ratio	6.75:1	6.75:1
Valve position	ohv	ohv
Inlet opens btdc	50	50
Inlet closes abdc	60	60
Exhaust opens bbdc	70	70
Exhaust closes atdc	40	40
Valve clear. (cold) in. (in.)	0.003	0.003
Valve clear. (cold) ex. (in.)	0.006	0.006
Ignition timing (degrees)	40	40
Points gap (in.)	0.012	0.012
Primary drive chain	$\frac{1}{2} \times \frac{5}{16}$ in. (74 pitches)	$\frac{1}{2} \times \frac{5}{16}$ in. (75 pitches)
Rear chain	$\frac{1}{2} \times \frac{5}{16}$ in. (108 pitches)	$\frac{1}{2} \times \frac{5}{16}$ in. (108 pitches)
Sprockets: engine (T)	19	22
clutch (T)	44	44
gearbox (T)	19	19
rear wheel (T)	52	52
O/A ratio: top	6.35:1	5.5:1
O/A ratio: 3rd	8.45:1	7.3:1
O/A ratio: 2nd	11.1:1	9.6:1
O/A ratio: 1st	16.1:1	14.1:1
Front tyre (in.)	3.25 × 19	3.25 × 19
Rear tyre (in.)	3.25 × 19	3.25 × 19
Fuel tank capacity (imp. gal.)	2.75	2.75
Weight (lb)	275	280
Carburettor settings		
main jet	120	130
needle jet	4/061	4/061
needle	5/065	6/065
slide	5/3	6/3
needle clips	third groove	third groove

From MAC 973, engine sprocket changed from 19 to 22T and cam lobe changed from five to three lobes.

From M 2770 and MAC 3228, close-fitting valve springs and modified top collar fitted to prevent surge.

From MOV 6253 and MAC 10149, increased bore to oil feed pipe.

From initial production of MOV and MAC to M 877 and MAC 413, straight-cut timing gears.

From M 878 and MAC 414 to M 1671 and MAC 1569 inclusive, 15 degree timing gears.

From M 1672 to M 1875 and MAC 1570 to 1840 inclusive, 11 degree timing gears.

From MOV 1876 and MAC 1841, all subsequent ohv models used 16 degree helical gear teeth.

All MDD and MAF, 16 degree helical timing gears.

Seven-plate clutch introduced to MOV/MAC following initial batch of WD machines in 1941, which included change of spring and carrier, and saw introduction of retaining ring locking plate and screwed plug retaining ball and spring in timing cover.

From MOV 6251 and MAC 10149, oil pump modification carried out which included the increased width of feed gears from 0.249 in. to 0.311 in.

From M 2637 and MAC 2993, improved rocker box introduced which required a suitable oil feed pipe to match.

From 1937, single side damper fitted to front forks.

From 1939, front brake cable adjuster transferred from lug on the fork leg to a stop on the front brake plate.

From late 1939, for 1940 season, a heavier link fitted to the MAC only when top spindles were increased to $\frac{7}{16}$ in. and on both MOV and MAC, a new type of steering damper knob was introduced.

Post-war MOV and MAC fitted with the heavy fork, although some 1946 models were issued with links of equal length top and bottom of $3\frac{7}{8}$ in. centres. However, later in 1946, $3\frac{5}{8}$ in. top links and $3\frac{11}{16}$ in. bottom links were fitted.

All MOV and MAC front brake drums were pressed steel until 1940 when they were to be in cast-iron for the WD model on. Brake shoe width also increased from $\frac{3}{4}$ in. to $\frac{7}{8}$ in.

MOV and MAC frames, from introduction until 1936, carried a one-piece rear wheel and brake hub; subsequently, all used QD wheels.

Cylinder head steady lug on frame MD 7391 on.

All fuel tanks to 1939 inclusive carried $\frac{1}{4}$ in. studs for kneegrip mounting plates. Subsequent tanks, WD and post-war, all had threaded $\frac{1}{4}$ in. holes for moulded rubber grips.

Special fuel tanks with tapered forward ends were used for lockstop clearance with Dowty Oleo forks.

Two-start oil pump from MAC 15444.

Model	**MAC SPRINGER**		
	1953–60		
Bore (mm)	68		
Stroke (mm)	96		
Capacity (cc)	349		
Compression ratio	6.75:1		
Valve position	ohv		
Inlet opens btdc	30*	50**	19***
Inlet closes abdc	60*	60**	49***
Exhaust opens bbdc	60*	70**	49***
Exhaust closes atdc	30*	40**	19***
Valve clear. (cold) in. (in.)	0.005		
Valve clear. (cold) ex. (in.)	0.005		
Ignition timing (degrees)	38		
Points gap (in.)	0.012		
Primary drive chain	$\frac{1}{2} \times \frac{5}{16}$ in.		
Rear chain	$\frac{1}{2} \times \frac{5}{16}$ in.		
Sprockets: engine (T)	21		
clutch (T)	44		
gearbox (T)	21		
rear wheel (T)	55		
O/A ratio: top	5.5:1		
O/A ratio: 3rd	7.3:1		
O/A ratio: 2nd	9.6:1		
O/A ratio: 1st	14:1		

Model	**MAC SPRINGER**
	1953–60
Front tyre (in.)	3.25 × 19
Rear tyre (in.)	3.25 × 19
Weight (lb)	355
Fuel tank capacity (imp. gal.)	3
Oil tank capacity (imp. gal.)	$\frac{1}{2}$
Carburettor	Amal 276 EY/IAT, $\frac{15}{16}$ in. choke diameter; later model Amal Monobloc 376/48
Throttle valve	3 (4 Amal 376)
Needle jet	105 (107 Amal 376)
Main jet	200 (130 Amal 376)

From mid 1954, prefix 11 gearbox superseded by prefix 14.

*M 17/5 cam **M 17/4 cam ***M 17/7 cam (requires change of bottom rocker)

Model	**MSS**
	1935–48
Bore (mm)	81
Stroke (mm)	96
Capacity (cc)	495
Compression ratio	6.4:1
Valve position	ohv
Inlet opens btdc	30*
Inlet closes abdc	60*
Exhaust opens bbdc	60*
Exhaust closes atdc	30*
Valve clear. (cold) in. (in.)	0.005
Valve clear. (cold) ex. (in.)	0.010
Ignition timing (degrees)	40
Points gap (in.)	0.012
Primary drive chain	$\frac{1}{2} \times \frac{5}{16}$ in. (68 pitches)
Rear chain	$\frac{5}{8} \times \frac{3}{8}$ in. (99 pitches)
Sprockets: engine (T)	23
clutch (T)	44
gearbox (T)	18
rear wheel (T)	46
O/A ratio: top	4.9:1
O/A ratio: 3rd	5.9:1
O/A ratio: 2nd	7.76:1
O/A ratio: 1st	11.25:1
Front tyre (in.)	3.50 × 19
Rear tyre (in.)	4.00 × 19
Fuel tank capacity (imp. gal.)	3.5
Weight (lb)	335
Carburettor settings	
main jet	180
needle jet	4/061
needle	6/065
slide	6/5
needle clips	third groove

Model	**KTS & KSS II** 1936–47	
Bore (mm)	74	
Stroke (mm)	81	
Capacity (cc)	348	
Compression ratio	7.6–8.4:1	
Valve position	ohc	
Inlet opens btdc	34**	35***
Inlet closes abdc	47**	65***
Exhaust opens bbdc	64**	70***
Exhaust closes atdc	29**	30***
Valve clear. (cold) in. (in.)	0.006	
Valve clear. (cold) ex. (in.)	0.010	
Ignition timing (degrees)	40	
Points gap (in.)	0.012	
Primary drive chain	$\frac{1}{2} \times \frac{5}{16}$ in. (67 pitches)	
Rear chain	$\frac{5}{8} \times \frac{3}{8}$ in. (99 pitches)	
Sprockets: engine (T)	21	
clutch (T)	44	
gearbox (T)	17	
rear wheel (T)	46	
O/A ratio: top	5.6:1	
O/A ratio: 3rd	6.8:1	
O/A ratio: 2nd	9:1	
O/A ratio: 1st	13.1:1	
Front tyre (in.)	3.00 × 21 (KSS)/3.25 × 19 (KTS)	
Rear tyre (in.)	3.25 × 20 (KSS)/3.50 × 19 (KTS)	
Fuel tank capacity (imp. gal.)	3.5	
Weight (lb)	333	
Carburettor settings		
main jet	150	
needle jet	4/061	
needle	6/065	
slide	6/3	
needle clips	third groove	

From MSS 1849, QD rear wheel fitted.
From 1939, for 1940 season, heavier fork links fitted top and bottom, and brake adjuster transferred to stop on brake plate.
From KSS 8373, suction filter fitted to crankcase.
From MSS 6301, taper main bearings fitted with 0.004 in. load when cold.

*M 17/3 cam (checking 0.025 in.) **K 17/10 cam ***K 17/7 cam (early)

Model	**MSS SPRINGER** 1954–69	
Bore (mm)	86	
Stroke (mm)	86	
Capacity (cc)	499	
Compression ratio	6.75:1	
Valve position	ohv	
Inlet opens btdc	19*	
Inlet closes abdc	49*	
Exhaust opens bbdc	49*	
Exhaust closes atdc	19*	
Valve clear. (cold) in. (in.)	0.005	
Valve clear. (cold) ex. (in.)	0.005	
Ignition timing (degrees)	36	
Points gap (in.)	0.012	
Primary drive chain	$\frac{1}{2} \times \frac{5}{16}$ in. (68 pitches)	
Rear chain	$\frac{5}{8} \times \frac{3}{8}$ in. (101 pitches)	
Sprockets: engine (T)	23	
clutch (T)	44	
gearbox (T)	18	
rear wheel (T)	46	
O/A ratio: top	4.9:1	
O/A ratio: 3rd	6.52:1	Prefix 14
O/A ratio: 2nd	8.57:1	
O/A ratio: 1st	12.4:1	
Front tyre (in.)	3.25 × 19	
Rear tyre (in.)	3.25 × 19	
Carburettor	Amal Monobloc 376/49, $1\frac{1}{16}$ in. choke diameter	
Main jet	240	
Needle jet	105	
Throttle valve	$3\frac{1}{2}$	
Pilot jet	25	

*Checking 0.030 in.

Model	VIPER
	1955–68
Bore (mm)	72
Stroke (mm)	86
Capacity (cc)	349
Compression ratio	8.5:1
Valve position	ohv
Inlet opens btdc	19* 55**
Inlet closes abdc	49* 65**
Exhaust opens bbdc	49* 75**
Exhaust closes atdc	19* 45**
Valve clear. (cold) in. (in.)	0.005
Valve clear. (cold) ex. (in.)	0.005
Ignition timing (degrees)	38
Points gap (in.)	0.012
Primary drive chain	$\frac{1}{2} \times \frac{5}{16}$ in. (67 pitches)
Rear chain	$\frac{1}{2} \times \frac{5}{16}$ in. (124 pitches)
Sprockets: engine (T)	21
clutch (T)	44
gearbox (T)	21
rear wheel (T)	55
O/A ratio: top	5.5:1
O/A ratio: 3rd	6.64:1
O/A ratio: 2nd	8.73:1
O/A ratio: 1st	12.62:1
Front tyre (in.)	3.25 × 19
Rear tyre (in.)	3.25 × 19
Weight (lb)	380
Carburettor	Amal Monobloc 376/61, $1\frac{1}{16}$ in. choke diameter (early models, 1 in. choke)
Main jet	270
Needle jet	106
Throttle valve	$3\frac{1}{2}$
Pilot jet	30

*M 17/7 cam (checking 0.030 in.) **M 17/8 cam, from VR 1262 (checking 0.030 in.)

Model	VENOM	VENOM CLUBMAN (as Venom except as below)
	1955–70	
Bore (mm)	86	
Stroke (mm)	86	
Capacity (cc)	499	
Compression ratio	8:1	8.75:1
Valve position	ohv	
Inlet opens btdc	55*	
Inlet closes abdc	65*	
Exhaust opens bbdc	75*	

Model	VENOM	VENOM CLUBMAN
Exhaust closes atdc	45*	
Valve clear. (cold) in. (in.)	0.005	
Valve clear. (cold) ex. (in.)	0.005	
Ignition timing (degrees)	38	
Points gap (in.)	0.012	
Primary drive chain	$\frac{1}{2} \times \frac{5}{16}$ in.	
Rear chain	$\frac{5}{8} \times \frac{3}{8}$ in.	
Sprockets: engine (T)	23	
clutch (T)	44	
gearbox (T)	18	
rear wheel (T)	46	
O/A ratio: top	4.9:1**	4.9:1***
O/A ratio: 3rd	5.91:1**	5.35:1***
O/A ratio: 2nd	7.78:1**	7.03:1***
O/A ratio: 1st	11.24:1**	9.25:1***
Front tyre (in.)	3.25 × 19	
Rear tyre (in.)	3.25 × 19	
Carburettor	Amal Monobloc 389/15, $1\frac{3}{16}$ in. choke diameter (early models, $1\frac{1}{8}$ in. choke)	
Main jet	330	
Needle jet	106	
Throttle valve	$3\frac{1}{2}$	
Pilot jet	30	

*Checking 0.030 in. **Solo, type 12 prefix ***Solo, suffix R, TT ratios

Model	VMT THRUXTON
	1965–71
Bore (mm)	86
Stroke (mm)	86
Capacity (cc)	499
Compression ratio	8:1 (with alternatives)
Valve position	ohv
Inlet opens btdc	55*
Inlet closes abdc	65*
Exhaust opens bbdc	75*
Exhaust closes atdc	45*
Valve clear. (cold) in. (in.)	0.006
Valve clear. (cold) ex. (in.)	0.008
Ignition timing (degrees)	38
Points gap (in.)	0.012
Primary drive chain	$\frac{1}{2} \times \frac{5}{16}$ in.
Rear chain	$\frac{5}{8} \times \frac{3}{8}$ in.
Sprockets: engine (T)	23
clutch (T)	44
gearbox (T)	20
rear wheel (T)	46
O/A ratio: top	4.4:1** 4.4:1***
O/A ratio: 3rd	5.3:1** 4.83:1***
O/A ratio: 2nd	6.97:1** 6.3:1***
O/A ratio: 1st	10.1:1** 8.4:1***

Model	VMT THRUXTON
Front tyre (in.)	3.00 × 19
Rear tyre (in.)	3.50 × 19
Carburettor	Amal 5GP2, 1$\frac{3}{8}$ in. choke diameter
Main jet	280
Needle jet	109
Throttle valve	4
Needle pos.	4
Pilot jet	25

*Checking 0.030 in. **Standard close ***TT close

Model	K, KT, KE, KN 1925–30
Bore (mm)	74
Stroke (mm)	81
Capacity (cc)	348
Compression ratio	6:1
Valve position	ohc
Inlet opens btdc	37*
Inlet closes abdc	52*
Exhaust opens bbdc	65*
Exhaust closes atdc	36*
Valve clear. (cold) in. (in.)	0.010
Valve clear. (cold) ex. (in.)	0.015
Ignition timing (degrees)	42
Points gap (in.)	0.012
Primary drive chain	$\frac{1}{2} \times \frac{5}{16}$ in.
Rear chain	$\frac{1}{2} \times \frac{5}{16}$ in.
Sprockets: engine (T)	20
clutch (T)	44
gearbox (T)	21
rear wheel (T)	55
O/A ratio: top	5.8:1
O/A ratio: 2nd	8.4:1
O/A ratio: 1st	14.5:1
Front tyre (in.)	2.75 × 21
Rear tyre (in.)	2.75 × 21
Fuel tank capacity (imp. gal.)	2
Weight (lb)	260

*Checking 0.012 in.

Model	KSS 1925–30
Bore (mm)	74
Stroke (mm)	81
Capacity (cc)	348
Compression ratio	7:1 or 8.5:1
Valve position	ohc
Inlet opens btdc	40*
Inlet closes abdc	56*
Exhaust opens bbdc	68*
Exhaust closes atdc	47*
Valve clear. (cold) in. (in.)	0.010
Valve clear. (cold) ex. (in.)	0.015
Ignition timing (degrees)	42
Points gap (in.)	0.012
Primary drive chain	$\frac{1}{2} \times \frac{5}{16}$ in.
Rear chain	$\frac{1}{2} \times \frac{5}{16}$ in.
Sprockets: engine (T)	20
clutch (T)	44
gearbox (T)	23
rear wheel (T)	55
O/A ratio: top	5.25:1
O/A ratio: 2nd	6.9:1
O/A ratio: 1st	9.98:1
Front tyre (in.)	3.00 × 21
Rear tyre (in.)	3.00 × 21

*Checking 0.012 in.

Model	KSS 1931–5
Bore (mm)	74
Stroke (mm)	81
Capacity (cc)	348
Compression ratio	6.5:1
Valve position	ohc
Inlet opens btdc	39*
Inlet closes abdc	69*
Exhaust opens bbdc	60*
Exhaust closes atdc	40*
Valve clear. (cold) in. (in.)	0.012
Valve clear. (cold) ex. (in.)	0.020
Ignition timing (degrees)	42
Points gap (in.)	0.012
Primary drive chain	$\frac{1}{2} \times \frac{5}{16}$ in.
Rear chain	$\frac{1}{2} \times \frac{5}{16}$ in.
Sprockets: engine (T)	20
clutch (T)	44
gearbox (T)	22
rear wheel (T)	56
O/A ratio: top	5.6:1**	5.6:1***
O/A ratio: 3rd		7.45:1***
O/A ratio: 2nd	8.1:1**	9.8:1***
O/A ratio: 1st	14.2:1**	14.18:1***
Front tyre (in.)	3.00 × 21
Rear tyre (in.)	3.00 × 21

*Checking 0.012 in. and 0.020 in. **Three-speed ***Four speed

Model	KTS		Model	KTT Mk IV	
	1931–5			1932–4	
Bore (mm)	74		Bore (mm)	74	
Stroke (mm)	81		Stroke (mm)	81	
Capacity (cc)	348		Capacity (cc)	348	
Compression ratio	6.5:1		Compression ratio	7.5:1	
Valve position	ohc		Valve position	ohc	
Inlet opens btdc	39*		Inlet opens btdc	51*	
Inlet closes abdc	69*		Inlet closes abdc	57*	
Exhaust opens bbdc	60*		Exhaust opens bbdc	71*	
Exhaust closes atdc	40*		Exhaust closes atdc	43*	
Valve clear. (cold) in. (in.)	0.012		Valve clear. (cold) in. (in.)	0.015	
Valve clear. (cold) ex. (in.)	0.020		Valve clear. (cold) ex. (in.)	0.025	
Ignition timing (degrees)	42		Ignition timing (degrees)	35	
Points gap (in.)	0.012		Points gap (in.)	0.012	
Primary drive chain	$\frac{1}{2} \times \frac{5}{16}$ in.		Primary drive chain	$\frac{1}{2} \times \frac{5}{16}$ in.	
Rear chain	$\frac{1}{2} \times \frac{5}{16}$ in.		Rear chain	$\frac{1}{2} \times \frac{5}{16}$ in.	
Sprockets: engine (T)	20		Sprockets: engine (T)	20	
clutch (T)	44		clutch (T)	44	
gearbox (T)	22		gearbox (T)	23	
rear wheel (T)	56		rear wheel (T)	55	
O/A ratio: top	5.6:1**	5.6:1***	O/A ratio: top	5.23:1**	5.25:1***
O/A ratio: 3rd		7.45:1***	O/A ratio: 3rd	6.34:1**	6.98:1***
O/A ratio: 2nd	8.1:1**	9.8:1***	O/A ratio: 2nd	8.34:1**	9.19:1***
O/A ratio: 1st	14.2:1**	14.18:1***	O/A ratio: 1st	10.97:1**	13.28:1***
Front tyre (in.)	3.25 × 19		Front tyre (in.)	2.75 × 21	
Rear tyre (in.)	3.25 × 19		Rear tyre (in.)	3.25 × 20	

*Checking 0.012 in. and 0.020 in. **Three-speed ***Four-speed

Model	KTT Mk I	
	1929–30	1931
Bore (mm)	74	74
Stroke (mm)	81	81
Capacity (cc)	348	348
Compression ratio	7:1 or 8.5:1	7:1 or 8.5:1
Valve position	ohc	ohc
Inlet opens btdc	40*	43
Inlet closes abdc	56*	70
Exhaust opens bbdc	68*	68
Exhaust closes atdc	47*	48
Valve clear. (cold) in. (in.)	0.010	0.012
Valve clear. (cold) ex. (in.)	0.015	0.022
Ignition timing (degrees)	42	42
Points gap (in.)	0.012	0.012
Primary drive chain	$\frac{1}{2} \times \frac{5}{16}$ in.	$\frac{1}{2} \times \frac{5}{16}$ in.
Rear chain	$\frac{1}{2} \times \frac{5}{16}$ in.	$\frac{1}{2} \times \frac{5}{16}$ in.
Sprockets: engine (T)	20	20
clutch (T)	44	44
gearbox (T)	23	23
rear wheel (T)	55	55
O/A ratio: top	5.25:1	5.25:1
O/A ratio: 2nd	7.6:1	7.6:1
O/A ratio: 1st	9.94:1	9.94:1
Front tyre (in.)	2.75 × 21	2.75 × 21
Rear tyre (in.)	3.00 × 21	3.00 × 21

*Checking 0.012 in.

Model	KTT Mk IV (cont.)
Fuel tank capacity (imp. gal.)	4
Oil tank capacity (imp. gal.)	1
Weight (lb)	290
Carburettor	Amal Type 57/002, $1\frac{1}{16}$ in. choke diameter
Main jet	250
Throttle valve	12

(For alcohol fuels, use 1000 main jet and twin floats)

*Checking 0.025 in. **TT ratios ***Touring ratios

Model	KTT Mk V
	1935–6
Bore (mm)	74
Stroke (mm)	81
Capacity (cc)	348
Compression ratio	7.75:1 or 11:1
Valve position	ohc
Inlet opens btdc	51*
Inlet closes abdc	57*
Exhaust opens bbdc	71*
Exhaust closes atdc	43*
Valve clear. (cold) in. (in.)	0.015
Valve clear. (cold) ex. (in.)	0.025
Ignition timing (degrees)	35
Points gap (in.)	0.012
Primary drive chain	$\frac{1}{2} \times \frac{5}{16}$ in.
Rear chain	$\frac{1}{2} \times \frac{5}{16}$ in.

Specifications

Model	**KTT Mk V**
	1935–6
Sprockets: engine (T)	20
clutch (T)	44
gearbox (T)	24
rear wheel (T)	55
O/A ratio: top	5.05:1
O/A ratio: 3rd	6.09:1
O/A ratio: 2nd	8.02:1
O/A ratio: 1st	10.55:1
Front tyre (in.)	3.00 × 21
Rear tyre (in.)	3.25 × 20
Fuel tank capacity (imp. gal.)	4
Oil tank capacity (imp. gal.)	0.75
Carburettor	Amal TT34, $1\frac{1}{16}$ in. choke diameter
Main jet	360
Needle jet	109
Throttle valve	5

*Checking 0.025 in.

Model	**KTT Mk VII**
	1938–9
Bore (mm)	74
Stroke (mm)	81
Capacity (cc)	348
Compression ratio	8.75:1, 7.8:1 or 11.5:1
Valve position	ohc
Inlet opens btdc	55*
Inlet closes abdc	65*
Exhaust opens bbdc	75*
Exhaust closes atdc	45*
Valve clear. (cold) in. (in.)	0.012
Valve clear. (cold) ex. (in.)	0.025
Ignition timing (degrees)	32
Points gap (in.)	0.012
Primary drive chain	$\frac{1}{2} \times \frac{5}{16}$ in.
Rear chain	$\frac{1}{2} \times \frac{5}{16}$ in.
Sprockets: engine (T)	20
clutch (T)	44
gearbox (T)	24
rear wheel (T)	55
O/A ratio: top	5.05:1
O/A ratio: 3rd	5.55:1
O/A ratio: 2nd	7.3:1
O/A ratio: 1st	9.6:1
Front tyre (in.)	3.00 × 21
Rear tyre (in.)	3.25 × 20

*Checking 0.020 in.

Model	**KTT Mk VIII**
	1939–50
Bore (mm)	74
Stroke (mm)	81
Capacity (cc)	348
Compression ratio	10.94:1 or 7.8:1
Valve position	ohc
Inlet opens btdc	55*
Inlet closes abdc	65*
Exhaust opens bbdc	75*
Exhaust closes atdc	45*
Valve clear. (cold) in. (in.)	0.012
Valve clear. (cold) ex. (in.)	0.025
Ignition timing (degrees)	30
Points gap (in.)	0.012
Primary drive chain	$\frac{1}{2} \times \frac{5}{16}$ in.
Rear chain	$\frac{1}{2} \times \frac{5}{16}$ in.
Sprockets: engine (T)	20
clutch (T)	44
gearbox (T)	24
rear wheel (T)	55 (alternative 56)
O/A ratio: top	5.05:1
O/A ratio: 3rd	5.55:1
O/A ratio: 2nd	7.3:1
O/A ratio: 1st	9.6:1
Front tyre (in.)	3.00 × 21
Rear tyre (in.)	3.25 × 19
Installed length of valve springs	$\frac{27}{32}$ centres
Carburettor	Amal Type 10TT, $1\frac{3}{32}$ in. choke diameter (std)
Main jet	400**
Needle jet	109**
Needle position	2**
Pilot jet	1–$1\frac{1}{4}$ turns open**

Dowty oleo legs should be run with SAE 20 oil and inflated to a pressure of 35 psi, variable according to the rider's weight.

*Checking 0.020 in. **For petrol/benzole fuel

Instructions for KTT Models Mk VII (Engine no. KTT 700 onwards) and Mk VIII (Engine no. KTT 800 onwards)

Valve timing
(Checked with .020 in. tappet clearance)
Inlet opens 55° before TDC
Inlet closes 65° after BDC
Exhaust opens 75° before BDC
Exhaust closes 45° after TDC

Tappet clearances
(Running) Inlet .012 in., Exhaust .025 in.

Valve springs
The installed length of valve springs is $\frac{27}{32}$ in. centres. This can best be checked between the top of the bottom valve spring washers and the underside of the top valve spring loop. This dimension is .562 in.

Ignition setting
Mk VII engines. 32° advance for petrol/benzol and alcohol. 30° advance for 70/75 octane fuel (pool).
  Mk VIII engines 30° advance for all fuels.
  These figures should be checked with .0015 in. gap in the contact-breaker points and with the back run of the magneto chain tight.

Sparking plugs
14 mm long reach.
For warming up KLG FE220 or 718C LR.
Lodge) Can be warmed up on racing plug.
Champion) Use least heat resistance.
For racing KLG 689LR, 646LR or 690LR.
Lodge. RL51, RL49, RL47.
Champion. NA14.
The racing plugs are arranged in order of heat resistance. Highest resistance first.
The machines are supplied with a warming up plug fitted and a racing plug in the toolkit.

Pistons
Mk VII engines. K.27/15 for petrol/benzol
    C. ratio 8.75:1
    K.27/15 for 70/75 octane fuel.
    C. ratio 7.8:1
    K.27/16 for alcohol fuels.
    C. ratio 11.5:1
Mk VIII engines. K.27/15 for 70/75 octane fuel.
    C. ratio 7.8:1
    K.27/16 for petrol/benzol.
    C. ratio 10.94:1

Gear ratios
Top 5.05:1. 3rd. 5.55:1. 2nd. 7.3:1. 1st. 9.6:1 with 24-tooth sprocket.

Lubrication system
Lubrication is carried out by means of a gear-type oil pump situated in the bottom timing case which consists of two separate pumps in one body, the larger of the two being the extractor pump which returns the oil from the sump to the oil tank. From the feed pump the delivery is taken to a check valve situated in the top of the timing case. The object of this valve is to prevent oil draining into the engine when the machine is standing. Should it be found, therefore, that the crankcase shows a tendency to fill up when the machine is stationary, this valve should be examined. The oil is then taken by suitable passages to a filter situated at the rear of the magneto chain case. This filter should be removed periodically and washed in petrol or benzol, bearing in mind that any particles of dirt will remain on the outside of the filter. From the filter, suitable passages and pipes deliver oil to a jet feeding through the centre of the crankshaft to the big-end bearing, a jet directed on to the top bevel gears and a jet directed on to the cam and lastly to a spring-loaded regulating by-pass valve situated in the bottom of the timing case. A screw and lock nut operating this valve will be observed at the rear of the timing case. To increase the pressure and, therefore, the quantity of oil fed to the engine, this screw should be turned CLOCKWISE and to decrease ANTI-CLOCKWISE. Do not alter more than $\frac{1}{4}$ turn at a time. The oil pressure is set correctly on all engines before leaving the works. The minimum pressure should be 8 psi, taken with hot oil at an engine speed of 6000 rpm. Give as much oil as possible while still keeping exhaust reasonably smoke free. The maximum oil pressure should normally not exceed 12 psi. Remove plug ($\frac{1}{4} \times 20$ tpi) from bottom of magneto chain case and attach pressure gauge pipe to this hole to check pressure.

Carburettor
Amal type 10 TT1 $\frac{3}{32}$ in. choke size.

Setting
For petrol/benzol.
  Main jet (Mk VII engines) 380
      (Mk VIII engines) 400
  Needle jet   109
  Needle position   2
  Throttle valve   4
  Pilot adjusting screw 1 to $1\frac{1}{4}$ turns open.
For 70/75 octane fuel
  Main jet 400 on both types of engine.
  All other adjustments unchanged.
For alcohol fuels
  (Mk VII engines only)
  Needle jet   113
  Main jet (Discol RD1 or JAP racing fuel) approx 800
  (BP racing ethyl, methanol or pure alcohol)
1000–1500
It is not necessary to use a double float chamber, as the standard type fitted will pass enough fuel to keep main jet fed.

Note
It should be emphasized that the main jet settings are only approximate, as the jet required varies with the locality and atmospheric conditions and should always be finally settled on the site.
With alcohol fuels, it is advisable to err on the side of richness, as little or no power is lost and cool running

is obtained. The ignition settings given should not be altered whatever fuel is used.

Tyre pressures
19 psi front, 20 psi rear. These are normal and should not be varied by more than 1 or 2 psi.

Note
When heating up crankcase or cylinder heads for bearing or valve guide replacement, etc, the temperature of the casting must not be raised above 160° Centigrade.

Timing
When timing, one rocker only should be in position at a time with no return spring.

Alcohol fuel with Mk VIII
If an engine is set up for use with petrol/benzol 50/50, the compression space is 35 cc which gives a ratio of 10.94:1. To one gallon of 50/50, mixture, add one pint of methanol. It would then be found that more power is provided. It is possible that it will be found necessary to increase the jet size by one or two.

Rear Oleomatic suspension
If the legs should be removed, on replacing, the centres between the two bolts must be 12 in. before finally tightening bolts. At the base of each leg will be seen a bolt running at right angles to the rear wheel spindle. On the head of each bolt is stamped an arrow.

The softest ride is obtained when the arrow on the head of the adjuster is pointing vertically up the strut. The average position for normal use will be found to be about 45° to one side of this position. It does not matter which way the valve is turned—either way will stiffen up the damping.

On no account should the adjuster bolt, viz. the one with the arrow on, be reversed in the unit, as this will blank off the oil passages, and the unit will become solid.

If at any time oil has been lost, top up with Mobiloil 'Arctic' through the inflation valve hole. A little more oil than is required should be introduced, then the unit should be carefully compressed, allowing the excess oil to be expelled. The inflation valve end of the unit is held uppermost during this operation. Refit the inflation valve and pump up with a good tyre pump.

Inflation pressures will vary slightly with different riders, but about 35 psi will be found suitable for a rider of average weight. Both units should be adjusted to the same inflation pressure. Pressure should be checked with both wheels of the machine on the ground and under its own weight. Allowance should be made for loss of air caused when removing pressure gauge.

Amal carburettor settings used for the TT
1938 Official 350 cc
$1\frac{3}{16} \times 1\frac{7}{32}$ in. jet block
Special RN1 carburettor 15/2312
520 jet
Valve 3
Needle position 2 with special RN7 needle
Standard length air tube
This setting used by Woods

Official 350 cc
$1\frac{5}{32} \times 1\frac{3}{16}$ in. carburettor
510 jet
Valve 2
Special RN7 needle in position 2
Standard length air tube
This setting used by Mellors

Official 500 cc
Woods $1\frac{7}{32} \times 1\frac{1}{4}$ in. Special 15/2312 RN1 carburettor
640 jet
Valve 3
RN7 needle in position 2
Air tube 1 in. longer than standard

Mellors $1\frac{3}{16} \times 1\frac{7}{32}$ in. special 15/2312 RN
620 jet
Valve 2RN7 needle in position 2
Air tube 1 in. longer than standard

All the above on megaphones

A special 350 cc Velocette used by Archer
which had a bored-out cylinder head used:
$1\frac{5}{32}$ in. bore TT 38 RN with
510 jet
Valve 3
Needle position 1

Unofficial entries on 1938 KTT
350 cc used $1\frac{3}{32}$ in. bore TT 36 carburettors
400 jet
Valve 4
Needle position 1 or 2
All these being on megaphones

KTT model
using $1\frac{1}{16}$ in bore carburettor TT 36
310 jet
Valve 4
Needle position 4 in conjunction with straight exhaust pipe

1939
Official 350 cc
Woods $1\frac{5}{32} \times 1\frac{3}{16}$ in. RN2
520 jet
Valve 3
Needle position 2
using RN7 needle
.109 in. needle jet

Mellors $1\frac{3}{16} \times 1\frac{7}{32}$ in.
520 jet
Valve 3
Needle 2
using RN7 needle
.109 in. needle jet

Official 500 cc
Woods $1\frac{3}{16} \times 1\frac{7}{32}$ in. special RN2
640 jet
Valve 3
Needle position 2
Special RN7 needle
.109 in. needle jet

Mellors $1\frac{7}{32} \times 1\frac{1}{4}$ in. special RN2
680 jet
Valve 2
Needle 3
using special RN7 needle
.109 in. needle jet

350 cc private owners KTT
$1\frac{3}{32}$ in. bore TT38 carburettor
410 jet
Valve 4
Needle position 2
.109 in. needle jet
Jet sizes on these varied from 400 to 430

Thomas and Binder had special heads, using $1\frac{3}{16}$ in RN carburettors with
510 jet
Thomas   Valve 3
         Needle 3
         Special RN7 needle
Binder   Valve 5
         Needle 2 with standard needle

Archer had special 350 cc using
$1\frac{5}{32}$ in. RN2 carburettor
Jet 520
Valve 4
Needle 2

Archer also had special 500 cc using
$1\frac{1}{8}$ in. bore RN2
Jet 540
Valve 4
Needle 1

1947
Official 500 cc
$1\frac{5}{32} \times 1\frac{7}{32}$ in. RN carburettor
660 jet
Valve 4
Needle position 3

.109 in. needle jet
RN4 needle

Official 350 cc
$1\frac{3}{32}$ in. TT carburettor
460 jet
Valve 4
Needle position 2
.109 in. needle jet

Special 350 cc (Foster)
which won the Junior race
$1\frac{5}{32}$ in. bore RN carburettor
460 main jet
Valve 4
Needle position 1

1948
Official 350 cc
$1\frac{5}{32}$ in. RN carburettor
Valve 5
.109 in. needle jet
Needle position 1
Standard RN needle
500 jet

350 cc KTT (private owners)
$1\frac{3}{32}$ in. TT carburettor
Valve 4
.109 in. needle jet
Needle position 2
400 jet

1950
Official 500 cc
$1\frac{5}{16}$ in. RN
470 jet
Valve 3
Needle position 3
RN11 needle
.113 in. needle jet

Official 350 cc
Salt $1\frac{5}{32}$ in. RN
         460 jet
         Valve 7
         Needle 2
         Standard RN needle
         .109 in. needle jet
Foster $1\frac{5}{32}$ in. GP
         420 jet
         Valve 3
         Needle 2 (six grooves weaker than standard GP)
Armstrong $1\frac{5}{32}$ in. GP
         340 jet
         Valve 3

Needle 4
516/045 needle
.109 in. needle jet

350 cc (private owners)
$1\frac{5}{32}$ in. TT
470 jet
Valve 6
Needle position 2
.109 in. needle jet
$1\frac{3}{32}$ in. TT
460 jet
Valve 4
Needle position 2
.109 in. needle jet

1951
Graham
$1\frac{3}{32}$ in. RN
570 jet
Valve 4
Needle position 2
.109 in. standard RN needle

Official 250 cc
$1\frac{5}{32}$ in. GP
220 jet
Valve 5
Needle position 4
.109 in. needle jet
Needle .103 × .093 in. tip
$\frac{1}{10}$ in. air jet

Official 350 cc
$1\frac{5}{32}$ in. GP
240 jet
Valve 3
Needle position 3
.109 in. needle jet (six grooves weaker than standard)
$\frac{1}{8}$ in. air jet

350 cc (private owners)
$1\frac{5}{32}$ in. TT9
400 jet
Valve 6
Needle position 2
.109 in. needle jet
$1\frac{3}{16}$ in. RN9
420 jet
Valve 7
Needle position 2
.109 in. needle jet

1952
Official 350 cc (Graham)
$1\frac{5}{32}$ in. GP carburettor
240 main jet
Valve 5
Needle position 2
GP6 needle
.109 in. needle jet
$\frac{1}{8}$ in. air jet

Official 250 cc (Graham)
$1\frac{5}{32}$ in. GP carburettor
220 jet
Valve 5
Needle position 3
GP6 needle
.109 in. needle jet
$\frac{1}{10}$ in. air jet

350 cc (private owners)
$1\frac{3}{16}$ in. RN9 carburettor
420 jet
Valve 7
Needle position 2
.109 in. needle jet

APPENDIX 2

Engine, frame and gearbox numbers

There are two sets of works record books, listing production figures. Since the nine volumes covering the period 1921–51 are in my possession, I can be reasonably sure that the figures given are correct. I have also had a brief look at the volumes that refer to 1951–71, when the factory closed. From these, I have listed the engine numbers for each calendar year. Their veracity can only be confirmed by a more detailed scrutiny.

The MAC records from July 1954 onwards, for instance, cannot be verified because they are inaccessible. My production lists for this model until July 1954 total 21,178 machines, but I also have a total figure (i.e. including post-July 1954) of 24,980. This figure may well be correct.

KTT records, commencing at engine no. 1 in 1928 and ending at 1090 in 1953 would indicate a total production in excess of 1000 machines. In fact, the total figure is 868 machines, including special works bikes produced in 1936–7.

Subsequent special machines for the 1938–9 works teams are not recorded. This suggests that either the information was omitted from the record book, or the previous year's models were uprated and rebuilt—which is more likely.

Also, certain frames which are not listed in the records, have been seen. Perhaps these were additional machines built and unrecorded. Perhaps they were spare frames taken from the stores to replace others damaged in use, or maybe they were used to convert a rigid (Mk VII) to a springer (Mk VIII).

Frames were produced in batches and stamped with consecutive numbers before being passed to the enamelling shop. Then they were put into the stores. They were taken from there at random, as required. Some frame numbers were never recorded in the book, since they were used subsequently to replace damaged items.

Engines were always stamped consecutively on assembly and recorded accordingly.

This system applied to all models produced at Hall Green.

Model D, D2, DL2, D3, DL3

Engine no.	Frame no.	Invoice date	
801	833	18–6–21	Frank Palmer, Leeds
1078	1148	29–12–21	
1079	1146	5–1–22	
1116	1187	21–4–22	

End of Model D production

Model E, E2, EL2, E3, EL3

Engine no.	Frame no.	Invoice date
1500	1506	30–11–21
2257	2275	Dec '22
2258	2276	Jan '23
2321	3686	Dec '23
2322	3688	Jan '24
2404	4129	Dec '24
2405	4131	Jan '25
2457	4207	Dec '25
2458	4187	Jan '26
2481	4203	14–8–26

End of Model E production

Model G, G2, G3, GS2, GS3, GC

Engine no.	Frame no.	Invoice date	
3001	2114	24–5–23	H. C. Webb & Co., Birmingham
3002	2225	Nov '22	
3068	3068	Dec '22	
3069	3088	Jan '23	
3628	3671	Dec '23	
3629	3674	Jan '24	
3703	3789		GC3 model for Gus Kuhn
3947	4046	Nov '24	
3948	4079	Jan '25	
3970	4110	28–4–25	

End of Model G production

Model A, B2, B3

Engine no.	Frame no.	Invoice date	
5001	5008	30–6–23	Pike & Co., Exeter
5164	5163	Jan '24	Model A phased out
5165	5165	Sep '23	Model B
5272	5301	Dec '23	
5273	5322	Jan '24	
5947	B7	Nov '24	

End of Model A and B production

Model S, Speed 249 cc engines

Engine no.	Frame no.	Invoice date	
2	—	Mar '21	Bradbury, Sheffield
39	1139	Dec '21	

End of Sports model production

Model AC and occasional B 1925

Engine no.	Frame no.	Invoice date	
1	25	Jan '25	Alec Bennett, Southampton
434–463	—		Engines only to S. America
492	459	Dec '25	
534	549	Jan '26	Schofield Goodman*, for Sydney
922	903	Dec '26	
923	892	Jan '27	
1228	—	Oct '27	

End of AC and B production

*In 1923 Veloce acquired the services of a Birmingham shipping agency named Schofield Goodman—no relation—who were instrumental in extending their overseas business, especially to Australia and New Zealand. This was a particularly good move because machines sold through the agency were paid for in full on delivery to their packing department. They remain in business to this day.

Model H, H2, H3, HS2, HS3, HC3, HSC3

Engine no.	Frame no.	Invoice date	
1	1	14–11–24	Premier Motor Co., Birmingham
31	22	Dec '24	
32	33	Jan '25	
272–281			Not issued
330	376	Dec '25	
331	377	Jan '26	
517	284	Dec '26	
519	311	Jan '27	
569	623	15–8–27	

End of Model H production

Model U Utility 14 December 1927

Engine no.	Frame no.	Invoice date	
2	3	Dec '27	
4	17	Jan '28	
1317	1317	Dec '28	
1318	1287	Jan '29	
1646	1992	Jul '29	Model 32 phased in gradually
1912	2165	Dec '29	

End of Model U and 32 production

Special machines, HSS, HCSS, HC3, 1925

1	39	6–2–25	Schofield Goodman & Sons, Melbourne, Australia
13	359	Nov '25	
14	386	Jan '26	
39	559	Dec '26	
40	560	Jan '27	

End of HSS type production

Model USS

1	86	Jan '29	Pike & Co., Exeter
262	2140	4–10–29	

End of USS production

GTP

Engine no.	Frame no.	Gearbox no.	Invoice date	
1	144	111	6–1–30	Thos. Parish, Preston
1946	1992	1924	Dec '30	
1947	2057	2008	Jan '31	
2753	2747	2720	Dec '31	
2754	2779	2762	Jan '32	
3862	3883	3879	Dec '32	
3863	3888	3891	Jan '33	
4477	4552	4468	Dec '33	
4478	4478	4465	Jan '34	
4989	4993	435	Dec '34	Four-speed
4990	5023	437	Jan '35	
5474	5526	924	Dec '35	
5475	5483	918	Jan '36	
6017	6051	1482	Dec '36	
6018	5998	1464	Jan '37	
6619	6650	2072	Dec '37	
6620	6681	2071	Jan '38	
7105	7149	2574	Dec '38	
7106	7108	2547	Jan '39	
7529	7582	2976	Dec '39	
7530	7563	2986	Jan '40	
7630	7648	3069	12–8–40	

End of 1940 season

7629			6–3–41	Not used, 1940 Veloce Ltd, for ARP
7631	7692	3084	17–7–41	Veloce Ltd, for E. F. Goodman

End of 1941 season

9001	7751		Jan '46	P. & R. Williams Ltd

Engine no.	Frame no.	Gearbox no.	Invoice date	
9247	7899		Despatched 8–4–46	S. Vidal, Portugal

End of GTP production, of which all post-war models were sold to overseas agents

Magneto ignition on all post-war models and on some 1934 models

MOV

Engine no.	Frame no.	Gearbox no.	Invoice date	
1	1		12–10–33	W. Tiffen
2	19	15	Aug '33	
433	571	497	Dec '33	
432	536	498	Jan '34	
1176	1922	1835	Dec '34	
1177	1953	1896	Jan '35	
1746	3508	3453	Dec '35	
1747	3515	3421	Jan '36	
2486	5227	5221	Dec '36	
2487	5279	5206	Jan '37	
3078	7140	7068	Dec '37	
3079	7152	4043	Jan '38	
3574	8970	4473	Dec '38	
3575	9059	8988	Jan '39	
4115	10737	10704	Dec '39	
4116	10739	10706	Jan '40	
4167	10921	10835	17–5–40	
6001	1630		31–5–46	S. Benard, Chile
6214	3329		Dec '46	
6215	3217		Jan '47	
6252	3397		May '47	
6253	4548		Apr '48	
6500	6062		Sep '48	

End of MOV production

MAC

Engine no.	Frame no.	Gearbox no.	Invoice date	
1				Pike & Co.
3	450	4/313		
64	605	493	Dec '33	
65	489	504	Jan '34	
751	1988	2013	Dec '34	
752	2071	2019	Jan '35	
1636	3422	3414	Dec '35	
1637	3487	3361	Jan '36	
2697	5255	5229	Dec '36	
2698	5231	5215	Jan '37	
4020	7105	7123	Dec '37	
4021	7186	7143	Jan '38	
5268	8549	8710	Dec '38	
5269	9096	9000	Jan '39	
6560	10730	10705	Dec '39	
6561	10770	10714	Jan '40	
6706	11000	10912	Aug '40	
6707	12123	11688	Jul '41	R. W. Burgess, Veloce Ltd
W6721	11325		Mar '43	Pike & Co.
W6735	3449		Jul '44	Pike & Co.

WD models

Engine no.	Frame no.	Gearbox no.	Invoice date	
11001	11001	10939	11–5–40	
12201	12201	12207	17–11–41	
12202–12321				Engines only, to contract 67974, dated 7–8–40 to 24–12–41

Post-war production

8001	1294		Mar '46	P. & R. Williams, Sydney
10050	3162		Oct '46	
10051	3342		Jan '47	
10150	3241		Dec '47	

1948 Programme with Dowty forks

10151			Jan '48	Motorcycling
10152	4074		Jan '48	
13797	7311		Dec '48	
13798	7282		Jan '49	
14407	7946		Dec '49	
14408	7938		Jan '50	
15888	9423		Dec '50	
15889	9470		Jan '51	
17778	11385		Dec '51	
17779	11340		Jan '52	Lou Branch
19214	13028		Jan '53	
19318	12744		9–12–54	The last rigid MAC sold to the Crown Agents (munitions)

MAC RS (rear sprung)

20001	1001		22–12–52	Leon Martin, Brussells
22565	3623		22–12–52	White, Wellington, NZ
22362	3403		29–1–54	
23162	5194		30–7–54	The last recorded MAC, subsequent factory records for this model have disappeared

MSS

1000				Works machine, AOF 435
1001				Works machine, punt and trailer, BOA 636
1002	21	30	19–5–35	Schofield Goodman, for Sydney
1142				Stripped for compilation of spares list, rebuilt by apprentices and used as works punt and trailer, BOM 49
1518	1577	717	Dec '35	
1519	1631	530	Jan '36	
1944	1836	1370	15–7–36	
2159				Olympia show model, invoiced to Stevens, London

End of 1935–6 season's models. Note, production figures continued up to 30–9–36

2259	3084	1990	Dec '36	
2260	2950	1991	Jan '37	
2996	4409	3363	Dec '37	
2997	4401	3419	Jan '38	
3842	5835	4185	Dec '38	
3843	5745	4894	Jan '39	

Engine no.	Frame no.	Gearbox no.	Invoice date	
4436	6199	5747	16–10–39	End of 1939 programme
4447		5704	20–10–39	Veloce for Army test
4517	6839	5822	Dec '39	
4518	6818	5819	Jan '40	
4678	6956	5927	3–7–40	Chief Constable of Bucks

End of 1940 season

Engine no.	Frame no.		Invoice date	
W4681	1550		29–6–43	Davis Bros, Chester
W4688	5547		26–1–44	Pike & Co., Plymouth

MSS post-war production

6001	7124		30–9–46	White, Aukland
6265	7253		Dec '46	
6266	8191		Jan '47	
7476	8870		Jun '47	
7477	9746			Commencement of 1948 models
8304	10496		25–6–48	

End of rigid MSS production

MSS RS

Engine no.	Frame no.	Invoice date	
10001	3389	2–12–53	Bill White, NZ
10002	3386	8–1–54	P. & R. Williams, Sydney, Australia
10908	6645	11–2–55	
11000	1005/35		BJG experimental scrambler
11100	4769		POH 341 experimental
11506	6443	31–12–54	Strom, Sweden

Some models dark grey, intermittent

12082	7634	23–12–55	Adelaide, Australia
12083	7625	13–1–56	Cottman, Melbourne, Australia
12084	7626	16–12–55	Williams, Sydney, Australia

The above all show models

12319	9254	22–11–56	Billy Tiffen
12277	8798	31–1–57	
12473	10276	13–11–57	Lou Branch
12474	10422	21–1–58	
12606	11736	31–12–58	
12607	11798	14–1–59	
12769	13707	30–12–59	Freddie Frith
12758	13802	1–1–60	
12915	16347	16–12–60	
12883E	15641	19–1–61	Cottman, Melbourne, Australia (bronze green)
12969S	1141/35	12–5–61	
12945	16514	12–4–62	
12980S	1148/35	27–9–62	
129828	17334	21–6–63	Venom Clubman
13079S	1213/35	20–12–63	
13063S	1206/35	29–5–64	
13124	18206	7–2–64	
13125	18268	4–2–65	
13158	18511	23–12–65	
13159	18759	28–2–66	Dark blue
13206	19157	30–12–66	
13207	19155	26–1–67	Coral mist

Occasional royal blue, dark blue, coral mist or plain blue

Engine no.	Frame no.	Invoice date	
13237	19538	22–11–67	
13236	19589	16–2–68	
13258	19798	31–12–68	Coil ignition
13259	19825	28–2–69	Coil ignition
13270	19989	30–9–69	
13271–13276			All sold in 1970 with coil ignition
13277	20268	26–8–77	Geoff Dodkin

Viper (VR) RS

Engine no.	Frame no.	Invoice date	
1001	7632	8–12–55	Green. Show model sold to Davies, Chester
1081	7991	30–12–55	
1058	7953	3–1–56	
1379	9225	14–12–56	Green
1335	5004	5–3–57	
1996	10267	15–11–57	
1597	10488	31–1–58	Show model
1938	11789	31–12–58	
1939	11669	12–1–59	Green
2557	13775	31–12–59	
2529	13752	5–1–60	
3628	16311	15–12–60	
3582	16271	14–4–61	Veeline

Red and black, intermittent

Engine no.	Frame no.	Invoice date	
4046	17199	4–8–61	Black and white
S3647	16428	11–1–62	Dark blue for Crown Agents
4150C	17614	31–12–62	Clubman
4151R	17244	31–1–63	
4286	17868	31–12–63	
4282	17878	3–1–64	
4413	18255	23–12–64	Clubman Veeline
4402C	18219	8–1–65	
4507C	18679	31–12–65	
4508	18695	22–8–66	
4550SP	19154	30–12–66	
4551	19198	25–1–67	
4584C	19540	20–12–67	
4585	16681	23–2–68	
4589C	19777	29–11–68	
4590	20223	1975	Ken Swallow
4591	20215	1975	R. F. Seymour

End of Viper production

Venom (VM) RS

Engine no.	Frame no.	Invoice date	
1001	7623	8–12–55	Dove grey. Show model to Stevens, London
1083	7823	30–12–55	
1084	8007	10–1–56	
1537	9165	14–12–56	George McClean, Dundee
1479	9091	4–1–57	Victor Horsman
1929	10233	19–11–57	
1930	10405	10–1–58	

Red and black, intermittent

Engine no.	Frame no.	Invoice date	
2692	11443	31–12–58	Slocombs, London
2614	11727	16–1–59	

Engine, frame and gearbox numbers | 185

Engine no.	Frame no.	Invoice date	
3750C	13798	31–12–59	Rex Judd
1369C	13694		
5068C	16306	30–12–60	Charles Freeman
4878	15997	3–1–61	
5485	17447	20–12–61	Veeline
5073	16859	22–3–62	Kings, Leeds

Veeline and Specials, intermittent

5562C	17553	31–12–62	
5556C	17565	15–2–63	Clubman
5759	17865	24–12–63	
5744C	17949	20–3–64	Veeline
5996C	18218	31–12–64	
5977C	18214	13–1–65	Veeline
6173C	18723	31–12–65	
6172C	18690	28–1–66	

Mk II Intermediate Clubman, like Thruxton but with standard engine

S6330	1245/35	30–12–66	Scrambler with special frame
6320E	19190	25–1–67	Endurance
6449	19550	21–12–67	
6444C	19531	7–2–68	
C6600		30–12–68	Coil ignition
C6601	19801	28–1–69	Coil ignition
C6683	19133	28–11–69	Coil ignition
C6623	20075	3–3–70	
C6723	20071	30–1–70	
6684–6722			Not issued
C6750	20157	29–7–70	Geoff Dodkin

Thruxton (VMT) RS

101	18340		Works experimental, Venom based
102	18237	30–6–65	Whittakers
255	18727	31–12–65	
S254	18718	7–1–66	
479	19156	30–12–66	
476	19186	31–1–67	M/C supply USA
686	19537	14–12–67	
673	19505	5–1–68	
871	19794	31–12–68	Coil ignition, black
V873	19807	27–1–69	Coil ignition, black
V1088	20051	31–12–69	Coil ignition
1068	20028	18–2–70	Coil ignition, black
1092	20009	16–2–70	Coil ignition, black, to Stevens, London
1094–1134			Not issued
1135	20047	19–2–70	Coil ignition, black
1208	20177	30–11–70	Coil ignition, black, to Bateman, Canada

End of VMT production

Model K

Engine no.	Frame no.	Gearbox no.	Invoice date	
1				Robers
2	15			OM 5536, Veloce for G. Denly
3	42			OM 6619, Veloce—punt
7	41		16–7–25	
74	83		30–9–25	The first KSS
141	167		Dec '25	

Engine no.	Frame no.	Gearbox no.	Invoice date	
142	158		Jan '26	

Occasional KSS, KS, KT

572	564		Dec '26	
573	593		Jan '27	

Larger percentage of KSS, KS, KT, KE plus odd KES

1376	1436		Dec '27	
1377	1461		Jan '28	

Mostly KSS, KE, KS with KN and KNS phasing in

2467	2570	2466	Dec '28	
2468	2541	2454	Jan '29	

Mostly KN, KNS with some KSS plus odd KNSS

3225	3510	3463	Dec '29	
3226	3530	3535	Jan '30	All KSS models
3464	3756	4742	30–9–30	

Specific end of 1930 K production

KSS 1931 production

3465	3807	3952	13–10–30	
3525				KB, Edwards for competition
3546	3908	4964	Dec '30	
3547	3904	4982	Jan '31	
3767	4162	5390	Sept '31	

End of 1931 production

1932 KSS and KTS models

3800	1317	5395	30–11–31	
3885	1356	5469	Dec '31	
3886	1391	5476	Jan '32	
4299	1757	104	26–9–32	Four-speed

KSS and KTS 1932–3 season

4300	1819	132	19–10–32	
4409	1900	224	Dec '32	
4410	1870	229	Jan '33	
4871	4450	763	Dec '33	
4872	4462	772	Jan '34	
5627	5262	1581	Dec '34	
5628	5286	1551	Jan '35	
6025	5636	2034	18–7–35	

End of production of 1935 ohc models

KSS and KTS Mk II (ohc)

7001	1348			Experimental KTS 21–10–35
7002	1526	512	20–2–36	Vienna
7005	1832	581		W. E. Tiffen Jnr, for competition
7746	2076	1982	Dec '36	
7747	3098	2007	Jan '37	
8372	4447	3368	Dec '37	
8373	4425	3383	Jan '38	
8934	5864	4904	Dec '38	
8935	5905	4772	Jan '39	
9203	6805	5846	Dec '39	
9204	6887	5849	Apr '40	
9243	6954	6017	24–9–40	

End of 1940 production

KSS Mk II post-war

Engine no.	Frame no.	Gearbox no.	Invoice date	
10002	7148			Veloce, sold s/h to Premier Motor Co., 1950
10001	7137		27–11–46	
10005/08/10/14/22/23/26/37				To touring KTS spec.
10050	7436		Nov '46	
10051	7922		Jan '47	
11300	9779		20–11–47	

Dowty forks introduced intermittently from August 1947

End of KSS Mk II production

KTP
(prefix KA)

1	3	3406	19–11–29	Jordan & Co.
114	161	3429	Dec '29	
115	135	3545	Jan '30	
1138	1137	4936	Dec '30	
1139	1138	4918	Jan '31	

1256/7/9–1268, 1271–75   Engines only to Establishments
                                           Motolincteurs

| 1304 | 1234 | 5389 | 30–9–31 | |

KTT

1				Engine only to Francis & Co., Durban, SA
2	2534	2376	1928	Galinberti, Milan (Show)
3	2637	2595	Feb '29	
180	3466	3428	Dec '29	
181	3529	3238	Jan '30	
270			Nov '30	Engine only
271	3868	5087	Mar '31	
337	4189	5398	Dec '31	
338	4199	5535	Feb '32	
342	4191	1	Mar '32	Four-speed
365	4225	5095	Jul '32	Sold s/h with three-speed box
366				On loan to Bert Parrish

The following engine nos. were all supplied to KDT, dirt-track spec: 46, 89, 96, 104, 105, 115, 118, 119, 123–6, 137, 138, 144–7, 149, 151–4, 185

Commencement of Mk IV production

401	4286	185		Tiffen, Carlisle
402	4238	37	Jun '32	
444	4282	112	Dec '32	
445	4284	226	Jan '33	
502	4349	674	22–9–33	

Commencement of uprated Mk IV with bronze cylinder head, deep tank, subframe, etc

503	4430	708	6–12–33
505	4372	765	Dec '33
506	4519	818	Mar '34
548	4822	1372	5–10–34

End of Mk IV production

Commencement of Mk V production

| 550 | | | Oct '34 | Schofield Goodman |

Engine no.	Frame no.	Gearbox no.	Invoice date	
551	25	1844	Apr '35	
607/614/615				Not issued
616	65	2048	Aug '35	Salisbury Garage, Douglas
618				Special, sent overseas
619				Not issued
620				Special, sent overseas

KTT Mk I, engine nos. 1–266; Mk II, engine nos. 267–333; Mk III, engine nos. 334–65; Mk IV, engine nos. 401–549; Mk V, engine nos. 550–620.

Mk VI special racing machines

621	6TT3		29–5–36	Veloce, for H. E. Newman
622	6TT4		3–6–36	Veloce, for W. T. Tiffen Jnr
623	6TT5		3–6–36	Veloce, for Loyer
625				500 racer supplied to P. & R. Williams, Sydney, Australia

Commencement of Mk VII production

700	7TT2		23–3–38	Schofield Goodman, for Sydney, Australia
701	7TT1		23–3–38	
702	7TT4	3778	7–5–38	Stevens, London
717				Not issued
739	7TT39	4488	4–10–38	Schofield Goodman for Christchurch, NZ

End of Mk VII production

Commencement of Mk VIII production

801	SF25	5298	10–5–39	Jordans, Hull
842/845				Not issued
851	SF55	5497	8–12–39	Schofield Goodman, for Sydney, Australia
901	SF81		23–1–47	S. Platel, Berne, Switzerland
912	SF76		Sept '47	
913–1060				Invoiced inconsecutively between January 1948 and December 1949
1061	SF191		Jan '50	
1086	SF269		Jul '50	Last of UK issue
1087	SF264		Apr '51	
1089	SF262		Apr '51	All overseas
1090	SF274		Mar '53	

End of KTT production

Frame prefixes

Prefix	Model
GB	GTP
MA	Early MOV and MAC, 1933 on
MD	Late 1930s MOV and MAC, 1936 on
MB	MOV and MAC, 1940 on and post-war
D	WD MAC
RS	Sprung frame, 1953 on
KP	KTP
KTL	KSS and KTS, 1934–5
MS	KSS, KTS Mk II and MSS to about 1938
MDD	KSS, KTS Mk II and MSS, 1938 on
KDD	KSS II and MSS, 1946 on
SF	KTT Mk VIII from inception

Gearbox prefixes (P) and suffixes (S)

Number	Model
3 (S)	KSS and KTS four-speed, internal mechanism, 1934–5
4 (P)	MOV and MAC, pre-war
9 (P)	MOV and MAC, post-war, rigid
5 (P)	KSS, KTS, MSS and KTT from 1935
10 (P)	KSS and MSS, post-war
11 (P)	Springer MAC, from 1953 until 11D no. 14 box introduced with MSS in 1954
12 (P)	Venom and Viper with intermediate ratios as KSS II, KTT Mk IV and Mk V ratios
14 (P)	MSS, 1954 on, wide ratio as all MSS models from 1935 until mid 1960s when intermediate ratios standard

APPENDIX 3

Production figures

Year	Models		Annual total
1921	D2 DL2 D3 DL3		277
	Model S		37
			314
1922	D2 DL2 D3 DL3		37
	E2 EL2 E3 EL3		757
	G2 G3 GS2 GS3 GC		67
			861
1923	E2 EL2 E3 EL3		63
	G2 G3 GS2 GS3 GC		559
	A B2 B3		271
			893
1924	E2 EL2 E3 EL3		82
	G2 G3 GS2 GS3 GC		318
	A B2 B3		674
	H2 H3 HS2		
	HS3 HC3 HSC3		31
			1105
1925	E2 EL2 E3 EL3		52
	G2 G3 GS2 GS3 GC		22
	AC and occasional B, including 29 engines only		492
	H2 H3 HS2 HS3 HC3 HSC3 HSS HCSS HC3		13
	Model K, including KSS		141
			720
1926	E2 EL2 E3 EL3		23
	AC and occasional B		388
	H2 H3 HS2 HS3 HC3 HSC3		186
	HSS HCSS		26
	K KSS KS KT		431
			1054
1927	AC and occasional B		305
	H2 H3 HS2 HS3 HC3 HSC3		50
	K KSS KS KT KE KES		704
			1059
1928	Model U		1316
	KSS KE KS + KN + KNS		1091
	Phased in KTT		2
			2409
1929	Model U with Model 32 gradually phased in		584
	USS only		262
	Mainly KN and KNS, plus odd KSS		758
	KTT		178
	KTP only		114
			1896
1930	GTP only		1946
	All KSS		321
	KTP only		1024
	KTT, including 22 to dirt track spec.		90
			3381

		Annual total			Annual total
1931	GTP	807	**1937**	GTP	602
	KSS with KTS phased in	339		KSS and KTS	626
	KTP, including 17 engines only	166		MOV	592
	KTT	67		MAC	1333
		1379		MSS	737
				KTT Specials	4
					3894
1932	GTP	1109			
	KSS and KTS	524	**1938**	GTP	486
	KTT	73		KSS and KTS	562
		1706		MOV	496
				MAC	1248
				MSS	856
1933	GTP	615		KTT	39
	KSS and KTS	462			3687
	MOV	433			
	MAC	64	**1939**	GTP	424
	KTT	61		KSS and KTS	269
		1635		MOV	541
				MAC	1292
				MSS	675
1934	GTP	512		KTT	49
	KSS and KTS	756			3250
	MOV	745			
	MAC	687	**1940**	GTP	101
	KTT	44		KSS and KTS	40
		2744		MOV	52
				MAC	146
1935	GTP	485		MAC for French military mission 1940–1	1200
	KSS and KTS	398		MSS	161
	MOV	570			1700
	MAC	885			
	MSS	519	**1941**	GTP for Veloce staff on ARP and other duties, plus one other for E. F. Goodman	2
	KTT	65		MAC, Veloce, for R. W. Burgess	1
		2922			3
1936	GTP	543			
	KSS and KTS Mk II	746			
	MOV	740			
	MAC	1061			
	MSS	741			
	KTT Specials	9			
		3840	**1943–4**	W/MAC	29
				W/MSS	10
					39

			Annual total				Annual total
1946	GTP		247	**1954**	MAC to July		598
	KSS, including 8 to KTS spec.		50		MSS		1506
	MOV		214				
	MAC		2050				2104
	MSS		265				
	KTT		1	**1955**	MAC		—
			2827		MSS		576
							576 + MAC
1947	KSS		1250				
	MOV		38	**1956**	MAC		—
	MAC		50		MSS		237
	MSS		1211		Viper		1379
	KTT		11		Venom		537
			2560				2153 + MAC
1948	MOV		248	**1957**	MAC		—
	MAC		3647		MSS		154
	MSS		828		Viper		218
	KTT		70		Venom		392
			4793				764 + MAC
1949	MAC		610	**1958**	MAC		—
	KTT		77		MSS		133
					Viper		441
			687		Venom		684
							1258 + MAC
1950	MAC		1481				
	KTT		25	**1959**	MAC		—
			1506		MSS		163
					Viper		591
					Venom		1146
1951	MAC		1890				1900 + MAC
	KTT		2				
			1892	**1960**	MAC		—
					MSS		246
1952–3	MAC (rigid)	1436 + 105	1541		Viper		99
	KTT		1		Venom		1318
			1542				1663 + MAC

1953
MAC
(springer)   2565

		Annual total			Annual total
1961	MSS	46	**1968**	MSS	22
	Viper	14		Viper	5
	Venom	417		Venom	151
		477		Thruxton	185
					363
1962	MSS	21			
	Viper	503	**1969**	MSS	22
	Venom	77		Venom	83
		601		Thruxton	197
					302
1963	MSS	99			
	Viper	135	**1970**	MSS	6
	Venom	197		Venom	29
		431		Thruxton	140
					175
1964	MSS	45			
	Viper	127			
	Venom	237			
		409			

Total production figures by model
(excluding LE, Viceroy and MAC from July 1954)

GTP & other two-strokes	14,771
Ohc, other than KTT	10,722
KTT	868
MOV	4,669
MAC	22,378
MSS	9,392
Viper	3,693
Venom	5,721
VM Thruxton	1,108
	73,372
Spare engines for French Military Mission	120
Balance of MAC from July 1954	3,802
Total	77,284

		Annual total
1965	MSS	34
	Viper	94
	Venom	177
	Thruxton	155
		460
1966	MSS	48
	Viper	53
	Venom	157
	Thruxton	224
		482
1967	MSS	31
	Viper	34
	Venom	119
	Thruxton	207
		391

These production figures are based on the engine number lists from the works and may not tally with information provided elsewhere. They are intended as a guide only.